Love, Coach

ALAN DICKSON

WESTBOW
PRESS®
A DIVISION OF THOMAS NELSON
& ZONDERVAN

WestBow Press books may be ordered through booksellers or by contacting:

WestBow Press
A Division of Thomas Nelson & Zondervan
1663 Liberty Drive
Bloomington, IN 47403
www.westbowpress.com
1 (866) 928-1240

ISBN: 978-1-5127-6975-3 (sc)
ISBN: 978-1-5127-6976-0 (hc)
ISBN: 978-1-5127-6974-6 (e)

Library of Congress Control Number: 2016921298

Print information available on the last page.

WestBow Press rev. date: 8/2/2017

Acknowledgments

I would like to thank my lovely wife, Chris, for all of her support and encouraging me to fulfill my dream of writing this book.

I would also like to thank my daughter Allison for all of her hard work taking my handwritten, sometimes barely legible, scribbled out pages and putting them onto the computer and editing. I couldn't have finished this book without her; it might still be a bunch of papers in a box in my cozy den.

Preface from Bill Bettinger, former Cedar Park Christian School Athletic Director and dear friend:

I am excited for you to read the story of Coach Dickson. You will find in these pages a life of leadership, coaching, inspiration, motivation, listening and learning. I found it to be an honor and a privilege to serve alongside Coach Dickson at Cedar Park Christian School in Bothell, Washington. As the school Athletic Director, I was inspired on a daily basis by Alan's willingness to be strong in grace. In particular, two scripture references may describe Coach Dickson's approach to teaching and coaching long after his Physicians attempted to predict his health-related demise.

> **2 Timothy 2:3, 4 - Suffer hardship with *me*, as a good soldier of Christ Jesus. No soldier in active service entangles himself in the affairs of everyday life, so that he may please the one who enlisted him as a soldier. (NASB) Romans 8:18 - For I consider that the sufferings of this present time are not worthy to be compared with the glory that is to be revealed to us. (NASB)**

As you read this life story, you will be encouraged to live for God - to please Him as the one who enlists you for service. Coach Dickson's story will undoubtedly help to answer questions you have about the purpose and plans for your own life. Do you want to be obedient to

God? This story will persuade you to be obedient, no matter what the circumstances or hardships you face. Do you desire to know God's will for your life? This story will guide you to seek God's will to be revealed in your relationships, your thoughts, and your courage. Do you want to have the right motives in your life? This story will direct you to pay close attention to your day-to-day decision making process. Do you want to advance God's kingdom? This story will inspire you to better understand your purpose upon this earth. Do you want to bring glory to God? This story will provoke you to consider that the sufferings of your present life are not worthy to be compared with the glory that will be made known to you. Do you want to help people succeed? This story will prepare you to look at others as being more important than yourself. Do you want to grow spiritually? This story will motivate you to grow in your faith and to wait eagerly for a hope that drives you to a changed life.

Enjoy your time reading through Coach Dickson's life story. More importantly, absorb the truths about leadership, coaching, inspiration, motivation, listening and learning that you will discover in this book. Coach will be happy to know that his story has an impact on you as you commit to influencing others.

Chapter 1

Early Coaches/Key Players

Why did I always have the feeling that God was there with me every day, all the time, directing my path? I was in church a lot due to the faithful, persistent prayers of my two grandmothers and both mom and dad believing church was important. My parents had to work long hours as a waitress and butcher, but they sure insisted our attending. Being literally raised by the two oldest of my four sisters, Pat and Sharon, these Victorian gals were very strict in enforcing my grandmothers' prayers for the five of us! So, every Wednesday night, Friday night, and Saturday night "prayer band", every Sunday and Sunday evening we were always there. Dad provided five dimes so that we could all take the four mile, ten cent bus ride to church. He picked us up after church and the two older sisters left with boyfriends. Sometimes Barb, Joan and I would hitch a ride with them and get treated to Bonnie Doon's ice cream and a burger, fries and cherry coke. The fifty's were great years! Ours was a simple but very content life.

My afternoons were spent at the playgrounds of Beiger School, as our house was just a short block away. I was able to compete with school kids in football (touch and tackle) on the fields. Softball games were played on one of three full diamonds. However, it was the basketball courts that caught my attention. This collegiate looking K-12 building had three full asphalt courts and one half court attached to the shop building (this one with gravel) but compacted enough that a basketball could be bounced on it! Often I would get a stick and mark the out of bounds lines so our games were more competitive. I felt at home, in ownership with these courts. Little did I know that I would continue to be at home amongst each court, or gymnasium I entered. This playground became a big part of my life for the next eight years.

That church world also was a big part of my life! I became a believer when I was eight years old and my sisters and I were attending a Saturday night "Prayer Band" service at Apostolic Temple in South Bend, Indiana. This was my favorite service. David Rowe was very compassionate about his vision to lead people into the Kingdom. His love for all just radiated throughout that building. Usually this Saturday evening service was a smaller group and I liked the informal, relaxed environment. Music was uplifting and helped you connect to the heavenlies. Elder David just had a special way to draw you out of your self and into the God realm. The other side, so to speak. Well, this Saturday night I felt drawn to go forward and "receive Christ". I got baptized that night and felt so renewed and special on the inside. "I really slept well that night!"

<u>Key Player #1 Elder David Rowe:</u> Elder David Rowe was never the "Pastor" at Apostolic Temple; yet he was the assistant pastor and he mentored me, a few times in high school and then college years. He did the marriage counseling for Chris and my wedding. We never lived near the Apostolic Temple Church; yet when we made our visits to see family we would attend the church and Brother David Rowe always called us into his office after the service to catch up on our (spiritual) lives. Occasionally, we would meet him at Bonnie Doons for a treat after church. Elder David was a real servant of the Lord as he ministered to us and we were never really members of his church. His compassion for souls always made a strong impression on me.

The next day at school: I sinned. I lied! I told a lie to a friend that I had a new, red bike. I was so tired of all my friends bragging about (it seemed to me that they were) their fancy bicycles. Mom and Dad just didn't have extra money like the parents who had executive, or sales jobs, etc. We had enough, barely, but my parents really loved us. However, a butcher and waitress only make so much. The five of us always had really quality clothes and we were given great medical and dental services. Our home was not very special, but it was always clean. Yet, we packed five kids into two bedrooms. I was the only boy and needed a room of my own so dad partitioned the bathroom off and I was excited to have my own place. I decorated it with my deerskin that one of the suitors of my oldest sister gave me. Also, I mounted my tomahawk given to me by Jack Vanlew (he always said he was half American-Indian). I was fascinated by him and his family who owned a nine hundred acre ranch down in Missouri. The other walls were decorated with basketball photos from sports magazines, which I got free from the librarian who would save them just for me. But my favorite pictures were of the Mishawaka High School football and basketball stars which I got from the local newspaper. These guys were my heroes.

Here I go getting ahead of myself again.....back to the "white lie". I thought I lost my salvation! That evening my older sister sat in our big living room chair with me and I told her about the lie. Sister Sharon was wise in her words: "Alan, it's OK! You will have battles throughout your life. Just repent, and keep believing in your conversion. He forgives daily." I was sooooo relieved!

Key Player #2 Sister Sharon: Throughout this book you will see how Sharon's powerful prayer life helped me through some serious situations. Soon though I got really caught up in being popular at school and in second grade I was showing off, not paying attention and distracting the class at times. I think the fact that some girls thought I was cute and boys seemed to look up to me as I was starting to stand out during recess games. My religious experience was losing its effect on me! It was fading. A very good, warm experience but was distant to me now.

Key Player #3 Miss Bartow, 2nd grade teacher: Thank God for Miss Bartow, my second grade teacher. She was so pretty and just so sweet! I loved her. Maybe I was showing off to get her attention? I literally had a "crush" on her! She certainly affected my life! She called me in for a "private talk" during recess. "Alan, you are so bright, charming and you are such a leader! But you are leading in the wrong way". I was shocked that this special person was not happy with me! I was heartbroken. I was affected. I said, "I will try hard to not do this again!" I slowly walked out of the playground a changed young boy. I loved Miss Bartow and wanted her to like me. I decided to please her. I don't think, in fact I know I didn't tell my family. And she never told them either!! As I look back this was critical to the rest of my life. God was directing me through a teacher. Now I wonder if she had a relationship with God? Probably, I never went back and thanked her I am sorry to report. Things went pretty well in school: grades were up and my next significant event in school was Mr. Witham, basketball coach for our fourth grade team. Our team for hoops was loaded with boys who shared a passion for hoops -spending recess, and after school on the playground. But I was an absolute fanatic! My parents worked until eight P.M. and I was on the courts until a few minutes before they got home, ignoring the repeated calls from my sisters to get home to eat dinner.

Bouncing ahead a few years in fourth, fifth, and sixth grades I was rapidly developing as a very skilled basketball player. Welcome to "Hoosier Hysteria"! It starts like a mustard seed in all those elementary school kids in the Indiana schools. It's all the dads and often moms talked about!

My dream was set in fourth grade and it grew stronger in fifth and sixth grade. I loved being on the playground of Beiger School. I knew every mark on those full courts. I cherished the main court with the real nets most of all. I made sure that when these nets wore out or occasionally stolen, I requested the custodian to replace and he did so immediately. All others featured chain nets. I loved the sound of the "swoosh" when the shot was made. My older sisters' boyfriends were both high school basketball players and took a liking to me and my passion for hoops. When they came a courting Pat and Sharon, they would take me down the street to the playgrounds and gave me instruction on the one-handed push shot and bank shots. Also, Sharon's boyfriend Lynn Williams (He later became a high school teacher and coach) taught me an awesome hook shot! Mishawaka City School District was composed of five elementary schools. Back in the fifties each of these schools had a basketball team supported by cheerleaders in full uniform for grades 4-6. It was a hoop-crazed team during the basketball season! My mom and 4 sisters (along with their boyfriends) attended every game. These games were on Saturday and began at 8 A.M.

Lynn and Sharon were no longer dating and Kenny moved to La Porte when he and Pat were married. Those mentors were gone, but I still had Mr. Witham. Our elementary teams at Beiger won almost all of our games (I think we lost one in fourth grade). My good friend and fellow player, John Stout would scout all players from the other schools that we knew and asked questions about their teams. Scouting teams in elementary school sounds absurd! This was Indiana though.

Key Player #4 Mr. Witham Grades 4-8 Beiger Bulldogs: Now, I'm ready for the next level! Seventh and Eighth graders played after school games and even two night games verses Main Jr. High (The other Jr. High) in the school district. These games were at Mishawaka High School and the high school coaching staff would be in attendance. Beiger school was nicknamed the Bulldogs (perhaps a forerunner of things to come). Mr. Witham would be a great coach for us. I was really glad he decided to move up to Jr. High and be at the helm of our team. It was destined that way for me. He was my first coaching mentor. All I wanted to do was prepare for basketball season! I had a burning passion to be on the court and compete. This feeling is so hard to understand even now for me, but that is where I was back then. The football coaches (Mr. Jim Tansey and Clarence Lindsy) approached me in P.E. class and said that going out for the football team would really strengthen me for basketball, especially defense and rebounding! I thought about it and decided to play even though I preferred the finesse game of basketball instead of getting smashed around by those huge eighth graders in football. Some had hair on their chests and full beards! Not a real exciting venture in my mind. I played football and this was not fun like when I played two-handed touch football on schoolyards. These guys were rough and unlike basketball, there were guys out there who went out just to beat up people (I believe). These were the guys who were bullies on the playground.

Mishawaka was a blue-collar town where sports were premier. Local heroes were made of football and basketball players. I think some of these tough guys came out just to "knock around" those aspiring to become sports heroes. No matter what - I did not love football in seventh grade. Being the back up quarterback was awful. Everyday the first team loaded with the overgrown eight graders ran all over our second team of mostly seventh graders. All day in school I was nervous thinking about football practice. I never felt so miserable in my life. I counted the days until basketball began. The basketball gym was my home and I couldn't wait. The football season finally ended and I had survived. No broken bones, not even a sprained ankle!

Seventh grade basketball went very well for me. That football experience helped me develop a real love for this hardwood game. My skill level was far advanced of the others; some were a bit more athletic, but no one spent more time on those outdoor asphalt courts than I did. Situation dictated a lot of this: we were a family of limited budget. I did not even have my own bike. Later that year dad came up with $35.00 for a really good, slightly used Colombia bicycle. I loved it! I could cover the entire town with my bike. Our city of 40,000 had eight beautiful parks and I could now travel these neighborhoods and compete with many different kids. There were Catholic Schools and I never got to compete against those boys in our regular school season.

That seventh grade season soon passed and I learned a valuable lesson from Coach Witham. After scoring 21 of our teams 27 points in a win verses Elm Road School, I thought I was (invincible). My teammates on that Beiger Bulldog team seemed to really be excited for my great game. Rushing home after the game I exploded through the front door and just couldn't hold in my excitement.

"Barb, you won't believe this, I scored almost all
the points in our game today! I think I had 21
points for the game. Oh, and we won 27-24!"

Unfortunately, my older sister, Barbara did not appreciate my boasting. Barbara always had a very balanced view of life. She was very wise for only being 1 ½ years older. And she was very close to Mr. Witham I think they were both of analytical mindset. In the big scheme of things Barb did not think that a seventh grade basketball game was that important to make yourself superior to all your teammates, your classmates who were all really good people. Wow. I knew by her countenance I was in trouble!

Next day at practice we were all shooting around and coach Witham walked out of his office. Being the science teacher at Beiger Jr. High, he also dressed for practice in the coach's office. This day he had a very somber face. His whistle echoed throughout the gym, and he said: "Everyone on the bleachers". He walked up to us, looking at each player then in a grave voice. "Boys, we have one player on this team who thinks he is more important than the rest of the team. Basketball is a team sport. Scores are only one part of the game. Defense, rebounding, passing, dribbling, scoring are all equal parts of the game. I never want to hear about how many points any one player scores again!"

I wanted to die, to just disappear. Thanks, Barbara. She ratted on me to Mr. Witham. Yet, deep down I knew she really loved her little brother. I was not angry at her.

After practice Mr. Witham came up to me with his normal kind smile: "Alan, you have a great future in basketball! I care a lot about you being a top player for Mishawaka High in a couple years. Look at today as a stepping stone to lead you into a greater future!" He smiled and patted me. Then he went back into his office. I got the message. Thank you, Barb. What a lesson, how priceless! I loved that man. In my later years after I began my coaching years I realized what a valuable coach I had, and I was proud to be a Beiger Bulldog!

Chapter 2

Eighth grade was a time of higher expectations for the students of Beiger Jr. High. It was a separating of the "sheep and the goats" in the school. If you had future plans that required higher-level education. This was the year to become serious about being prepared for that next level: High School. Football and basketball also took on a more serious tone. In fact my attitude toward football took on a drastic change. I looked forward to it. During the summer when talking to one of my friends, Rob, I asked him a serious question.

"Rob, you really seemed to enjoy the contact part of football last year. To me it didn't make sense to risk injury. Didn't you ever think about that?" Rob replied: "Alan, what is the worst thing that could happen to you? You could die on the field. That doesn't happen too often! And if it did, you would be carried off – a hero!"

For some reason that statement of confidence for this game really made sense in my young adult mind. From that moment on I took on a very aggressive attitude toward the game. Love of contact would become a key part of my football skills. When the season began, I made a point of standing out in the blocking and tackling drills. And when I caught passes from my tight end position, if I couldn't run past a defender I loved to try to bull them over with a hard hit and then spin away to gain a few more yards. I was now bigger and stronger and I now loved the sport! Little did I know it later would be a big part of my future. Only God knew that at the time. As I reflect on my brief friendship with Rob, I realize what a key player he was on my future. Unfortunately, he drifted from sports himself and hung out with some of the gang kids that were started to form in the area. Looking back I feel badly that he dropped out and took on different interests but I am glad I listened to Mr. Witham's words of staying on track and having good friendships. Yet, this teammate helped me love football.

The beautiful fall in Northern Indiana was slowly giving into colder nights and winter was approaching. It was October 31 and football came to an end. Basketball was right around the corner. Coach Witham saw me in the halls on that Monday after the close of the football season:

"Alan, come to my room after school, I have a
ball for you. Practice starts next week."

How did he know the ball he gave me in 7th grade was worn down to the rubber? When I arrived in his room he handed me a really new looking leather ball!

"Alan, I expect you to wear this out and come
see me when you do for another one!"

This gesture from Mr. Witham fired up my passion to be the kind of player he thought I could be! Mr. Witham really believed in me. He imparted a confidence that carried over to my high school career.

The future was very bright and I was a very happy young teen. However, I had a few friends from the neighborhood that would hang out on the playgrounds and smoke, etc. – maybe playing marbles – but not really sports. The Traylor brothers and Vince were trouble. Friendly but dangerous, these guys were dangerously enticing. I smoked a few cigarettes with them, even went to the Traylor's house for an overnight on one occasion. Mom and Dad thought they were good kids. Their mom was a nurse and the dad worked at the V.F.W. as a bar tender. The only problem was both parents worked late, very late. The Traylor's house was free for teens to party until 2:00 A.M. I only participated in smoking, but beers were available by the older brother Jim. Thanks to early church experiences, the Lord was with me there and my spirit was fearful. It's like I had an angel on one shoulder and a demon on the other, which do I choose?

Once again Mr. Witham came to the rescue. He saw me smoking with these guys on the playground. Apparently, he saw us when working late from his second floor science room overlooking the playgrounds. The next day he asked to see me in his classroom again. It's like God was always there guiding me through coaches, mentors, teachers!! Mr. Witham spoke in his serious tone:

"Alan, you need to make a choice! Your high school
academic and sports career is at stake. You need to
separate yourself from some of your friends."

I did and I spent my time with some really quality friends who have been with me for eight years at Beiger School. Among these friends were John, the principal's son, who ended up being the Valedictorian of our senior class. Phil Hughes a really wholesome Christian friend who was a star lineman on our football squad. And David Fisher, a track star who ended up as associate superintendent of Mishawaka Schools after several years as the principal of Beiger School. I continued these healthy relationships throughout my high school career. In fact, my four years of high school were totally focused on academics and football and basketball. My high school years were guiding me into my call and I began to sense a purpose for my life.

Thank you Mr. Witham for being there for me, he cared and I was determined to please him. He never mentioned it again and I was on track for 8th grade football and basketball. It wasn't as easy as the 7th grade and it was quite a challenge scoring. Now this year some of the players were really developed physically and I was still developing – but at a slower pace. Some of these guys were full grown! I stayed on track; believing in Mr. Witham's words and eventually I finished both seasons a key player on both football and basketball teams.

Social dynamics in the eighth grade started becoming more

solidified. Many of the students looked forward to high school as an opportunity to prepare for college; another large group of students looked forward to gaining a high school degree and solid vocational training that would enable them to land a real good job in one of the several factories in the South Bend-Mishawaka area in the 50's and 60's. Then there was another group that had no definite goals but sort of went along on the school journey but really cared more about hanging out at lunch and after school. They liked being there but never really got rooted toward any future goals. They wanted to have some fun socially then land a job after school. Often, these guys would end up in a gang, which was at that time more of a party association. But, there would occasionally be gang fights at the drive in restaurants after games or at games. These guys chose this avenue for their social life and status. This was typical of the late 50's and early 60's. I witnessed one major brawl at Merrifiled Park on Saturday night so my friends and I climbed a tree near by and witnessed the clash between the Shieks and the Cobras. There were zip guns, brass knuckles and clubs. I actually did not like any aspect of this "tumble" and I was so glad the police came right away and broke it up. I knew then that Mr. Witham protected me from that path, or maybe that goes all the way back to Elder David's spiritual guidance.

Chapter 3

Moving up to Mishawaka High School in the fall of 1959 was the beginning of my dream: a chance to be successful in basketball and football and move on to college ball. Ninth grade started off with an awesome experience. Our frosh football team was loaded with talent from the Jr. Highs that fed into Mishawaka High. Our numbers weren't huge, but there was talent at every position and a tier of quality subs for each position. There was never a let up during the games. Most importantly, we were led by Coach Mike Jellicoe who stressed team unity and mental and physical toughness. He told us that we were a family. We were one. If one of us were being attacked and had to fight, all of us needed to jump in and help our teammate! This left a strong impression on me. We went unscored on for the first eight games! And we scored over thirty points in every game. The last game of the season was against Elkhart High School and they scored a touchdown against us, but we stopped their attempt for an extra point. We won 27-6! It was a fantasy type season – one that elevated the promise for next season's varsity program.

Basketball that frosh year was very competitive. I bounced from first team to second team, as once again our team was talented. Our football coach, Mike Jellicoe was also our hoops coach. I loved his honest, open communication with us. But he was in charge and we respected him – especially after that football season.

My sophomore year began with a lot of promise! A very heralded coach, Robert Heck, took over the football program.

He was previously head coach on the college ranks and played professional football. Mishawaka had a strong tradition of success in the high school sports. The Cavemen had won two state football championships in the early 50's and in 1955 the basketball team went all the way to semi-state. That team was one of the very best in Indiana basketball, probably in the top four of all time. (Indianapolis Attucks with Oscar Robertson). Muncie Central, South Bend, Central and Mishawaka had captured all the public's eye. I remember each player on that team, even the manager. LeRoy Johnson (a 6-6 leaper) was the center. He later played for Indiana University and the (Harlem Magicians). There was also Dick Coppens, John Ronchetti, Jim Carnes, Jim Ganser and George Hixenbaugh. These guys were my heroes; I wanted to be like them! There was standing room only at most of their home games. I remember peeking into the lower gym doors – just to get a glimpse of the game against Indianapolis Crispus Attucks featuring Oscar Robertson. The game was a thriller and Mishawaka was leading for most of the game. Led by the famous Oscar Robertson, Attucks made a stunning comeback and stole the game from the Cavemen in the final seconds. The intensity of that high school game ignited my passion, my dream to help lead Mishawaka High to the top in Indiana high school basketball. That desire was still there when the football season opened on August 15, 1960.

Coach Heck had a passion to make our school one of the premier football programs in the state. At his meeting with us he announced that we were all going to be committing to the time that it takes to be successful. There would be summer conditioning run by the captains at Rose Park at 7:00 AM three days a week. Two days a week weight lifting would be held at the high school. When the season began August 15, 1960 we were going to have three a day practices for the two weeks before school began. The season went well. We competed in the tough Northern Indiana League that was composed of the eight large South Bend High Schools, La Porte, Michigan City Fort Wayne North, and Elkhart Central. In most of our talented frosh team were subs except James Pittman, a super talented running back, who was a Walter Payton type talent.

Bob Heck was also our J.V. basketball coach. He was really a great football mind but in basketball we ran the pick and roll offense. We just free-lanced and I excelled at that type of play. It was fun and coach Heck was a great person to be around: such an optimist. Well, his upbeat, positive attitude became a valuable asset to me as I faced a tremendous health challenge during the last quarter of the last game that sophomore season. My life took a very serious turn – I was forced to slow down and look at the reality that life was way bigger than just sports and school.

You see, academically I kind of floated through my 9th grade year – mostly B's and some A's I remember thinking "That was easy, if I try hard enough I could get all A's". Sophomore year I began striving for perfection in the classroom and also pushing myself on the court, I became seriously ill. Playing at Concord High School I passed out running the wing lane, on a fast break. I just laid there; I was exhausted. Without telling anyone, I had been bleeding internally from my large intestine for nearly a month. Sometimes I would fill the toilet with just bright red blood. When I arrived home I told mom and the next morning I was checked into Saint Joseph Hospital in downtown Mishawaka. I was there for two weeks while they diagnosed my condition. It ended up being acute ulcerative colitis.

During this stay at Saint Joseph Hospital in Mishawaka, I realized my life was on "pause". My roommate was a big strong, older Belgian farmer. His farm outside Mishawaka was nearly 100 acres and he was injured in a serious barn fire and several of his prize Belgian horses died. He shared many wise thoughts with me. First of all, he reminded me that I was blessed with such a loving family and extended family. I had 5-6 visitors daily. Aunts, uncles, nieces, nephews, and my sisters and brother in laws visited regularly. Classmates started visiting and one day nearly 20 showed up and brought me an X-Large milkshake from Bonnie Doons! I hurriedly ate it and unfortunately that evening I had a relapse. Dr. Reed chewed me out the next day. I will never forget all the cards the M.H.S. students brought (nearly one hundred). Being quiet and reserved at school, I never expected anything like that! Classmates took turns bringing my homework to my room – and I amazed my teachers by achieving all A's that six week's grading period. During that hospital stay, I wrote one of my best papers: "A Hidden View". A story about a boy hospitalized by a terrible automobile accident and while in his urgent care room, he noticed a beautiful bird outside his window. The bird came every day for a couple hours and rested on the same branch just outside his window!

It was nearly six weeks before I was released. Dr. Reed wanted to make certain I had no more bleeding before releasing me. Coach Heck visited regularly throughout the six weeks. He was a man of faith and a loyal Catholic. All the Catholic boys on the football team were encouraged by Coach to attend church each Sunday. He would even drive them if they had transportation problems. One time when we were alone I asked him "Coach, why did you play me in some of those varsity games?" He replied with his kind smile, with sort of a wink in his eye. "I knew you would be very important to our future." This blew me away. I didn't really think I was that good that year. Pastor Worthy Rowe also visited regularly and prayed for a complete healing for me. He knew how important getting my strength back was to me. I wanted to continue my dream in sports!

The 1960-61 school year at Mishawaka was overall not very significant for me. Still recovering from my illness and striving to regain my overall strength, I was not able to perform as I desired. Yet I gained a lot of game experience in football and basketball. I sure enjoyed my time in classes with all those wonderful students who showed such genuine concern for me when I was hospitalized. Mishawaka High was a special place for me.

Senior year at Mishawaka was a time of great promise! Our senior class was dynamite. Thirty-two of us had an A- average or above. We had talented drama students (awesome plays and skits during assemblies). Word was around the school that this class was one of the best MHS had in a long while. I had worked my way up into all honor classes. It was a great year for me. I was voted Vice President of the class, National Honor Society, V.P. Spanish Club, and had potential to start in football and basketball games. Most of us had spent all twelve of our school years at Mishawaka schools, we were a close-knit class and we strongly desired to make our school and town of 40,000 proud. At that time Mishawaka High was the center of this factory town. And you can be certain that sports were the main interest and center of attraction. MHS was a three story brick building with beautiful architecture surrounded by beautiful landscaping and mature maple trees. The gymnasium housed 5,200 people and the football stadium was like that of a medium sized college. Locker rooms and concession booths were under the stands that held a crowd of 13,000!

Physically I grew to six foot three. And now weighed 190 lbs. I had the size for college ball; I just needed to perform! The ball was in my hands! Our end of the summer practices, the annual inner squad scrimmage (maroon and white game) was held and I was determined to make a statement. And I did! I caught eight passes, (one for a touchdown). On defense I made five tackles at my end position. It was a really hot and humid end of August evening and I nearly passed out again. But I knew I was OK. I knew I was totally healed, but my Dr. Reed (also our team Dr.) insisted on walking me the short two blocks to my home. I was impressed how dedicated he was: I believe he was truly happy that he was able to administer medically to my healing, imagine a family doctor escorting a former patient home. I remember feeling very important. He went on and on about how well I played. I told you this blue-collar factory town was sports crazy!!

When the season opened, we were ranked number three in the preseason A.P. polls. Mishawaka High was on the map and I was excited to be part of it! The first game was at home and over 8,000 were in attendance. Gary Emerson was the competition and they had beaten us my junior year. The game started with a statement: A thundering kickoff by my good friend Phil Hughes! He booted the ball right through the uprights on the kick off. I remember wondering at the time if that was three points for us, but of course the ball came back out to the 20-yard line. At the end of the evening the Cavemen were on the map. Final score: Mishawaka 48 – Gary Emerson 6.

This team had talent. That undefeated, nearly unscored frosh year was no fluke. We went on to win seven straight games and were ranked number two in the state right behind Evansville Reitz whose quarterback was Bob Griese (a future Hall of Fame QB for the World Champs Miami Dolphins). We ended the season losing 29-27 to Laporte and 13-12 to South Bend Washington in the final seconds. But Mishawaka High School was on the map. Our last game against Washington the stands were overflowing with 13,000 in attendance. And this was high school football! It was a memorable season! I had a very good season by catching twenty-five passes and scoring three touchdowns. My selection to the second team All League (Northern Indiana Conference) game me a lot of satisfaction.

Basketball season went pretty well. We finished 13-10 and I played three or four outstanding games as I rotated at starting with two other forwards. My season was inconsistent, as I seemed to lack a consistent confidence. As I look back my previous coaches gave this confidence to me. Coach Smith was sarcastic at times and I think I was too sensitive, and not used to this type of approach. After scoring eighteen points and grabbing ten rebounds against E. Chicago Roosevelt on Friday night (the game was broadcast live on WSBT – the South Bend channel), I was ready to have my season take off! I was grounded the next night as we played a home Saturday night game against Marion. I threw a turnover pass on a fast break and coach yanked me out and literally pushed me on to the end of the bench. Playing just thirty seconds that game, I was humiliated and most of my confidence was squelched.

Timeout!

Coach was a great guy, and I kept in touch with him through the years. I know he respected me as a student/athlete. He nicknamed me Al and he said he named a son after me. I think he was frustrated with me and believed that I needed to be "tough" every night.

Chapter 4

Basketball season was coming to a close and our season was up and down; however we made a terrific run in the sectionals of the state tournament. Sixteen teams battled for the chance to move onto the State Regionals. Mishawaka High athletes had a tradition of fighting strong – especially in the state tournament! And this sectional tourney was no exception! We clawed our way into the championship game against highly talented South Bend Central.

"March, march on down to fame. We're out to win this game. Our coach and all the team are just what they seem. So give a loud cheer for Mishawaka. Hear all those Boosters talk! Central High may fight to the end. But we will win! Rah! Rah! Rah! Fight on Mishawaka; Live up to your name Raise high all your standards, Spread 'round you all your fame. We're marching to Victory. Won't stop till we're there. So fight, Mishawaka, fight, And win this game"

This song would fire up the Cavemen to go all out for our school, student body, staff, town's people and our families. It was now a mission, a battle for our town to win! Early in the season we had given South Bend Central Bears their toughest battle in the league only to lose by three points. I was thrilled with my play that game garnering fourteen rebounds against their young but talented 6-10 center, DeWitt Menyard. This South Bend Central team was always loaded. And this year they had a pair of sophomore guards Mike Warren (U.C.L.A.) and Jimmy Ward who could dunk at 5-8! For some reason Coach only played me a few minutes this game. I never was comfortable with his reasoning. Yet, I maintained my respectful demeanor during the game and questioned only myself. My early dreams of going to the state tourney in Indianapolis, playing before 18,000 fans at Hinkle Field House seemed a blur. I wanted a huge section of the stands to be packed with my classmates and fans of all ages decorated in maroon and white. Why couldn't God have made this happen? Easy for Him to do!! A distant fantasy. I remember picturing myself receiving the "Trester Award" for the top scholar/athlete competing in the finals.

That all didn't happen, but I played an important role on a basketball team that had a respectable season in the tough Northern Indiana Conference. I did show flashes of being a really solid forward at 6' 3" and a good passer and tough defender. I had three really good games with 17, 18, and 16 points. One game I even had 18 rebounds. Yet my final stats read 7.5 points and 5.4 rebounds. Why did I think something good was going to happen?

For some reason I had faith that I would be playing at the next level. It seems like I had this seed planted in me a long time before. I never felt alone with this vision. I just wasn't sure how it was going to happen. Dartmouth football coach Bob Blackburn, sent letters frequently requesting me to fill out an application. Our highly ranked football team had drawn attention from many colleges. I wasn't a star but a very solid tight end and defensive end. I received Second Team All League and was very satisfied with my season catching 25 passes and scoring 2 touchdowns. In addition, I received some letters from South Carolina, Ball State and a few other smaller schools. For some reason I knew God was in control.

As I look back, I am amazed that I wasn't panicked. Having helped over twenty-five players record college scholarships – and six D-1 full ride scholarships as the Girls Coach at Monroe High School in the Seattle area, I realize how challenging it can become. Yet, I had hope and peace it was all going to work out: something good was going to happen.

Springtime was beautiful in Mishawaka and I enjoyed watching the track meets at the high school. Several of my classmates were at one of the meets and a few of the kids in my honors English class were discussing their college selections. One girl (Ruthie our Homecoming queen) asked "Alan where have you decided to go next year?" That's when it really hit me. I don't have a plan. Dad and mom had nothing saved for my college – they were great providers but as a butcher and waitress, there was not a lot of room for savings. Yet, God was always there and I was NEVER ALONE and I knew there would be a college opportunity. Looking back I am amazed at the peace and trust I had that "all would be O.K.".

To better understand the situation: I was a definite college potential student/athlete with a 3.75 G.P.A. in honors classes; National Honor Society, vice president of my senior class and even vice president of Spanish club. But I needed a full ride! I was a definite contributor to a highly ranked high school football team (3rd in State!). Our fullback, Tom Fern was named to the High School "All American" squad. Both of our quarterbacks made the "All State" team along with Bob Griese from No. 1 ranked Evansville Reitz. Has any team ever had two quarterbacks so highly ranked? Coppens was an all-around player (offense and defense) and Witkowski a superb passer. In reality I was their no. 1 short yardage receiver, and played both offense and defense. But I wasn't named to any special honors! And I was soon to receive un-warranted favor.

It was the middle of April, 1962 and I had about 20 letters of interest from Bob Blackburn, football coach at Dartmouth University. His staff followed our conference (Northern Indiana) and he was aware of the talent that we had on our team by the way the letters were written. And I was one of the few starters who had the G.P.A. for the Ivy League. Air Force Academy sent a questionnaire and a follow up letter. As I look back perhaps Coach Heck or one of the assistants were trying to land me a scholarship. Taylor University, Wabash and Hanover College all showed interest by sending letters and applications. Phil Hughes, my close friend and football buddy and I made a recruiting visit together to Hanover. He drove and we had a ball visiting the campus. It was during spring break and the campus was mostly shut down. The visit was somewhat uninspiring and we both weren't impressed when we saw a couple students in dorms brewing 'home brew' beer. It would have been fun going there with Phil, playing football with him and I would have played basketball also at Hanover. We both told the coach we'd let them know and send back an application if interested. It just didn't seem right for either of us.

May 15, 1962 and still no set college plans for me. However, the next Monday I received a letter from the Athletic Department at Butler University inviting me to visit the school within the next couple weeks. The letter was waiting for me when I got home from school. All I had to do was call the athletic office and set an appointment with Coach Tony Hinkle!!!

Tony Hinkle was the man who molded Butler University's remarkable athletic tradition. Coach Hinkle was the varsity head coach for football, basketball and baseball. In addition, he was a teacher and the athletic director. He was a legend back then and later when he was in the Hall of Fame the Butler University Fieldhouse became the "Hinkle Fieldhouse".

Butler basketball had just come off a 22-6 season and really made a name for the school in the 1962 NCAA tournament. They had beaten No. 8 ranked Bowling Green with a future NBA star Nate Thurmond; Butler won by a single point. Then Butler had to face Kentucky, ranked third in the country. This game was four days later in Iowa City. Butler scrapped and scrambled, but Kentucky eliminated the Bulldogs by twenty-one. Butler finished the season 22-6. This was Hinkle's best record.

Well, I was on cloud nine and just felt like I was in 'basketball heaven'! I was going to make a phone call that afternoon: after I called mom at her job at the South Bend YMCA, where she was Food Services Director. She was ecstatic and told me "make that call right away!" I did and the athletic secretary set the appointment for that next Saturday morning. All that week at school I heard the news around the hallways and cafeteria that I was being recruited by Butler University! Anything sports related at our school was BIG! I have no idea why I walked the halls so confidently; however after talking to so many of my classmates at the class reunions that followed, I was reminded that I was so quiet, humble and nice. My confidence was very internal. But that day it was external!

<u>Butler</u>

Dad told me he had filled up the gas tank of our 1958 Chevrolet Impala Hardtop Super Sport. It was a sweet looking car and I got to drive it on my visit to Butler University to meet Coach Hinkle. Two weeks earlier I accompanied my good football buddy, Phil Hughes on a recruiting trip to Hanover College on the border of Indiana and Kentucky. It was a great visit, a small college, but quaint and they made both of us feel very wanted. I was recruited for basketball and football and Phil was to play football and compete in the shot put for the track team. He drove one of his dad's cool hot rods and we had a ball, but for me it wasn't happening there as I said earlier.

This Butler visit was what really was exciting me! I washed the white Impala Friday night when dad got home. Denny Wood, a sophomore at M.H.S. called earlier in the week and said his mother game him permission to ride along. Denny was a three-sport athlete with a bright future and I spent hours during the past three years on the courts with him. He always said he really looked up to me, but deep down I saw more talent in him than I ever had; at least in my mind. So Denny arrived at 6:00 A.M. and mom had one of her special breakfasts for us. There was a sense of excitement in our home that Saturday morning. A second pot of coffee was brewing on the stove as Denny and I enjoyed the eggs, breaded steak tenderloins, bacon w/hash browns and pancakes! As dad was a butcher, we always ate top quality cuts of meat. Although my parents were not college experienced (dad was really bright but only finished 6th grade). He says he quit school to work on the farm so his brothers could all get educated. A noble, but suspicious motive as I look back. Mom graduated from the historic French Lick High School and loved writing and her English classes. She had very high grades, but married at 18 and they had the five of us. My hard working parents really respected the school system and stressed how fortunate we were to be in the Mishawaka City School system. Mom always praised me for my good grades and dad just expected them. One time as a sophomore I brought home four A's and one A-. Dad wanted to know what happened in the biology class that I received the A-. I thought he was being rude but maybe he was trying to motivate me by sarcasm?! I liked mom's positive reinforcement style. (Dad reminded me of my high school basketball coach – in fact Coach bought his meat at dad's store). Mom was more like the loving coach Heck.

Well, we finished the delicious southern style home cooked meal mom had prepared and I remember Denny's remark: "I love your mother's cooking: she must have learned that growing up in French Lick Indiana!" (You see, at that time we considered any city South of Indianapolis the South and French Lick set nearly on the Kentucky border. Of course Larry Bird was still a young kid and not yet known. (He later played at Springs Valley with two of my second cousins who were twins). Kind of interesting connection as Larry ended up being my idea of a pure team player, the kind that I wanted to develop as a coach. And you could add, "He was all that and much more!"

Key Player #5 Wayne Forrest: We planned on leaving at 7:00 A.M. for the two-hour drive straight down Highway 31 from South Bend to Indianapolis. My younger brother-in-law Wayne Forrest, another key contributor in my basketball development, made me a very accurate map that led us right to the Butler Campus. Wayne was an organizer and coach type. He would often encourage us to go to the local Merrifield and Dodge Parks to play against teams of older guys: top flight former high school and college stars. Wayne, Denny Wood, and myself would do this on several weekends. Wayne supported me by attending almost all of my high school football and basketball games. His presence strengthened my resolve to achieve.

Denny and I never had enough basketball after nearly every high school home game we would get three other friends and have our team of five drive north of town to the "Barn". This barn housed two full basketball courts. A farming family converted it for their son who was a local star at Washington Clay High School in South Bend. He was now in college but they allowed anyone to play any time at night "Just shut the lights off when done". Usually we played until 12:30 or 1:00 A.M. and my parents never worried. Mom and dad really trusted Denny and me and that's really all we did that late – PLAYED BALL! My friend Gene Smith (who was only 5-2 but was quite an outside shot and tough on the ball defender) drove us there and dropped each of us off at our doorsteps each evening. Gene was the high school manager of basketball. Gene was a loyal friend and was irate at Coach when he would not play me enough. We were locker partners for four years (and he was the manager for all four years). He knew he wouldn't ever make the team and he had the same basketball passion as the rest of us: so he became manager and got to work on his high lifting set shot before and after practice. Gene made a great locker partner; he couldn't reach the top shelf so he kept all his books in the bottom of the locker. He was energetic, fun and not afraid of anything! It was a harmless and fun relationship.

My junior year I had a "crush" on the homecoming queen (who was a senior); Gene was in business ed. and had classes with her and set me up with a date to the senior class play. I was too reserved to ask her myself. Thanks Gene-O! However, it was nearly graduation time and she was staying home to work at a local factory and my focus was on going off to college. However, that was a beautiful evening and we enjoyed a few weeks together at school. She was a princess, but I was on a mission.

Well, Denny and I headed south on Highway 31. We drove directly to the Butler Field House. We had both been there before, as Mishawaka High School would send the varsity basketball team each year to the state finals. Each player received an all day pass and food money for three meals. The coaches and teacher chaperones drove us down in vans. It would be a true final four. Teams 1 and 2 would play first, followed by teams 3 and 4. Then a five-hour break and at 6:00 that evening the losers would play a consolation game followed by the STATE CHAMPIONSHIP at 8:00 P.M. Remember, at that time (1962) the state tournament was single elimination and all schools were entered into the same tournament, regardless of size and record. It was a classic high school basketball event!

The Butler Field house is a staple of Indiana basketball love, and it's changed very little since it was built in 1928. Coach Tony Hinkle was a legend. He was soon to be inducted into the "Coaches Hall of Fame". He was unique in that he especially valued those few athletes that could play two and sometimes even three sports. Ken Freeman, from my high school, started in all three sports (football, basketball, and baseball). So as we sat in the parking lot and I was collecting my thoughts – I realized this coaching legend might actually believe I could be the next Ken Freeman! My frosh year at Mishawaka, Ken Freeman assisted Coach Jellica for a week of summer practice and I really respected him. I thought we resembled each other. Both of us were 6-3, lanky and 190-205 lbs. And blonde and fair skinned with 1960's crew haircuts.

As Denny and I entered the front door of the field house, a wonderful presence surrounded me (Denny later shared that he sensed the same feeling). We walked straight down the hall and Hinkle's office was on the right side: just as the athletic office secretary described. We walked in and I introduced myself and my best friend Denny Wood. I told them he was only a sophomore but had a bright future in all sports (football, basketball, and baseball). Hinkle gave a smirk of a smile and said "Well Dickson, let's get you signed up and then we'll look forward to your friend joining us in a couple years!"

I was elated: it was going to happen! This was too easy. Actually, I was flabbergasted! But did not show it!!

Time Out!
God was really in control – He was right there: I
can't explain how but He made things happen.

Coach Hinkle was making an offer to me!! Looking back and
spending those years at Butler I learned that Hinkle's recruiting
system was the "network" approach. Former players (which were
numerous) became coaches and they referred the athletes who fit
into "Hinkle's system".

Key Player #6 Coach John Chelminiak: Key Player coach John
Chelminiak, an assistant football coach, was a primary contributor
to this offer. I regret to this day that I never went back and personally
thanked him. I said hi at a game, but why did I not thank this man,
send a card or something? What a major player in my life!

Coach Hinkle introduced us to a couple of his football assistants
(he only had five, a trainer, and Charley the equipment manager).
Then, he talked briefly about academics and to think seriously about
course of study, and to ask many questions when you talk to your
counselor. It was a short talk – and he told us to take a tour of
campus and he would send me a letter of recruitment next week. I
still remember Tony Hinkle jokingly asking: "Do you fellas want
Coach Heddon and me to walk you around or do you want to enjoy
the campus at your leisure?" (I loved his casual approach).

Tuesday morning the letter arrived: I was given a full tuition
scholarship, room and board and books paid. Here we go!! Butler
University, here I come!

Chapter 5

A New World of College

All those hours of sitting at my desk in my room at the front of our small, but very cozy two-bedroom bungalow on Fourth Street in Mishawaka sure paid off! Admittedly, I would organize all my homework then stare at the wall and dream of my future. During those periods of time when I was done dreaming of the future my thoughts would come back to sports and some of the girls that I was attracted to at school. My parents would be very quiet in the family room as they watched T.V. I can't remember once watching T.V. on a weeknight. I always ate, and did my homework. My dad had set the tone for my studies by building me the strongest desk in the world. Dad proudly proclaimed to me: "Alan, this desk will never break and you can stand on it with your 200 lbs. and jump up and down. It is cherry wood and was made with the sides of our coal bin in the old house!" I loved my dad; he was a true hardworking American who got a lot out of his sixth grade education. He was tough but a good man. Dad always said that he had to learn how to do everything to survive: fix and repair cars, electrical repairs at work and home – he even built our house in Niles, Michigan when I was little. After moving to Mishawaka, Indiana he purchased an old house remodeled it and added a large family/dining room.

I will never forget this story: Dad was doing a repair on the car and wanted to teach me – just as his dad taught him. I was standing there bouncing my ball and really not paying attention, Ray Dickson became furious! "Give me that ball!" He then booted it over to the next-door neighbor's house. And then dad shouted: "You will not amount to anything if you don't quit playing ball all the time!" I understood my goals were different than his and I still loved him.

Let's get back to the desk: I treasured that desk and it was helpful in keeping me focused. Writing this chapter I had to Google popular T.V. shows in 1962 and the following came up: "Dennis the Menace", "Lassie", "Bonanza", and ABC had Bell and Howell "Close-Up". There were others, but those I recognized. What came to my mind was the simplicity of life back then. Things were black and white – just like our televisions.

My satisfying but simple life was taking on a new adventure. It was August 15, 1962 and I needed to report to Butler for pre-season football. We left on a Wednesday and that was dad's day off. We crammed the 1962 Impala Super Sport with all my clothes and headed once again down Highway 31 to north Indianapolis and Butler University. I was excited yet content knowing specifically that all I had to do was show up at the dorm and get my key. All the arrangements were made and a letter of confirmation was sent to me by the Athletic Department. I felt blessed and secure. Cruising down Meridian Street, I noticed all the beautiful mansions that lined the street. Landscaped yards, brick patios, and mostly brick homes – they must have been four to six bedrooms and multiple baths. When Denny and I traveled this route a few months earlier, I was so focused and I just wanted to get to the Fieldhouse that I didn't notice anything on the way. The northern suburbs of Indianapolis were beautiful.

Wow! All of a sudden we turned onto College Avenue and the Greek fraternities and sorority houses looked like European castles! Dad and I at the time just thought they were rich people's homes. Looking at the campus map I received on my earlier visitation, I located the men's dorm; it was proper just like the campus. I stood up slowly as I crawled out of the car and just stared at the magnificence of the limestone building. In fact most of the campus was built in limestone. It was like a 'New World' to me. As I stood there I will never forget the warmth of the late summer air and the beauty of my new home. After growing up in a modest two-bedroom home in a very middle class neighborhood of a blue-collar factory town, this new environment was like 'heaven on earth'.

Dad and I unloaded the car and carried my bags into the dorm. I checked into my room and after unloading everything I walked him back to the car. He had to drive back to Mishawaka and work early the next morning – so he was anxious. He got into the car, rolled the window down and as our family tradition was we always kissed our parents at bedtime or going away for any length of time (like overnight). Well dad stuck his head out the window for a kiss and I reached out my hand to shake his hand.

All because I didn't want any football players who might be looking out the dorm window to see me kissing my dad 'goodbye'. "How Stupid!" I should have continued the tradition as I did later in life. I felt badly for a few hours, and then I focused on getting my stuff in order as breakfast was at the cafeteria at 7:00 a.m. and practice reporting time was 8:30. I went to my room and still felt in awe of Butler University. My room was very quiet as only the football players who were living in the dormitory were there. My roommate was a basketball player, Francisco Denting, and he wasn't to arrive for two weeks when school started. Naturally I took the safe bed by the window. We had a basement room and I loved it.

Breakfast was like a banquet of fresh fruits, sweet rolls, pancakes, waffles, hash browns, ham, bacon, biscuits and gravy, sausage, and cereals (hot and cold). It was like a modern day buffet. Of course there were all kinds of juices, milk, tea and coffee.

I was a little nervous for practice so I did not overeat. Here's what I remember about that first meal. I was swept up by this charming upper classman who made me feel like a million bucks, a high draft choice. His name was Charles Anderson and he was a co-captain and a started at left tackle. He was so impressed that I was from Mishawaka H.S. and played tight end, and also basketball. He predicted that since our high school team was so good that I was going to be another Ken Freeman (who was my size and started 3 sports for 3 years at Butler). I told him that I wasn't going to play baseball, but that didn't slow him down. He excitedly introduced me to the other veterans as the next Ken Freeman. I was honored but a bit over whelmed – especially when the others said: "Dickson even looks like Ken Freeman!" Ken had graduated the previous year and was still on campus as he was going to assist with our frosh team as he finished his master's degree.

Soon I found out that I was being rushed by a fraternity recruiter and I am sure he liked me, but also he was trying to corral as many good football players as he could for Sigma Chi (they were the predominate football fraternity on campus). I was naïve and really did not know much about college life, as I was the first in my family to go away to college.

I remember Grandmother Dickson telling me (when I went to her house to cut her grass and say good bye a few days before leaving)…… not to join a fraternity. "You will become a wild drinking guy and forget what you went to college for!" My grandmother's both were very religious, two of my Dickson uncles went to college – and she was more aware of things than I was. Yet, even with this word from Grandmother Dickson, I joined Kappa Sigma. Boy did the beautiful welcoming come to a screeching halt! Anderson was still a good guy and friendly: One reason I joined as he said he would be my 'big brother' and watch over me and guide me through freshman year. I don't recall a lot of that, but what I do remember is immediately the pledges were headed together and informed they were the worker bees for several months. Just as all the actives had done. I was not prepared for this. I hated it!! In a month I informed "Mr. Anderson", as the actives are addressed, that I needed to leave as it was against my personal beliefs. He respected that and said that we would stay friends and enjoy our time on the team together. What a relief!!!

Frosh football was just amazing. Everything was better than I could ever expect. Our team marched through the league at a torrid pace beating Ball State 28-6, Indiana State 32-0, De Pauw 28-7, St.

Joseph 30-6, and I can't remember the other scores. Our coach was Pop Hedden - he was also the frosh basketball coach and the no. 1 recruiter for Tony Hinkle. Our first game was against Indiana State. Remember Ken Freeman and Don Benbow (a former All American at Butler who played with Freeman) were our assistant coaches. They really added a lot of class and motivation to Pop's old-fashioned tough guy approach. It was rumored that Coach Hedden would eat raw hamburger steak and grab the biggest guy on the team (that would be Tim Anderson – a 6-5, 290 lb. right tackle) and he would eat the meat in front of us as his conclusion of the pre game talk; and then grab this huge tackle and slam him into the locker bay – we were then told to "Go Kill those guys!" and rush down the tunnel leading to the Butler Field. It happened as predicted – Anderson was ready – and we all jumped up and the ordeal was over. Actually I thought it was a bit humorous. Coach Hedden was 5-6, very round, bald headed, but had a normally charming personality and nice smile. We won that game and our frosh team cruised through the season undefeated. My most memorable game was Ball State at Muncie, Indiana. Mom and dad came to the game. I started, we had a great team, and I would be opposing the All American full back from my Mishawaka High School team, Tom Fern. However, he told a friend of mine that he was third string as they were loaded at that position. Being highly motivated for that rival game, I had the best football game of my life: six tackles from my defensive end position (2 solo quarterback sacks). Also, I caught three passes before I got injured early in the second half. It was a horrible ankle injury and I was sandwiched by two blockers and bulled over by the burly fullback. Trainer Gene taped me up tight as Coach Pop Hedden said: "We need Dickson back in there!" I hobbled back in the game but lasted only one play. We won 28-6!

Basketball started early in October for those on scholarship and walk-ons. My roommate had a tuition scholarship for basketball. During the last week of football, Francis (my roomie) told me he was cut from the freshman team. Remember in the 1960's frosh could not play varsity at NCAA schools. Butler had a varsity (12 players), a junior varsity team that only played a few games and they were used as practice players. They were scholarship guys that did not make varsity at that point. Then, there was the frosh team.

Two of Coach Tony Hinkle's varsity coaching staff were running the basketball drills and scrimmages. The varsity and junior varsity were in the Fieldhouse – and the back gym held the frosh players. Long time assistant coach Bob Deitz was running the practices until the football season ended, and Dietz determined most of the rosters. He knew what type of players would fit into the Hinkle system. I knew I was getting a full ride for playing two sports, but I was concerned about making the team if they were cutting guys on scholarship. I talked to the frosh coach. He seemed to love me since my dad took about ten photos of him after Ball State game. He probably liked me because I always played hard. Anyway, I was elated when he told me that I was penciled in and would play a lot in basketball (this was definitely God's favor as I know he never saw me play high school ball). The next week five football players were invited to join the basketball team from our frosh football squad. Only the quarterback, Joe (a standout hoopster from Indianapolis Washington) and I survived the first cuts. We were the only two from football to play both sports (Butler preferred multisport athletes).

As I reflect on those early Butler days, I learned during my first few months as I listened to those close to the program (sports publicity director, equipment manager, the trainer): Butler recruited chiefly by referrals. And there were so many coaches out there in Hoosierland that were coached by Butler that he had a huge edge on the other Midwestern schools! This confirmed to me that Coach Chelmiciak delivered for me. He convinced Hinkle that I was to be the next Ken Freeman. Now, I know why Hinkle closed my meeting with him by "we're hoping to have you play year round for us: football, basketball, and baseball!" "We'll see!" I said this knowing I only played part league ball (actually more fast pitch softball than baseball). And in the spring in high school I practiced hoops. I never liked looking ridiculous swinging a baseball bat wildly at a sharp breaking curveball.

Chapter 6

"I felt at peace at Butler, as if God put me there."
Arriving back to my dorm room after another great meal (I was given meal tickets that allowed me to eat as much as I wished), it was difficult to hold back my excitement of being on the Butler squad as my roommate had been cut. He was on tuition only scholarship, as twenty-five frosh basketball players were on partial scholarships and twelve were kept. Scholarships at Butler were complex back then. We were D-1 in basketball and D-2 in football and other sports. Most players had tuition only scholarships. Just a few of us I later learned had full rides. Also, those with tuition scholarships had to do work projects for the University. My scholarship did not have that requirement. As I learned all this, I felt very blessed. My roommate, Francis, was on a tuition scholarship, but he was very depressed over not being able to participate. He told me that he was transferring at semester break. Grace College was in his hometown and he was going to transfer there to play (He did leave at break and was a starting point guard there for three years).

Assistant coaches at Butler were almost always Hinkle graduates. They were truly loyal to coach Tony Hinkle just as his players usually made strong bonds with him. Frosh coach Pops was no exception. He was fiercely loyal to the Hinkle way and he demanded hard work and absolutely no cockiness or shades of disrespect. He was short in stature but was burly, with a bald head that radiated especially when he smiled with satisfaction. I loved the guy, and I had his favor – guess I fit "the mold" as a "Bullpups" (nickname for frosh athletic teams).

Just as the frosh football team won the Indiana Collegiate Conference, our basketball team only lost one league game. We ran the Butler offense (A High Post motion offense) to perfection and we could all pass and shoot and scrapped on defense and rebounded the old fashioned way of blocking out and playing tough. We lost a game at Indiana State University and that was all! Guess what? Coach told me I was his sixth man and I would play more minutes than the starters. Like I said if you played your guts out – he was your loyal friend. Just like in football! I blocked so hard from my tight end position that they always ran the "power 6" play right off my block. Coach told me my job was to mow down the defensive line on my side. I took him literally and even "growled" like a bear when double-teaming with our huge RT tackle. He kept his word and I started every game for our undefeated football team. In Basketball he was equally loyal.

I remember this incident as if it were yesterday: Jeff, a highly touted high school star from Evansville was banging his slender 6-7 frame against me as we ran down the court. I imagine he was ticked that Pops had him on the second team. I was playing with Larry and the first unit. I told Jeff I would smack him if he didn't stop, he jeered and had a cocky look on his face. I just finished a tough and highly physical football season and was not going to let any gangly hoops star out muscle me. Larry was definitely the super star of our team He went on to start the years as the varsity point guard: he called for a high post screen and I got the opportunity to set a very physical screen on Jeff. He was flattened and Larry scored. Humiliated and frustrated, Jeff turned and cold cocked me with a wild swing at my face. It split the lower part of my tongue, but I didn't say anything just grabbed a towel as I was led downstairs to Gene Paskit, our trainer. Coach was irate and he suspended the cocky forward. They taped the tongue and I returned to practice to Pops' delight!

There were a couple other significant remembrances of that year:

One was the preseason game against the "Old Timers". Our frosh vs. all those former Butler stars. The most notable old timer was Bobby Plump, who was Jimmy in the classic movie "Hoosiers". My greatest thrill was I got to guard him for one quarter. He passed a lot and I was thankful for that!

The other was the Notre Dame game and the frosh teams from both schools were playing prior to the varsity game. My mother rode down to the game with my brother-in-law, Wayne Forrest. Like usual I came off the bench early in the half and hit my first shot, an elbow jumper. That game I took four shots and made all four, and went four for four at the line! By the end of the second half the gym was packed (18,000 cheering fans). Our Bull Pups won by four and I had a perfect shooting night! Mom, Wayne and I went to the popular burger place near campus "The Huddle" and enjoyed their famous patty melts. They dropped me off at the dorm and drove back home.

Basketball was over and I concluded a storybook freshman year in sports: My grades were over a 3.0 PT average and I got the only A in frosh composition class! Spring was beautiful on the Butler campus. Trees were budding beautiful flowers and there were flowers planted everywhere. A special area was "The Gardens" a beautiful walk down a stone walk from the Campus Club. Birds were singing all over. The air was even warmer than back home in northern Indiana. A river meadowed thru "The Gardens" and it was so peaceful! Romance was sure in the air as many coeds were now doing their studies on blankets in the closely trimmed spacious lawns in the Gardens.

Timeout:
I need to mention that during Orientation week, I got a glimpse of the most beautiful girl that I had ever seen.

Arriving early for the lecture by Dr. Usher, I found a seat six rows up near the door. As I settled in and opened my leather briefcase (my primary gift from high school graduation family get together) and took out notepaper and a pen. Just then Marta Christine Fassnacht walked in and took a seat two rows in front of me. I was drawn to her look and her spirit seemed calm and loving. Maybe it was just how pretty she seemed. Dr. Usher rambled on and on and I respected how this beautiful girl seemed so respectful as she listened. I couldn't remember a word he said – my mind was on this coed! That was in early September and now it was April and I never saw this girl again on campus. Until…..I was sitting in the C. Club with a couple friends (Bill, a football player from South Bend St. Joseph and a high school rival and Ron, a religion and music major). There it happened, two beautiful girls walked thru the club and I blurted out: "That's the girl from Orientation week 1".

Ron answers me: "I know her, she's in the dance department; her name is Chris". The next day he asked her if I could call her at the dorm. She consented and I called. Back then all dorm phones were in the halls – you called the dorm and the phone would ring in the hallway, someone would answer and I asked for Chris in room 110. The person answering brought me Chris and we talked a bit and she said she was a blonde and I said no…..I'm looking for a Chris with auburn hair. She exclaimed in horror: "You are looking for my roommate she is shorter and auburn hair". The first Chris seemed nice, and when I was told they were both walking through C-Club – I knew they were both very good looking. Yet….I was seriously attracted to the girl in Lecture Hall A, second floor of communications building on Orientation Day 1. When the second Chris got to the phone, I knew this was the girl of my dreams. In fact, she was even better….she had a sweet spirit. She was very different in so many ways. We talked nearly two hours that night, the next day we met for a coke in the C-Club and we were both attracted to each other. We even studied together on a blanket in the grassy lawns of the Gardens.

After Spring Break, dad suggested that I drive his Impala Super Sport back to campus and he would use my 1954 Chevy hardtop. It was a good solid car but the 1958 Chevy Impala Super Sport would be a real flashy car to take to Butler. It was a special make: All white, with Aqua interior, auto shift on the floor. Very sporty for back then! Ray Dickson was a very self-sacrificing man who gave his all for his kids!

Timeout!
Was this a mistake?

Dad originally told me that I could not take my car to Butler my first year until I showed that I could finish that year with high grades and do well in sports. He was smart for his limited education. Ray Dickson was street smart! Now, the year is only three-fourths over and he's offering me his car.....something's not right here. I did not even suggest it. Dad was becoming proud of what I was accomplishing with my life. At least he no longer gave reference to my lack of interest in home and auto repairs. (I did love cutting the grass and washing the car for dad). Simple physical, grunt jobs were good enough for me, as my real focus was academics and athletics. Still is!!! I loved all my years of teaching and coaching: The profession God had chosen for me.

Love was in the air, and I definitely was part of it! Chris Fassnacht and I had our first real date in that beautiful car. We went to the popular drive-in just north of campus off Rte. 31. We had great conversation and unfortunately I concluded the dining by spilling my cherry coke on my leg. Another date the next week, I drove to the girls dorm and drove her to the Gardens and we parked down there and talked some more – we had so many things that we shared with each other especially our families. Chris liked to smoke and I joined her for a couple Marlboros. This evening concluded with some warm kisses – no coke to spill tonight.

Finals were right around the corner and I became busier with some spring football workouts and studies. We didn't see each other much those last few weeks; yet I did see Marta Christine hanging with different boys when I passed through the C. Club. Was my storybook, first year college coming to a halt? A loneliness settled in my heart as I began remembering the coke dates and warm, down to earth conversations. Romance was totally new to me. Never read romance novels or dated heavily in high school. My dates previously had been very selective with some very pretty girls, but nothing long term.

That next summer I worked at Yellowstone Trailer Co. in Elkhart, Indiana. My brother-in-law, Kenny Wenger had worked there for years and they agreed to hire me as summer help. It was tough labor as I was challenged to keep up with the local Amish laborers who were really quick with their hammers as we built sidewalls. This job enabled me to have saved several hundred dollars for spending money at college. I did make one phone call to Chris Fassnacht in July and she seemed very excited that I called. She had a high school girl friend there, but we still talked for nearly an hour.

Summer soon came to a close and I had packed and headed back to Indianapolis and the mid August football drills. Sophomore year looked really good for me. I was selected as one of the 'Top Sophomore' prospects for the 1963-64 season! We went 8-1 for the season: undefeated in the league and only lost in the Grantlant Rose Bowl to Morehead State. Only one player from our undefeated frosh team played regularly – Dicky was a shifty runner as a punt returner and kick off returner. However, the other seven of the "Top Sophomore Prospects", we played regularly as substitutes for the seniors and juniors that Hinkle usually preferred to play.

I earned my letter sweater and was very satisfied. Earlier I said that romance was not a familiar game for me. Basically, I was confident in my appearance, but reserved in my approach. I think I believed that "whatever will be, will be," because God was in control. Therefore, I did not pressure Chris, but I thought we'd just naturally connect. When I did come across her in the C-Club she seemed attracted to this guy on the frosh football team. Immediately, I pulled back my emotions for her and focused on studies and rehabbing my inured ankle from football. The basketball season was already started and I was one of the three footballers who was expected to turn out that week. I pretty much had to sit out the drills, but it was amazing watching Tony Hinkle run practice. All of his drills led into his offensive and defensive schemes. He was a patterns master and eventually was heralded as a "Hall of Fame" college coach. Academically, I took two classes from Coach Hinkle and they were titled "Theory of Football", and "Theory of Basketball." What a wealth of information he packed into those classes! Basketball that sophomore year was very disappointing – the frustration really mounted when I kept reinjuring my ankle after attempting several comebacks. Highlighting that season was being able to watch "Hinkle, the master" run his practices and teach his motion offense, often referred to as "The shuffle". Always moving, always cutting, finding sharp, well planned passes; the players looked like they were performing a dance.

Timeout!

Is this leading to another bad idea, like the car at campus? That spring, Joe Purnich, Joe Dez and I all decided to join the Kappa Sigma fraternity. I liked it much better than the one I joined my frosh year that was mostly football players. Joe P. was a quarterback in football and a guard in basketball; I played tight end and defensive end and Dezelan was the center on offense in football. I guess we were highly recruited by the fraternity because of our sports successes. We had a great pledge class and I became the leader. My personality really became more outgoing and carefree. Drinking was a big part of the social life at Kappa Sigma. The president each spring hosted "Tuckers Wine festival" at a local gravel pit (they called it a swimming beach). I was very popular at the socials, which were mixers with the sororities. With my cool Chevy and being a Butler athlete, it was easy to get dates with some of the sweetest girls in the sororities.

Being socially active and not completely used to this freedom to drink as (remember my parents did not drink and none of my friends in high school), consequences piled up. I now lived in the fraternity house and had very little supervision. Was I on a downward spiral? Not familiar with the effects of alcohol ended up being a detriment to my future success at Butler. There were times when I would miss spring football meetings and practices and never once was called in by a coach. There was not a lot of accountability by the football staff either. Circumstances made it very easy to slide through the weeks that spring of 1964.

A friend told me that Chris Fassnacht was no longer going steady, and we ran into each other in the C-Club. We started dating heavily and I soon gave her my fraternity pin. Being "pinned" is like pre-engagement at Butler. She told me in our many talks that she knew that I was the one she could marry in the future. However, at that time I was not certain about her longevity at Butler. She told me that she was serious about becoming an American Airlines stewardess. My mind was on my dilemma, and not my student/athlete role at Butler. My grades slipped as I became careless in my study habits and life style.

Timeout!
Alan Stop the slide! You are losing!
A series of events occurred that spring that caused me to realize that what my professor in British Literature told me: "Alan you are now behind the eight ball in my class!" I was not aware of what this meant so I asked a fraternity brother and he told me bluntly: "You are going to fail his class no matter what you do the rest of the term." "Yikes!" I moaned, "I have never got an F in my life!"

My skipping that 8:00 A.M. class caught up to me. I thought if I just got an A or B on the final I would pass with ease. It did not work that way in his class. British Literature was a five credit semester class and in my major I would need to take this class over and the new grade would stick.

The slide was not over: Chris and I were in the library and I was completing a report for my "theory of track and field" class. We decided to head to C-Club for a coke. So I just ripped the final two pages of my library magazine out and put them into my notebook; I would finish this back at the house. Well, when I turned my report in the two pages of the pamphlet were accidentally stapled to the reports and "Butler University" was stamped on them. Dr. Walker, the track coach, called me into his office three days later and told me the following: "Alan, these pages were stapled to your report, did you take them from the library?" I answered him honestly and the slide became more severe….

Chapter 7

When you crossed over that line, when you became so self-pleasing and ignored His wisdom that used to bless your decisions – you were headed for trouble! Peace was being replaced with shame and regret. Self-confidence was still there, but it was from within my own mind – not the overwhelming confidence that I had experienced with God as my co-pilot. Things were different:

Time-Out: What am I doing?
I was not experiencing that overwhelming calmness
that permeated my spirit when I arrived at campus.
I had confidence from the All Powerful Person
from above who was always right with me.
I now was getting my personal strength and attitude
from my past accomplishment and successes and not
looking toward my heavenly source as my strength. I was
on the wrong path: The self-pleasing path to who knows
where? Would things get worse? Maybe I could turn
this around......I was overwhelmed and confused.

Back at Butler.............

Coach Walker did turn me in! I was scheduled to meet with the Ethics Board for scholarship students that next Monday. I sure didn't expect all this formality from what I originally deemed a minor infraction of library rules. That certainly was immature thinking on my part. I had really believed the issue would be dropped and Coach Hinkle would just call me in for a verbal reprimand. However, Butler was a first class institution of higher learning and academic justice would prevail.

Timeout: I got a break!

Apparently God was still right there: He allowed me to learn and the reprimand was not too severe. Since my record was good at Butler and this was my first infraction of any type, I only lost my board for one semester. No more free meals for one semester. The tuition and room would still be paid by the scholarship.

And the second semester of my junior year the scholarship would return to a full scholarship as long a I maintained a 2.5 or above G.P.A., and of course no miscues. My football buddies and my close friends at the Kappa Sigma fraternity encouraged me to be thankful that it wasn't worse. There was no cloud on my school record – just a financial take-away for one semester.

Timeout: What voice was my mind listening to?

Nevertheless, I kept thinking how could this happen to me? Rather than being grateful – I was upset. My pride was affected. My spirit had been tainted this second year at Butler. I was still Alan Dickson, with my personal qualities intact, but I was different inwardly. I did not recognize this then.

Timeout: Poor judgment continuous!

What I failed to realize is that I was taken care of as well as I could have been. It was a minor infraction that I let after my judgment.

Being "pinned" (going steady) to Christine Fassnacht was the most important thing in my life at this time. I remember that first glance at her during frosh orientation: I felt an excitement that I had never experienced. She would be my girl. It was now one and one-half years later and I claimed her for a permanent relationship. Everything else was definitely secondary. She was beautiful, fun, loving and easy to be with. We really "clicked" and it became a serious relationship right away. We often had serious talks, sharing our hearts to each other regarding God, family, and even philosophy of life! We seemed very compatible. There was, however, one serious roadblock: I was totally committed to this relationship, but it appeared that Chris seemed to desire the social life of college and maybe she was not as serious regarding our future as I was at that point. I was patient with her, but the fact that she spent hours in the C. Club hanging out with so many different guys and friends didn't seem right to me!!

Timeout: More Turmoil!

I chose to break off the relationship. Friends were always giving me reports of her social life. Maybe it was my pride, but this was not the way I expected the relationship to go. After much mental torment and anguishing over the situation, I called her that evening after 10:00PM (The campus rules for girls was a weekday 10:00PM curfew). She came to the phone in the hallway of the dorm and I told her what so many fraternity brothers and football buddies reported to me. Then I hesitantly said she did not value the relationship as I had hoped. So I broke it off and asked for my fraternity pin to be returned! It was decorated with pearls and other valuable gems. "Maybe we will get back together again", I suggested. And hoped.......When we first met for a coke date in the C. Club in Spring of 1963 we both later said that we felt we were meant for each other. So why is this happening now?

<u>Key Player - Sister Sharon:</u> The break up really affected me emotionally; in fact, I was in despair (I did not understand!) it was a serious relationship for me. My immature solution was to buy a bottle of Cherry Vodka from a little bar west of campus known to serve minors. I also grabbed a six-pack of Pabst Blue Ribbon (The KS Fraternities' favorite brew). Returning to campus where the campus security police allowed students to drink in their cars, I listened to the radio in my 1954 red Chevrolet. After becoming intoxicated, I was later told by my fraternity brothers that my car looked like a red streak racing around campus. Then I disappeared. My friends were concerned, they really seemed to care for me as I was the President of my pledge class at the fraternity. My leadership skills were starting to evolve, but not as God had intended.

I had driven to a downtown section of Indianapolis where I was so angered at what I had done that I beat my fists on the brick wall of a downtown building. I heard a voice; a calming, sweet angelic voice that said: "Alan, go home. Everything is all right!" A covering of love enveloped me. I knew I was safe in His presence. I sobered enough to return to the car and ventured carefully back to campus. Bloodied fists and glassy eyed I crawled into the top bunk of my bedroom at the Kappa Sigma House. For some reason a sweet presence engulfed me as I slept. Everything was going to be all right! There seemed to be an angelic presence in that bedroom.

Timeout!
Trouble at night, but peace came in the morning
At 8:00 AM Saturday morning my sister, Sharon Weldy called. I was awakened by the pledge on duty, Jon Marsh, a frosh basketball player. "Alan, what happened to you? We saw your car flying around campus last night! Are you OK? Your sister, Sharon is on the phone."

Sharon's first words echoed: "Are you OK?" I was up all night

46

praying for you!" I was overwhelmed, but very thankful, and then I proceeded to tell her the story. It was easy talking about your shortcomings to a person who had the heart of God. After talking to Sharon and eating breakfast I called Chris and we decided to meet at the Garden's lawn and study together as it was to be such a beautiful day. Chris brought a portable radio so we could listen to rock and roll music and the Indy Time Trials. She was so overwhelmed at what happened and my sister's timely phone call. She agreed that Sharon's intervention sent Angels to protect me. At this moment I was convinced Chris and I should be life partners.

Our relationship continued, she still had my pin, but soon another "bump in the road" was upon us. Chris decided to not return to Butler as a dance major: the demands seemed too great. Rather than switch majors and continue at Butler, she had heard American Airlines was recruiting in Indianapolis. She applied and was accepted. That left me returning to Butler in the fall minus the first real love of my life: my soul mate.

In the fall of 1964 I returned to Butler and met with the coaching staff and they agreed to red shirt me and give me a fifth year on my scholarship. Now I had options. Maybe I would transfer to another school, or decide to play out my years at Butler. They had moved me to middle linebacker and pulling guard on offense. Even though I was excelling at these positions, I let my flesh get in the way by telling myself that I was potentially a great blocking tight end with great hands. Rather than trusting that God was leading my coaches, I began to trust more in myself. My perception was clouded and voices in my mind were challenging me to show them that they were misjudging my true talent.

The spiral downward continued. Chris was now in Dallas training for the airlines job. I was not patient and made a recruiting trip to Ball State and they encouraged me to transfer and play my final two years there. I continued to work hard at the practices. I was no longer playing for God, family, and my school.....I was playing for myself. As a red-shirt player going against the top units I wanted to show them.

Weekends were tough for me. Chris asked her roommate at the dorm to keep an eye on me and she sure did! On weekends where we had no fraternity activities Marci and I went out drinking.

<u>Key Player, Indy police officer:</u> One Saturday evening I drank too much and we were at the Tepee Drive-in in downtown Indianapolis. Across the four-lane highway was the river that ran through Indy. I became so sick that I stumbled out of the car and crossed the highway and slid down the riverbank to vomit. After feeling better I crawled up the bank, and saw a police officer standing at the top of the bank shining a flashlight on me. When I reached the top I begged him to not report me to Coach Tony Hinkle. I pleaded: "Coach Hinkle will take my scholarship, and I will have to leave school!" He did not, but rather walked me safely across the interstate to my car.

At practices I was starting to really shine at middle linebacker. Perhaps my basketball skills and long arms were a natural for the pass defense where I really excelled. Loving contact and the ability to read the quarterback, made me a natural 6-3 and now 230 lbs. Just as I was starting to shine in football again and was taking a greater interest in my literature studies at Butler, another bad choice doomed me.

Timeout!

What were you thinking Alan? Were you even thinking?
Chris was coming to Indianapolis and I was going to drive her
to Bloomfield Hills, Michigan to meet her family. This means
I would be missing the game vs. Bradley University. They had
their No. 1 passer in the nation and I shined that week in
practice. However I reasoned: "They won't miss me, there are
100 players dressed and sitting on the bench. They'll think
I have a cold or something. I will tell Dezelan to tell them if
they are looking for me that I was sick back at the frat house."

Bad call Alan! When the players arrived to the dressing room at 11:00AM for the 1:00PM game, Coach Hinkle and Coach Hauss were calling out my name in the locker room. They had decided to take me off red shirting and start me!

Chapter 8

When I checked in by phone Saturday night after completing the six hour drive to Chris' home, my football fraternity brothers could not stop reprimanding me. Now I knew that I was really behind the 8-ball! I blocked my mind of the football problem that was awaiting me when returning back to campus, and had a great time spending the weekend at the home of my girlfriend. Deciding to skip my two Monday classes and leave Monday morning for the long drive back to campus, I had plenty of time to think: rather than face the situation that I created for myself back at Butler.

Back to the long drive to campus from Bloomfield Hills, Michigan, this gave me lots of time to think.

"I can turn all this for good," I thought.

My plan was to transfer to Butler's No. 1 rival – Ball State University. Butler had dominated the Indiana Collegiate Conference during the past several years and I was certain they would welcome me. In fact the Varsity Coach was good friends with my high school coach, Bob Heck, and had told him that they were interested in me if I chose B.S.U. instead of Butler!

Timeout!

What was I thinking? My situation had not changed that
much. Why was I going to leave and not trust God?!?!
The one semester probation and reduced scholarship
caused me to run rather than work my way through
the situation. My thinking was flawed.
I returned to campus that Monday evening. I finished that
football season and had very little interaction with the staff as
I now was looking in a new direction (unfortunately one that I
had planned – I did not consult God or my family in anyway).

Timeout!

It is amazing what pride and ego can do to damage you.
At the end of the semester I withdrew from Butler.........
Walking away from that full ride scholarship that I was so blessed
to receive. (Today, I look back at that being so irresponsible of me –
and ungrateful.) I hardly said good-bye to my fraternity brothers,
football and basketball teammates, and my friends on campus.

Ball State did offer me an opportunity and I had this vision
that I was going to be a premier tight end there; and a stalwart on
defense....But the opportunity at B.S.U. was not a guarantee of
any sort – it was a gamble. My pride was leading me in the wrong
direction. At Ball State I would have to pay my first year and then
if I made the traveling team (TOP 33); I would be on scholarship
(possibly full). What a gamble!

Timeout!

When I told the coaches about my transfer they did
propose a marriage apartment arrangement if Chris
and I decided to stay. What was up with me??

After meeting with the coaches there at B.S.U., I was given the opportunity to stay at Coach Freeman's house. He was a varsity assistant. His son Timmy was also sitting out that season as a transfer. Tim was a three hundred plus defensive tackle. The plan was set and it was now January, so I would return home to Mishawaka to work and save money for tuition and board the next year.

Chris was now working in Chicago at American Airlines. She requested that location to be close to my home in Mishawaka, Indiana. Hometown Finance Co. offered me a job as assistant manager. It was a salary and easy hours. Just had to take loan apps and collect on bad loans. This was hard for me as I often felt sorry for those poor people in South Bend who took high interest loans just to survive. I wrote good applications but was a poor debt collector. In addition, I would take night classes at Indiana University (South Bend Campus) to keep my credits moving forward. Chris and I were able to spend many weekends together as the drive to Chicago was less than two hours. However, soon I decided to propose to Chris and exchange the fraternity pin for a diamond engagement ring. My future was challenging but exciting. Yet, little did I know that moving on your own; not consulting God could lead down a bumpy road. I remember asking her to marry me as we were walking to her apartment from the parking lot. I felt we needed to both make a total commitment. She seemed both excited, but somewhat unsure of that serious of an arrangement. Her face looked nervous, but we were engaged and I felt secure that this was my true love.

Soon summer was ending and the Ball State staff did arrange for me to house at the home of their freshman coach, Tubby Smith. I enjoyed the classes and the opportunity to do drills and workouts with the Varsity football squad. Being ineligible to compete that year, it was hard to watch the games. That winter a couple of former Mishawaka High athletes and I formed an Intermural Basketball team: Denny Baldwin (a scholarship QB in football there and a great high school basketball player), and Mike Hughes (high school football standout) became great friends and we had a lot of fun as we dominated their Intermural Basketball League. It looked as if my college basketball career was over so this Intermural League was a great opportunity to play hoops again.

Being a few hundred miles from Chicago while at Muncie Indiana, Chris and I seemed to be growing apart and I became concerned when one of her roommates told me she was out dancing a lot at a local club. After hearing this a couple times; it really bothered me. I asked Mike Hughes to drive to Chicago with me as I needed to break off my engagement. Driving all the way to the N.W. suburbs of Chicago from Muncie, Indiana was a trek.

Timeout!
When you know God is involved, why doesn't everything go smoothly? Maybe we weren't walking with Him.

I had called Chris and told her to be there as we were coming. Mike and I stopped at a bar on the way and drank a beer – I think I needed to get my courage up! Mike Hughes was two years behind me at Mishawaka High and his older brother told me he always looked up to me as a football and basketball player. In my mind I think the inflated ego was still ruling me.

Timeout!
Why didn't I pray and counsel with her?
Chris met us at the door of her apartment. I asked her to come outside to the parking lot as Mike uneasily returned to the car.
"Chris", I said. "We cannot stay engaged because you have disrespected this engagement! I want my ring back!"

She got tears in her eyes and started crying. She gave me the ring and I started walking back to the car. Chris came sprinting to me and jumped on my back. She was 5'3" and 105lbs. And I was

6'3" and 220lbs. She blurted: "Please, don't leave let's talk!" It didn't happen.

Timeout!

I was just trying to straighten her out. I expected a
reconciliation call the next day. Mike and I drove back to
Ball State that dark night. Chris and I didn't talk again
for two months. (Are you just on your own? Has God left?
Where's the peace? Isn't anything working out anymore?)

I really missed her but I accepted the fact that maybe I should look around and I did date some BSU girls. Mike Hughes later fixed me up with his girlfriend's best friend and this seemed a good fit, a Mishawaka girl. Over Christmas break Chris called me at home in Mishawaka. She wanted to come to town and visit. After a wonderful dinner my mom prepared, Chris and I told mom and dad we were going out for a couple hours. I knew she'd like a rock in roll band; we went to a club in South Bend (I was not comfortable going to a bar in Mishawaka, my image was still important to me). It was great to be back together, but we both drank too much. We got back to my parents home around 1:00 A.M.

As I drove Chris to the bus to go back to Chicago and her American Airlines job the next morning, I told her that I was dating a frosh at St. Louis University who was a Mishawaka girl. I was confused and unsure of my feelings, but I knew I was in love with Chris. Just as when we first met. I was meaning to pay her back with this statement, which was true at the time. However, in reality Chris meant way more to me. I was looking for a different "fit" for my wife – but my heart was still with Christine. Well, apparently I really hurt Chris after telling her this and I did not hear from her until nearly three months later and the call came with some shocking news.

Timeout!
God had to mold both of us into the couple that He
intended us to be from our first meeting that frosh year
at Butler University. What Satan meant for evil, God has
repaired and blessed. We were both so in love, but the
world can sure cause you to take the bumpy road.

After returning to Ball State spring drills began and I was
motivated to shine. After all, my Butler team dominated at Indiana
Collegiate League and I felt Ball State was lucky to have me. Soon
I realized that I was in a battle to prove myself. But, I began to
second-guess my decision to transfer from Butler. All they did was
take a portion of my scholarship for one semester, and they put
me at middle linebacker and offensive guard. I was a determined
blocker and had this mentality to shine at linebacker. What was I
thinking?", I thought. I even gave up the opportunity of continuing
my basketball career at Butler.

Timeout!
Why didn't I make it work at Butler?
They were committed to me.

After three months when I did hear from Chris, she was in a
hospital near Park Ridge, Illinois. She went in for a minor surgery
and the doctor told her she was three months pregnant. That was
a Friday, so I left for Chicago, Illinois. We needed to talk! Surgery
went fine and she was still pregnant. After a long and thoughtful
drive home to Indiana that evening, my brother-in-law, Bud Weldy,
met with me for breakfast that Saturday morning. His advice was
everything will be fine if you marry as long as you both put God
first and bond your love through Him. Chris and I met later that

weekend at a Pancake House and talked for several hours and I shared what Bud had said. Chris' comment was that she always wanted to be close to God. And her dream was to have a Christian family. On May 7, 1966 we were married. Bishop David Rowe conducted the wedding. Guess what his marriage counseling was: "Put God first and you will have a wonderful marriage."

Well, I finished up my studies at Ball State and made a decision to transfer again to Bethel College in my hometown of Mishawaka, Indiana. Bethel had four former high school stars returning: hopefully, I would be the fifth starter. My good friend from high school, Denny Wood was on the basketball team there and he convinced me that I could be the missing link in rebuilding the Bethel Pilots! It worked!

Chris and I settled into our new house; the den apartment of this brick mansion on the cliffs of the St. Joe River in downtown Mishawaka. Bethel did not offer athletic scholarships, but I was able to get a job at Dodge Motor – working the midnight shift in the foundry. One of the board members of Bethel College was the personnel director at the large factory. Denny Wood was also able to get a job there. He was a night custodian and I worked in the foundry at the dip tanks and the paint booth. My new schedule was work from midnight to eight in the morning. Then I went home and showered for my nine o'clock class. After classes, I studied at school until basketball practice then home for dinner, more studies and bed at 8:00 P.M. and up at 11:15 P.M. and off to the foundry job at Dodge. The schedule was grueling but I felt a peace that my life was on track: The direction of my new life was secure. In His guidance. It was as though I was where He wanted me to be. Bethel College was perfect for me.

Key Player Don Granitz: Coach Don Granitz was a mature man of God and he was very happy to have me.

Timeout!
My passion for basketball was reborn!

I loved basketball; it was my true passion. After a couple games I was inserted into the starting line-up and we had a super year. Bethel College's best season to date. Our team averaged nearly 93 points per game without the 3-point line. We had amazing scorers – very skilled shooters and ball handlers. I had a really solid year averaging 14.8 PTS and 10.2 rebounds per game (50th in nation NAIA schools). We had six players averaged in double figures. I was so thankful to be on the court again. (I was injured in football my sophomore year at Butler and could not participate in practices, only watch). I played so hard no one was going to out hustle me at practice and the games: every loose ball and re bound was mine! I was not going to blow this opportunity. This was my passion, and I fully realized it.

Most importantly, Coach Granitz mentored me as a player, a young father and as a future Christian leader. He was such a blessing to me. And Bethel College (especially my English professors) made me feel protected for the one and one-half years there. These professors were highly intelligent and with genuine Christian principles. The chapel services and the Christian environment provided an opportunity to heal and get prepared for His service.

<u>Notes on Bethel:</u>

<u>Key players:</u> Coach Don Granitz, Dr. Rainer English department (No. 1 men's basketball fan and score keeper)

The nurturing I received from Coach Granitz and Dr. Rainer was key to my success as a player and student becoming a starter for Bethel College meant so much to me as my real passion was to be a high school coach and have a strong relationship with my team (just like Coach Jellicoe – my frosh year at Mishawaka High School). Playing with the Holmes' brothers from Madison Township High

School, Jack Edison from Greene Township, Denny Wood and Jim Sili from Mishawaka High School (they were two years behind me at Mishawaka). And don't forget Everett Walterhouse who was the seventh leading scorer in the state of Indiana that year; an ex marine, who had played three years for the marines team before attending Bethel College. We were loaded, and Coach Granitz led me to believe that I was the missing link and they could use my two years of basketball experience under Coach Hinkle at Butler University. And my three years of collegiate football, prepared me to battle on the boards as I ended up in the top 50 rebounders in the nation at 10.2 per game (N.A.I.A.)

That year at Bethel was so rewarding. I fought my way back; I turned my spoiled athletic career around. Sure I ended up at a small Christian College instead of nationally known Butler University. Sure I had to work two years on the night shift at Dodge Manufactory Corporation in Mishawaka. I was so satisfied. God gave me the strength, drive, and passion to complete the task. These experiences those two years were so meaningful to my future in my career.

Timeout!
I believe the two years of working nights at the
factory, taking College classes, and playing basketball
at Bethel brought me back to trusting God.

Coach Granitz and Dr. Rainer inspired me to have an impact on the world.

Just as I played so hard – like never before at Bethel. Every loose ball was mine. I owned that ball whether on the backboard or bounding on the floor! Then, I really enjoyed the team plays that we executed that year at Bethel. I believe Jack Edison, our point guard, was the key. He could have scored 20 plus points per game, but he would rather gain 10-12 assists per game. He was unselfish and we became such as unselfish team. The Holmes brothers, and Denny

Wood were all pure shooters. Denny was also a clever passer – just like Edison. By the way, Denny offered to come off the bench so I could start! We were best friends from high school and he read my mind and knew I needed that. He still averaged 12.0 off the bench. That entire team played as one. We didn't realize but our 93.2 PPG was a record for several years and we were the team that got Bethel Basketball on track. Later in the 70's, 80's, 90's Bethel won a number of National titles. I believe that team helped build the foundation of a national power in the NCAA division. Equally as important to me, my foundation was rebuilt to enable me to minister as a teacher and coach. My confidence was renewed and my faith was strengthened as I realized God was there all the time helping me when I needed Him to continue the call that He placed in my life.

Chapter 9

Spring in Mishawaka, Indiana is a dramatic change from the harsh winter months; however, my job working the night shift at the foundry kept me very warm and then I skirted home for a hot shower and to the warm classrooms and of course the gymnasium. It was a grind but I gained so much from playing a vital role as a starter on a college team with great teammates and a coach we all loved. Coach Granitz was a true missionary at heart and the love he showered us with won us over. It was a fantastic experience!

Timeout!
Remember Bethel College was founded as a Missionary School.

As the flowers broke forth with their beauty and the trees began to blossom – I became aware that I needed to spring forth and pursue my career. College would be soon over and all I needed was a student teaching experience that summer to be a certified teacher. It was 1968 and Chris and I began a mass mailing of resumes and letters of interest to nearly thirty Detroit area school districts. Most of these districts would not have actual openings until May or June when teachers resigned, transferred to other areas or retired. However, we did receive six or seven encouraging return letters asking me to complete an application. Curiously, I received zero interest from the

City schools of Detroit (my main interest was inner city teaching). I wanted to make an impact on the lives of inner city students.

Timeout!
Why pick Detroit area? My very large and very close
family all was around Mishawaka, Indiana.

Chris and I had a peace about moving to the Detroit area. Her parents had a beautiful ranch home on two acres and a cottage right on Lake Huron. They had no other grandchildren and the extra help would be really helpful. While I was finishing my final days of classes at Bethel, Chris received a phone call from the Avondale School District in Auburn Heights, Michigan.

"Hello, is this Mrs. Dickson? This is Hobart Jenkins from
Avondale School District, in Auburn Hts., Michigan. Is
Alan there?" "No, he is at school finishing up his classes!"
she replied. "Well, we are very interested in talking to
Alan about a teaching and coaching assignment at the
Senior High. We like his size for an English teacher!"
When I got home that afternoon my wife greeted me at the door very excitedly. And she had a smirk on her face when she told me about the remark about my size for an English teacher.

"Guess what, Alan? You will be teaching remedial
English classes." I thought to myself: "this will work
fine....I might be able to do something for the kids.
It will be another challenge....and it's a job!"

Timeout!
The seed of molding lives was placed in me back then and grew
for the next forty years. And it's still there in my retirement
days. It's my calling.....it is what gives me the most satisfaction!

During my two years of going to Bethel and working at the Dodge Mtg. Corp. Foundry – we were able to pay for all my schooling and take care of our own two boys (Matthew and Marc). In addition, we had enough money to make $65.00 a month payments on a beautiful 1965 Chevy Impala Super Sport Convertible: Royal blue with a white top. It was just a couple years old.

Now it was time to pack that car and go check out Avondale Senior High School, and hopefully sign a contract. I would be so thankful: a salary, sick days with pay, and all the benefits plus great school vacations. Working so hard to complete school while working nights at Dodges' taught me what the real world was like. I really entered the teaching world with the attitude that I was a public servant commissioned by God to make the world better. Now to get my first job became a must do!

After returning from the visit at Avondale, we returned to our small apartment in Mishawaka as I had one final hurdle before getting my degree in August. Student Teaching for me was the only class I needed to complete to get my teaching certificate at Bethel. I was assigned a classroom of students who had all flunked during the school year. This was going to be tough. It was summer school and the class ran from June 10 – August 4, 1968. I just needed to complete this class and I was ready to take on that job at Avondale Senior High in Auburn Heights, Michigan. I was ready and excited for this challenge.

I walked into South Bend Adams High School that Monday morning. I was to meet with the regular teacher at 7:30 A.M. and my class began at 8:30 A.M. Basically he told me that he would be there everyday, but he would be in the teachers' lounge. As the student teacher I was put in charge on Day 1. The class was composed of thirty kids who really did not want to be there. The material was not exciting to most of those students: Grammar and Composition 101. Students in the class were racially diversified, and some had participated in various student riots the previous year. The class challenged me that first week and it took all my courage to show up each day, but I knew God was there with me – He gave me a vision of my future and a passion to complete this assignment and move on to the next! I have to admit that this hot, humid summer was taxing on my body, as I stood in front of these students for two hours of Grammar and Composition daily. It was standard to wear a dress shirt and tie and I would sweat through my shirt daily, as there was no central air conditioning back then. All I really remember is standing behind the podium and looking out at a group of students who were just waiting for me to say something wrong. My only incident that summer was when this African American girl said I was racist because I didn't call on her first when others had their hands up. She started talking back really loudly and I about fainted. Just then the Assistant Principal in charge of summer school walked by in the hallway and called her outside telling her:

"Mr. Dickson is a fine young teacher and does not
have one racist bone in him. Show him respect
or you will be dropped from this class."

Then, he called me into the hall and told me that she was guilty of throwing acid in a Vice-Principal's face during the student riots a year earlier. She never smiled at me the rest of the summer, but I continued to assist her and she passed the class. Overall, I felt very successful with that difficult student teaching experience. It was hot, humid in the room, students hated Grammar and Composition, and their skills were very low. Nothing would ever be as difficult as this assignment. Now I was ready for Avondale Sr. High School.

Timeout!

Thank you God for sending ministering angels to get
me through a very tough inner city student teaching
assignment. I hope I had some impact on those
students. As I now reflect, it is all that really mattered;
besides of course improving their writing skills.

Chapter 10

Welcome Home

Those first two years at Butler with the glowing blessings poured upon this student/athlete from blue-collar town of Mishawaka, Indiana were absolutely wonderful. The downward stride from favor that third year and the regrettable transfer to Ball State are behind me now. My final year at Bethel College guided me back on course. I'm now where God originally intended me. He was there with me all along the journey. He guided me back on track and turned Satan's detour into His glory. It was quite a journey, but I wouldn't trade it for the entire world. I was at Avondale Sr. High School in Auburn Heights, Michigan: Teacher and Coach. In fact, I was assigned three coaching jobs. Through all the previous highs and lows, I was now ready to give my all to my new world.

Avondale School District was located about twenty miles north of Detroit. This was September 1968 and Detroit was just reeling from the effects of racial riots of that time. I was appointed head ninth grade football coach that first year. The school failed previous levies the past two years and this would be the first year with football in a while. They had Varsity and Junior Varsity teams, but nothing at the junior high level at that time. So, we started with a team of inexperienced football players (they had only played flag football). Our league was the Oakland A League (comprised of basically 4-A and 5-A schools). The Varsity had been 0-9 the previous year, and there was a loser mentality flowing through the school. Always having been blessed with faith and optimism, I relished this challenge!

Timeout!
God was smiling down on me. Angels were all around blessing my work. Ministering to me.

Likewise, I had a challenge in the classroom those first weeks of school. The first week went very smoothly; some of the experienced teachers and the principal mentioned that I was so relaxed and a natural teacher. My confidence grew rapidly that first week. My discipline was excellent considering four of my five classes were loaded with potential dropouts and students from "the wrong side of town".

I loved this challenge and it was obvious God had given me "the gift" because it was working. I attached myself to the kids and they knew I cared about them. It was a family atmosphere. It was too good to be true. Toward the end of the second week (actually, it was a Friday morning), something happened that rocked the boat!

My second period Basic American Literature class was filing into the second floor classroom. This group was probably my least friendly and polite group (I think I am being very generous in my description). A large number had failed this class last year. It was a REPEAT! They weren't excited. Now, I could have come up with some creative projects, but this was my second week of my first year. I was definitely by the book. White shirt and tee, jacket on until later when it was sweltering from late August and Early September heat. No air conditioning – to survive you had the screenless windows open halfway. This was the dilemma! The third young man filing in was John Hartly, a very unhappy student. Everyday he glared at me, like he hated teachers. I believed I could help and motivate this class. I greeted John in a friendly voice as I did others. When John walked to his desk in the back row (He wanted that seat and

I felt safer with him there), he flipped the book on his desk out the window. Unfortunately, I viewed the entire act. What am I to do?!?

Remembering back on that day: Avondale Senior High School was about 20 miles north of Detroit, Michigan. In 1968 the student population came from a combination of middle class factory workers, upper middle class and upper class executive, sales, etc. However, there was perhaps ten percent from a "Red neck type of family". I was alerted of this when I interviewed. The school was not very racially diversified! The "red neck" types had settled in the town area of Auburn Heights years ago. As the Auburn Hills area was becoming more expensive and suburban. These small, rough looking small houses in town seemed out of place.

My first year was going beautifully. I felt called to teach, I was very comfortable in the classroom. This was so much better than that dirty foundry at Dodge Mfg. and the Amish trailer factories where I worked during the summer at Butler. Grammar was my expertise and Literature was interesting to study and present. The pay was $6,900 and I picked up another $1,100 coaching three sports. (9th grade football, 8th grade basketball, and J.V. baseball at the high school. We appreciated the pay, but rent was higher in the suburbs of Detroit then back home in Mishawaka, Indiana.

Back to my second week incident – Out of the corner of my eye I noticed John, a tall, dark haired young man looking at me out of the corner of his eye. He seemed up to something. As I greeted the students, John only grunted as a return greeting. I kept my eye on him. He literally tossed a literature book out the window, then he sat down with a smirk on his face.

Timeout!
"Why did this have to happen now? Everything was going so smoothly. Maybe I was never called, I didn't want to be a 'police' type teacher".

Now I have to do something. I went over to John's desk and quietly asked him why he tossed the book. "John, if you go get the book right now, I will drop the issue if the book is O.K." I quietly spoke the words to him. John responded by boldly stating that he did nothing and don't call him a liar! I told him either step out in the hall and go to the office or I will call Mr. Marzell, assistant principal to the room (each room had a classroom phone). I called Mr. Marzell and he came to the room and escorted John to the office.

Mr. Marzell, the assistant, was previously in the Detroit Catholic Schools and believed in strong discipline. He was very moral and spiritual, a man of character. I was an optimist out to change the world. This situation was tough.

After meeting Mr. Marzell after school, he told me the dad came in and was a tough red neck type who said his son does not lie and he refused to pay a .50 cent fine for the "repair" of the book. Making a long story short, John was never held accountable (The school board supported his dad). Mr. Marzell and I both seriously considered going to another district or dropping out of education. We both stayed, we had families and could not just quit. In a few weeks things were back to normal; John's class never really came around. But, my other classes were rewarding, and my ninth grade football team was really rolling!

Timeout!
I survived Satan's plot to discourage me. My
passion came on very strong later that year.

Avondale Sr. H.S. had not won a varsity game that year. The Junior H.S. dropped football five years ago. The football guys had to join flag football clubs. So my first team was comprised of inexperienced aspiring athletic athletes. Yet, I saw their size, builds and their determined look. They were hungry. We had sixty-five 9th grade boys sign up to play. Wow – 65 – and one coach to manage these numbers. Once again I was ready for the challenge!

Basically, I ran practice from the center of the field during station work. I would run back and forth to opposite ends of the field to guide linemen and backs at opposite ends. Needless to say, I was exhausted, but it felt good! The second week the husband of my wife's high school friend volunteered to help. Eddie Buckaweitz was so enthusiastic and his specialty was kicking (my worst skill).

Timeout!
I don't mean to brag here – I just now
realized He's guiding my passion.

Bingo! We won our first six games! The seventh game was against the powerhouse of this Oakland A League (mostly 4-A schools). We lost that game. We were tough and executed our power offense I learned at Butler University very well. But Utica was loaded with superior athletes. They had a 10.0 100 yd. dash trickster running back kick offs. He scored on a reverse on the opening kick-off. We fought the entire game and eventually lost 33-14. We played as a team and were beaten by a better squad that night. Both teams were undefeated, our A.H.S. 9th grade squad was drawing more fans than the Varsity, so we were given the game under the lights. It was classic.

A humorous incident about Utica's athletic director and my father-in-law occurred that night! Both teams were warming up and the fans were filling the stands. It was a perfect early fall Midwest football evening. The competitive juices were flowing through my veins and it seemed to fire up the team. Utica seemed very organized and polished as they zipped through warm-ups.

Meanwhile in the press box George Fassnacht, my father-in-law, and the Superintendent of Utica Schools were in a vigorous debate over who was going to win this battle of the unbeaten! George offered to make a $100 bet, but of course the Superintendent backed off. My wife was humiliated at this (incident). Our A.D., Dick Bye was great at breaking up the tensions in the press box.

Utica scored at the opening kick-off. Welcome to the real world of coaching Alan. I was not full of pride – just confident and believed in my players. I never quit and neither did the guys. The final score was 33-14. We left it all on the field and were way thrilled to have a winning of six to one season!

Timeout!

Thank you Lord for being there with me guiding my first experiences coaching my very own team! I rapidly knew coaching was my passion and I was in the seventh heavens. All that great coaching I had at Mishawaka High, Butler, and Bethel College, had prepared me for this work.

I can't wait to share this story about my ninth grade football squad: My frosh year at Mishawaka High my coach Mike Jellicoe taught our undefeated and nearly unscored on football squad to be like a family. We were told to be so close that if one got in a fight – all of you were to join the fight! Realizing that coach was speaking figuratively, I thought others would take it to the sauce! Not my football squad, I repeated that same pep talk to my team and they apparently took it seriously. It was a warm Friday afternoon one week before the Utica game. There was an assembly at the junior high and a visiting rock band was part of the festivities. A large contingent was with the band and as this group was leaving the building a couple of the band members picked a fight with Teddy Clark (our smallest lineman – but definitely the toughest!) Well as coach said "You all jump in!" The battle became huge! I was called by the principal's secretary to get down there.....NOW! The principal at my school covered my class and I rushed down there. I was the only person who could call this off. The junior high principal was a former high school coach and as I told him what I had said to the team, he liked the concept, but not the incident. However, he protected my team and me from any consequences. And we all wrote it off as a learning experience. The fight was more of a showing type and no injuries occurred. Oh for the old days of reason and old-fashioned judgment in the public schools.

Chapter 11

The second year at Avondale High School found me promoted to Junior Varsity basketball coach, offensive coordinator of the Varsity football team, and Varsity baseball Coach. Life was good! Principal Joe Coe gave me my own classroom and I now felt like a major contributor at the school and the community. A strong passion for coaching and working with the students in the classroom fueled my energy. My social life was my wife and I socializing with the coaching staff and teachers after the football and basketball games. We were not attending any church as I mostly rested on Sundays and neither Chris nor I felt drawn to attend. We did go to church with my family in Mishawaka, Indiana when we visited on a weekend.

In early March that year Bud and Sharon Weldy with their children visited us for the weekend. I believe they were hoping to help get us into a church. Sunday morning we went to visit a church in the western suburbs of Detroit. Bud knew the visiting evangelist who was speaking that day. Scotty Teets was a compassionate speaker and as he concluded his message to about four hundred in attendance, he spoke the words "Somebody here needs to come forth as God has called you and you will lead many to the Lord". For some reason I believed it was me. Yet, I was not ready, my life was full and very enjoyable as it existed. Standing with Bud and Sharon my mind was bombarded with the preacher's words. Maybe I should have gone forward. There was a pulling at my heart. It was that same drawing that I experienced as a young boy at that Saturday night prayer band.

Just as we were ready to leave Scotty Teets walked right up to me in the back of the church and said, "You were the young man that I was talking about. My sister Sharon also mentioned that she felt like God was talking to me! In my heart I witnessed to the same.

We went out to eat, and the Weldy's left for Indiana. All that Sunday afternoon I thought about the evangelist's words. "God has called you to do a mighty work." My wife Chris was not experiencing my same feelings. I made a decision to attend the evening service to hear the evangelist again. As I was leaving Chris was very upset that I was going back. In all fairness she probably thought I was going to quit teaching/coaching and become an evangelist or Pastor. (We don't all get called at the same time, her time was coming). That evening at the conclusion of the service, I went forward and prayed. A young man from the University of Michigan graduate school ministered to me at the altar. Then, a remarkable spiritual experience followed as I walked around the church, with hands raised to heavens and "spoke in tongues" for nearly an hour. Never once did I open my eyes! I saw a vision of Jesus and the clouds opened and He stood in front of me in a very bright light. This was real and I never doubted the experience. When I came back to myself from over an hour of communicating with God by marching around those aisles with eyes closed and hands raised, hardly anyone was there. The pastor and a few others said it looked like I had a glorious experience, I sure did! I wanted to thank the University of Michigan student for sticking with me and not letting me leave the altar when God didn't seem there at first. His counsel was vital to my future. He was gone. The evangelist was gone. When I drove home that night, I was filled with the Holy Spirit that was so vital for my challenges ahead in my life.

Chris was not ready for my newfound passion for Christ. (Satan's messengers must have really affected her thinking). I was not really going to do anything different, but I was "on fire" for God and it was exciting for me. However, she was fearful that I was a threat to our marriage. A spiritual battle arose as I was not patient with her confusion.

In a few struggling weeks, I compromised and cooled my passion. Yet, I could not understand why Chris did not want a very spiritual husband.

Timeout!
I was a novice Christian and knew nothing of the battlefield of the mind, inherit in the Christian walk. Yet God was still in control; He was right there once again!

Soon I became very ill during the baseball season. The infirmity in my colon that threatened my health as a sixteen-year-old student/athlete came back and was ravaging my body. I had met with a specialist and was given a heavy dose of prescriptions to heal the colon. After a few weeks I seemed to be worse. After an examination with another specialist at a local hospital, the doctor scheduled me for removal of the large intestine. He said the disease had spread throughout my large intestine and was affecting part of the small intestine. This was a Friday and surgery was scheduled for the next Tuesday. Sunday morning Chris and I were sitting on the couch watching T.V. the boys were in bed and we discussed my prognosis. All of a sudden Chris blurted out to me: "You find one of those churches like the one you grew up in and go and get healed!" Then she proceeded to empty all my prescription medicine for the colon into the toilet and flushed it! Next, we looked in the phone book for a church. We found two near us and I was not certain which one to visit for prayer.

Timeout!
I was taking thirty-two pills a day, and we just flushed them away. They were expensive. What was she thinking? Chris calmly said, "The medicine is not helping you! Let God heal you! Looking back I can now say that her Christian Science background led to her faith in healing.

It was now Sunday afternoon and I decided to follow her leading. At six o'clock I headed north on Livernois Rd. as both churches were in that direction. Just as I approached Sixteen Mile Rd, I heard a voice: "Go to the church on the right"

I immediately followed that voice and after a few blocks down the road, a beautiful white country church appeared on the right hand side (Troy Christian Apostolic). Music was flowing from the organ and piano from inside the church to the parking lot. I definitely felt the presence of the Lord as I left my car in the lot. As I entered the building I walked straight up the center aisle as the service had begun a few minutes earlier. Being drawn by the presence of the Lord as I entered His Chapel, I knew that I found peace in the midst of my trial.

This particular Sunday evening service was a youth revival service. It was perfect for me; many passionate teens shared their testimonies. There was an honest and open atmosphere and I enjoyed as the young people shared. At the conclusion of the service, David Abbott, the youth pastor introduced Pastor Spencer and they had an altar call that requested any person who needed a touch or even a miracle form God to come forth. I never hesitated as I went to the front with ten others. When the elder laid hands on me and asked what I needed, I shared my health situation. David Abbott said to me in a very confident voice: "Alan, Brother Stanley has had many miracles in his ministry!" My faith elevated within my mind and spirit as he spoke that sentence. When asked by David Abbott if anyone would like to share a possible healing, two of us spoke to the audience. When it was my turn, I shared that I didn't know if God healed my serious intestinal bleeding, but I was so thankful that I felt close to the Lord once again. After the service I asked to speak to Pastor Stanley. While in his office I asked him: Should I fast tomorrow to promote my healing?" He replied: "Alan, that is not necessary, but it would be an option. Follow God's leading." I did fast the next day at work and as the morning passes as I was teaching my classes, my faith grew as I was experiencing no pains. At the end of the school day I went to the baseball field to coach my Varsity squad. While sitting in the clubhouse watching a team scrimmage, my manager Keith Weston offered me a stick of gum, which I quickly devoured. Then I quietly disposed of it as I was fasting; I explained to Keith why I didn't continue to finish chewing the gum. He seemed very interested in my prayer experience and the concept of fasting (that I observed at an early age in my home church).

A major miracle occurred at that Sunday night youth service~ I was healed! I never bled again. This was miraculous. Now, I believe it was Pastor Stanley's faith that rubbed off on this young teacher/coach. The next Wednesday evening there was a mid week service and I couldn't wait to attend. Chris and our two boys came with me as I shared my healing testimony. It seemed to inspire the entire church. In fact, we later learned that all eleven that went forth that night were healed.

Equal to my passion to coaching and teaching was my new passion to share Jesus with others. Later that spring I was asked to serve as youth pastor in the Troy Church. Several of my students at Avondale Senior High had recently been saved at a Baptist Church near the school and they seemed drawn to me. At a Sunday evening service I packed eight of them into my Chrysler station wagon along with my two sons Matt and Marc and we drove to the church. Four were on my football squad that previous year and they asked others to join including three cheerleaders and another boy. All of them shared a testimony that night and I was so high on God's spirit as my sons and I drove them back to the school to meet their parents.

Timeout!
I realized right then that there is no greater feeling than ministering to youth wanting to experience more of the Lord. A large percentage of Avondale High's students were touched that year by the revival God was blessing the school and local churches. I felt a part of all that was happening there.

God really blessed me and Chris at Troy Christian Apostolic. Jeannine Jezierski ministered to my wife at her weekly bible studies. In fact, Chris received the Holy Spirit at one of those fellowships. What a lift to our marriage as Chris seemed to ride on a new level of joy and our marriage was stronger than ever! We were one like never before. Many of the men of the church were great friends for me and especially Fred Jerzierski as he took me under his wing. Jeannine was a talented pianist and Fred was an accomplished organist. Their entire family sang Christian music specials. They were such a blessing to many.

Timeout!
Once again "God is right there". Those next couple years helped strengthen the foundation of our marriage. Jeannine and Fred Jerzierski mentored us personally for those years and have continued to be our close friends through the years.

Chapter 12

Principal Joe Coe encouraged me to pursue a M.A.T. degree from nearby Oakland University. Avondale Senior High had a high percentage of struggling readers and he thought I'd be the perfect one to take on the challenge to bring these students up to par. I accepted the challenge and this opened new doors for my career. My mentor teacher Dr. Richard Baron nominated me to be a reading intern at Oakland Schools. My district released me for six weeks to study and research at their facility in Pontiac, Michigan. Next, Oakland Schools recommended me to the University of Michigan to be their reading specialist for the speech and hearing clinic/camp located in Northport, Michigan (twenty-five acre camp on the beautiful shores of Lake Michigan).

Our entire family had our own cabin and all our meals were served at the lodge. We thoroughly enjoyed the experience, but it was exhausting as you only had Sunday off. It was more than designing individual reading instruction for those campers needing reading improvement. I loved the three summers there. Chris did not have to cook because all our families' meals were provided by Ruthie (the camp cook). She would prepare a tray of food for the family and Chris would drive down to the lodge and get the meal three times a day and return to the cabin to eat with our children. As a camp instructor I was required to head a table in the lodge and provide language development opportunities during the meals. These opportunities for discussion and making announcements during mealtime were an enrichment opportunity for developing the speech and language abilities of the campers. Not only were the meals homemade and delicious, it was an all you can eat affair. The atmosphere was frisky and full of life as the campers (ages 8-18) were finished with morning classes and they really enjoyed the fellowship and of course the meal. Our view out the window was awesome as we were situated on a hill overlooking an expansive Lake Michigan.

After dinner we had a one-hour rest period of naps and reading. Then, we had an afternoon of outdoor enrichment activities with basketball courts and tennis, hiking trails and swimming on our own beach. Twice a week we would do field trips. To me, I had a dream job as I was able to encourage down trodden campers who struggle at school. The staff of one hundred University of Michigan grad students was unified in the passion and love to help the nearly two hundred campers at Shady Trails. It was a wonderful three summers as I gained so much valuable teaching experience. An added bonus was the campfires with several staff as we shared our life stories and I discovered so many had a close relationship with the Lord.

Professionally the time at Shady Trails allowed me to complete a research project with Dr. David Doly (the camp director) and this became my first published work: "Training Parent Surrogates for Reading Instruction".

In my third year at Avondale Senior High I became very involved with my mentor professor, Dr. Barron of Oakland University. My passion for leading instruction was growing so strongly that I stepped down from all coaching activities to complete my Masters in Secondary Reading and develop the best reading comprehension program in the state of Michigan. Principal Joe Coe subbed my classes as I scouted school districts in the Detroit area to check out the top secondary reading programs. There were not that many, but I observed three or four that gave me great ideas. As a result, I came up with a proposal for funds from the school board, and my master's project was actually the proposal. "Reading with Power" was a comprehensive secondary reading program in booklet form that included research, and a total semester curriculum with specific daily lesson plans. It was passed unanimously and I was given this large room with an office and storage areas, reading carrels and spacious seating arrangements to be very inviting to students and guests. That first year we had over one hundred teachers and educators visit our Reading Center at Avondale. Most of these visitors purchased a copy of my "Reading with Power" booklet. The key to the success of this program is that we were able to take the stigma off the "remedial reading" room by developing a beautiful facility and also serving the top students in the reading center by offering a reading techniques class for college prep students. In addition, I utilized three student teachers each semester to work with the students in small groups. Dr. Barron of Oakland University provided these helpers from his Reading Instruction classes.

Timeout: A Battle Needed to be Won!

It is so amazing to see God bless our efforts and give us a creative mind to be able to bless others. Now, I know that when I hit a roadblock on the development of this program – I had to battle the complaining of the school's reading director. She argued that what they had been doing for the past twenty years was effective. My (argument) then was that it basically was helping just a few kids and they were embarrassed going to literally a closet for reading support. Fortunately the principal was my main support and our ideas were widely supported. The reading director ended up on our bandwagon and supported our ideas when we presented to the school board. God was with me on this educational project to the very fruition of a dynamic learning experience for over two hundred students a year.

Timeout!
The destroyer of our souls was going to attack!

79

In early March of 1972, I was invited to a celebration at Oakland University for all the students receiving the Masters Degree in Education. At that reception they served a delicious punch in two bowls. Being very involved in my church now I had not drank any beer or wine for nearly two years (since I was healed). I began enjoying the punch with all the treats they provided; soon I switched to the alcohol punch. They looked the same. Of course, voices in my head told me: "Alan, it's OK, just enjoy yourself." And I sure did. I finished several glasses of this drink. I am not certain what it was (probably vodka based). It was getting late and I headed home around 11:30 P.M. I was light headed a bit but not really drunk, so I thought. I was driving our beautiful 1965 Chevy Impala Supersport Convertible. It was a beautiful evening, but as I approached I-75 my vision became blurry. Soon I realized that I was traveling in the wrong lane – traffic was coming at me! Rather than try to turn around and exit I chose to continue on to my exit as headlights were coming right at me. Fortunately it was now after twelve midnight and there was less traffic. At Fourteen Mile Rd. I exited and this was a major intersection at the Oakland Mall. I had my window down as I now was grasping for air and I ran right through the intersection at John K. Road and Fourteen Mile Rd. I hit a car, just the tail end of it, but I totaled my beautiful car. The only thing I remember was no one got hurt, but the man was upset that his gas tank got knocked off his car and he just filled it. While he was ranting I was walking around this busy intersection confessing: "I'm sorry, I did not mean to drink too much!" Several spectators from all the stopped cars were there now. The police arrived and I gave my name and showed the drivers license, and insurance.

Timeout: He was Right There!

Timeout: He was Right There!

God came to my rescue again. Our band director, (Rob Moore) arrived at the accident scene and told the officer that he taught with me at Avondale High School and he would drive me home. Mr. Moore was just coming home from playing in a nightclub. Can you believe the officer let him take me home and I did not receive any ticket at all? The accident was a miracle that no one was hurt and the fact that I survived the traffic going the wrong way on a major Detroit area freeway was amazing!

As I reflect back on that incident, I remember that Kathy, our lady custodian at Avondale Highschool was a weekend gospel singer and evangelist, had prayed over my car in the parking lot of the high school. She told me she always prayed over her cars and those of friends! At the time I thought it was corny but now I'm a believer.

Timeout!

God bless you Kathy for following the leading of the Holy Spirit and teaching me that He will send His angels to protect us!

Chapter 13

Timeout!

So Alan thought: However coaching was in his D.N.A.
Those five years at Avondale Senior High were tremendous
growth years for me and my family. My teaching career was
enhanced with the opportunities for growth, and now possessing
a Master's Degree I was really eager to advance my education.
In fact, Dr. Barron said my master's thesis was such that it could
be developed into a doctorate dissertation. I was really pumped
hearing that! My focus now was all educational: coaching was
on hold for the past year and the near future (so I thought).

It was early March and Dr. Barron sent me notice of two school
districts searching for a secondary reading specialist. Back then
most reading specialists were elementary teachers and consultants
for elementary schools. The first district was Red Lion, Pennsylvania;
the other was High School District #211 in Palatine, Illinois. Chris
was somewhat interested in the Red Lion District because it was
Amish Country. It would be a great place to quietly raise our then
four children. However, God had specific plans for me! Both districts
requested interviews after my resume was sent. The Palatine High
School job intrigued me as it was twenty-five miles NW of Chicago
and less than two hours from Mishawaka, Indiana – where my

family lived. In addition, they would pay for my doctorate degree as part of their teacher contract. This was what I desired at the time. The salary the first year was actually $1,000 less the first year, but later in the contract teacher's pay was significantly higher than the Avondale School District.

I interviewed and I had such a peace about taking the job that I accepted at the first interview. They told me that they had sixty-five applicants, but I was now their first choice! It was important to my future plans that I made it clear at that interview that I wanted to be hired as a reading specialist dedicated to developing a top quality reading program for Palatine High School and work on my doctorate: no coaching for the next couple years. They agreed and the job was finalized. In the long run I liked the possibility of being the District Reading Coordinator as High School District #211 had several large high schools. Job changes and moving your family were all very stressful. Yet, Chris and I were at peace and excited for this move to Illinois. As you will soon see God was in this move.

Before moving on to my Illinois teaching job, I must mention how fortunate that I was to be mentored by Mr. Joe Coe, Principal at Avondale Senior High School. His encouraging words on nearly a weekly basis really motivated me to give my best each week. He made me feel like a "top notch" teacher. I was not going to let him or the students down no matter what! Just a few days ago my wife googled Joe Coe's phone number and I felt led to thank him for his influence on my life. His goal as a principal he told me "was to provide the best learning situation for the students at Avondale". And he tried to motivate teachers to feel the same. When I dialed his number, I recalled that he shed a couple tears when I told him that I was leaving the District for an Illinois school. I felt so good that I called him that day after 45 years.

As I became more experienced in later years and wiser in my teaching techniques; I realized the truth that "your words are powerful!" Thank you, Principal Joe Coe. On a side note: Mom had died in 1971 after four short months from liver cancer; as she and my

dad were living in a very comfortable 1,500 sq. ft. apartment above
the five car garage on my sister Sharon and Bud's three hundred acre
farm in Niles, Michigan. Dad also was battling colon cancer but he
seemed to be improving at the time. This picturesque property was
highlighted with a beautiful brick Georgian from the late 1800's.
My brother in law totally remodeled and expanded it into a 5,000
sq. ft. mansion type house. Therefore, being closer to my sisters
became very important at the time. Chris' family had relocated to
Pennsylvania, so this also made the decision to move easier.

God was certainly guiding the move to Illinois; everything went
so smoothly as my wife and I just had our fourth child (Eric John
Dickson) and our organizational skills were pretty nonexistent.

Timeout!

The dramatic miracle of healing at Troy Christian
Apostolic Church in Michigan sure prepared my
FAITH for the upcoming JOURNEYS.
The move to Illinois was the beginning of my FAITH
JOURNEYS. After the five years at Avondale Senior
High, and our experiences living in Detroit, I began
maturing in my Christian walk. I was now aware that
God had been my co-pilot all along the way: His help was
certainly put to the test as this relocation took place.

The journey began when Dr. Barron walked into my classroom
with two letters of job openings that I might want to consider. I really
wasn't looking for a new job, but I was ambitious and Dr. Barron
thought this would be a worthwhile opportunity. In the past I had
confided in him that part of me would love to live in a small country
town and be very involved in the community. The first opening was
a Reading Specialist high school job at Red Lion Pennsylvania. (A
small Amish community outside of West Chester PA, a suburb of

Philadelphia). The other was for a Reading Specialist position at Palatine High School; Palatine was twenty-five miles North West of Chicago, Illinois. The pay was $12,329.00 for a teacher with a master's degree and five years of experience. This was in the year of 1972. This was exactly $1,000 less than I would be making at Avondale. However, the pay scale was much more in future years. Also, they paid for all advanced education (including a doctorate degree). At the time my desire was to make a big splash in the field of high school reading instruction (kind of a new educational frontier in 1970's) and eventually teach at the college level. The icing on the cake was that Palatine was only one and one-half hours from the Dickson Clan in Mishawaka, Indiana. Christy, my dear wife, had a fascination of living in rural Amish Country, but a strong leading from God led me to Palatine High School.

As I said, Palatine District Township #211 was comprised of five large (5-A) high schools. It was an excellent district with highly motivated students – nearly sixty-five percent went on to four-year colleges in the 1970's. My resume was armed with flowering letters of recommendation from: 1.) Dr. Richard Barron. 2.) Dr. Florence Coutler of Oakland Schools (where I was a reading intern). 3.) My principal of Avondale, Joe Coe.

I was soon called in for an interview and was told that I was their top choice of sixty-five applicants. What was most impressive was the salary in a few years rose rapidly; and the district paid for all advanced degrees – even a doctorate!

Palatine Township High School District #211 was a highly desirable school district for aspiring teachers. It paid more than neighboring districts – much more! Teachers retired at seventy percent of their top salary at age fifty-five. Needless to say, much of those benefits were due to the teamsters belonging to the AFL-CIO teachers union. The interview with Dr. Bruce Altergott was very enlightening. He shared that he was a Christian and that his mission was to have the most positive and highly skilled teachers employed by the district. Right then I knew God was in this move to Palatine

High School. After lunch I was given a tour of Palatine High by the principal, Mr. Len Newendorp and the English Department Chairman, Meredith Newburg. Driving up to the school I was impressed by the classical appearance, it reminded me of my high school in Mishawaka, Indiana. On top of that, the town of Palatine was very impressive with beautiful, well-maintained houses and tree-lined streets. The school was the centerpiece of this village, situated right on the N.W. Commuter R.R. line to Chicago.

I met Miss Newburg at the front doors of the school. She was a tall, large boned lady who had a very elegant and authoritative appearance; yet when she spoke, I could tell she was a very wonderful lady. She asked about my wife and children and gave me a beautiful description of the village of Palatine. Miss Newburg and I met Mr. Newendorp in the principal's office. I did reiterate to him that I was taking the job to build them a top-quality reading program, like I did at Avondale High in Michigan. Coaching would not be an option, as I wanted to take advantage of the opportunity to get my doctorate completed and open the doors to a future university or college position instructing future teachers and reading specialists. Dr. Barron at Oakland University who mentored my master's thesis – told me that my paper 75 pgs. with much detailed research, could be expanded into a doctorate.

Timeout!

God had other plans and He was there to redirect my plans (when would I learn to consult Him first?)

Back to the tour by the department chairperson. Her position was full time as this 5-A high school had 125 teachers that year and nearly 30 of which were English teachers. The meeting in Dr. Leonard Newendorp's office was very brief: He welcomed me aboard and said he respected my decision to not coach right away. He did, however, say they would love to have me join the coaching staff in the near future.

My reading lab was situated on the third floor (no elevators), and it was adjacent to the spacious, well-equipped library – a great plan! Yet, this room was not as impressive as my Avondale reading center. However, the room was best described as a huge den with beautiful mahogany dark wood walls. I was spoiled with lots of space and room for six learning stations in Michigan. I would need to be creative here – and the room had a spread 'presence' to it! God's Holy Spirit permeated every corner of this third floor developmental reading center. I knew that I was where He wanted me. Right across the hall was a spacious art room and our two rooms were the only ones on the third floor alongside the Media Center (library).

A long desk, which looked like it belonged in a famous lawyer's office, was centered in the front of the room. As we walked toward the desk, Meredith seemed very pleased to tell me:

"Alan, there is a letter on the corner of the
desk that Mr. Pethick left for you."

Glancing at the letter, I noticed that it was lying on the top of a black leather Bible. At that moment God's presence grew stronger in the room.

Timeout: Destined by God!

Mrs. Newburg and I visited and the
principal stopped by and said:
"Is he taking the job?" with a big smile I nodded "yes"
and he wished me a happy rest of the summer.

The English chairperson gave me the key as I said I wanted to stay awhile and browse the room. As soon as she left I quickly sat down behind that big desk and opened Mr. Pethick's letter to the new teacher, Mr. Dickson.

This letter made me weep! The Holy Spirit shot through my veins.

"Alan, I have heard great things about your teaching in Michigan. I know that you are a genuine Christian, and I have prayed to be replaced by a believer. I left a Bible on the corner of the desk as students have often liked to read a few passages after they completed their work. You need to meet Mike Bourban.

He was a student last year who gave his heart to the Lord and has organized a very large Bible study for the high school students at Palatine. (Mike was radically converted from drugs and alcohol and his life has been very dynamic as a living testament of God's mercy). He is highly respected by students and faculty alike. I will bring him to see you in the fall."

Timeout: How did Mr. Pethick know I was a Christian?

Mr. Pethick had been the teacher of the Reading Lab (developmental reading) for fifteen years. He was perhaps one of the kindest men that I had ever met. The district really respected him as a teacher. Formerly, he was a missionary with the Presbyterian Church. He was now seventy-two and ready to head to Denver for retirement and whatever God had next for him. He touched my life in one short meeting.

Chapter 14

Walking down the steps of the Palatine Township H.S. District #211 Administrative Center, I looked up at the clear Chicago area skies the sun was shining brightly and I felt the comfort of His presence engulfing my spirit. Knowing you're following the leading of the Holy Spirit is an awesome experience; it's a taste of the heavenlies right here on the earth. No fear about the relocation to Palatine – it was all in His hands! I had just signed a contract to serve this district and I was determined to be a light in this huge school district. District #211 was the fastest growing high school Chicago suburban district as it was composed of five high schools of around 2,000 students each. Perhaps this district would be my final destination. A place where I would leave an imprint on the school's academic success, and hopefully the lives of the students.

Well, now it's back to the Weldy farm for a night of one of Sharon's home cooked meals, visit with dad and of course some of my sister's famous German chocolate cake. I loved my visits to her warm and welcoming country estate. I left early Sunday morning to head back to Sterling Heights, Michigan as I had school the next day.

At Avondale Senior High that Monday I had shared with my closest teaching and coaching friends my excitement for the new job. However, I also had the daunting task of informing my beloved principal that I would be leaving. A meeting was soon set up with his secretary right after school and it was a tough time for both of us. He was the man that guided me through my first five years of teaching and coaching.

<u>Key Player Joe Coe, Principal</u>: A man used of God, I believe. He was there to prepare me for a long tenure as a teacher, coach, and a minister to the youth.

Timeout!

I gained so much confidence and practical teaching concepts from my teaching under Principal Joe those five years. A foundation was laid preparing me to be effective in this ministry God had prepared for me.

This after school meeting was going to be emotional. After conversing with Joe Coe, he asked me how would I be able to leave these Avondale kids that seemed to cling to me and would miss me immensely. I responded as if prompted by the Holy Spirit.

"Joe, there are students and athletes at Palatine High that may need my gifts. And, I believe that I am leaving the school with an excellent developmental reading program."

The response I received was disheartening: rather than Joe Coe accepting the fact that I could further my education and have new opportunities, he seemed discouraged and I noticed tears in his eyes. I felt horrible but I still had that inner peace.

Now I was ready to move on. Chris and I ran a rental ad in the Detroit paper and quickly signed a rental agreement with a wonderful single executive who seemed to be the perfect tenant. We quickly packed and put all our belongings in one of Uncle Bud's large farm trucks. He had offered to store our furniture in his pole barn while Chris, the four kids and I spent the summer at the University of Michigan's "Shady Trails Camp".

With our Sterling Heights home rented and the furniture safely stored in Uncle Bud's pole barn, we spent the weekend at the farm

before the job at the University of Michigan's camp, Shady Trails. Friday evening after dinner Bud looked up at me as he spoke:
"Alan, you need to find housing in Palatine
before you leave for camp."

Timeout!

God had orchestrated all the details up to now. Now
He would need to work out one more detail.

Needless to say, we left early Saturday morning for the N.W. suburbs of Chicago. Our first stop in the quaint town of Palatine (25 miles N.W. of Chicago) was at the first realty office that we came to on Northwest Highway. The agent greeted us with:
"Good luck fellas! Rentals in this town are rare.
We have zero available. But, check the local papers
there may be some that came out recently."
Bud seemed unwavered as he said to me, "Let's just drive around and see!"

After driving six or eight blocks we were just two blocks south of the high school. Bud pulled over to the curb and said, "Let's pray!" He prayed aloud and I tried to muster up enough faith to support the prayer. As we concluded and looked up, we both noticed a man staring at us from across and down the street. Bud in a determined voice said; "Let's go talk to that guy." We approached him and Bud asked, "Sir, are you aware of any houses for rent in this town? My brother-in-law signed a contract to teach at the high school and needs a house to rent for his family."

He told us his name was Roman and he just bought this house (right next door to his) and he was painting it to rent out. It was a very nice bungalow with a large porch, full basement; however, there were only two bedrooms and a living room. We would make it work! He agreed to rent it for $175.00 a month and would hold it all summer with no deposit. He signed a simple piece of paper stating the house would be available August 25, 1972. He wanted no check until I moved in; he was 'old school ' and said his word was good. Bud and I were rejoicing all the way back to Niles, Michigan. Chris, the kids and I could leave for camp Monday morning with no immediate concerns.

Timeout: God does care about our daily needs – housing included!

Shady Trails was a nationally known speech and language camp situated on twenty-five beautiful acres, right on the shores of majestic Lake Michigan. It was located just twenty miles north of picturesque Traverse City. This would be our second summer there and we were excited to return. Matthew was seven, Marc six, and Melissa and Eric were three and one years old at the time. What a wonderful place for kids to spend the summer! They were able to participate in the many outdoor activities and attend some of the classes that I taught as the camp Reading Specialist. Melissa learned how to read that summer by attending one of my morning classes. She was barely three! Chris looked forward to a summer of being served delicious homemade meals by Ruthie and her staff (the camp's cooks). Chris would drive our big old blue Chrysler wagon to pick up a tray of food for the kids and her to eat in our cabin. As a staff member I was required to eat and supervise speech instruction during the meals. Campers gave announcements and carried on conversations with the staff at the individual tables. One or two staff members assisted at each table. I learned a valuable teaching technique called the "Wang Ho" game at dessert time (as extra desserts were handed out to the winners of this game). At the count of three the instructor would say "Wang Ho" and each camper would hold up fingers any number 1 to 10. I would then add the number and then count around the circle until I reached the camper that had that number and if there were three desserts left, the next time three campers would receive the treats!! By the way, in my many years of teaching middle school, I would utilize this game to share treats in my classroom for rewards at the end of the class period. Believe me, it came in handy!

As my summer at Shady Trails was winding down, I reflected on my role there. Although it was very exhausting, the rewards were beyond measure. So many of the campers (it was an all-male camp) were lacking self-esteem and confidence. My God given gift of a strong belief in young people's potential to overcome language and reading difficulties (barriers) enabled me to see where I helped contribute to the academic and social development of those campers that I instructed in my reading cabin there. I felt tired, but very satisfied form my work at the camp.

My camp duties concluded after the final campers departed Shady Trails. Many were bussed to the Traverse City Airport as campers came from all over the U.S. Our station wagon was soon packed and we returned to the Weldy Farm as my mind now became occupied with my new assignment at Palatine High School. After driving straight to the farm, Sharon had a welcome back dinner of beef and homemade noodles.

Chapter 15

When we arrived at our rental home in Palatine, Illinois the next morning, we were in complete delight over the fresh painting job and the beautifully finished floors; needless to say, the place was immaculate inside and freshly landscaped outside. This village in the Northwest suburbs was reminiscent of some quaint, tree-lined towns in Vermont and Virginia. The house was custom built, two large bedrooms, one bath and a huge living room and dining area. The kitchen was also very nice. This fine man from Romania fixed it to a tee for us and held it all summer at no cost! Just a note scribbled on a piece of paper saying rent of $175.00 begins on Sept. 1, 1972. Bud had driven behind us in the farm truck; we were able to unpack and settle in as tomorrow was the teacher in-service training.

Little did I know that God led me into a "dream teaching assignment" As the teacher meetings concluded, I climbed the three flights of stairs up to my reading center and sat at the desk glancing over my class rosters. Yes, it was true, each class of Developmental Reading was exactly twenty students and listen to this: each student had to have two teacher referrals and a minimum of a "B" average in English courses. These were college bound students desiring to read more efficiently and enhance their study skills. The presence of God I sensed when I first entered the room last spring after the interview was even stronger! Something good was about to happen in this school year and I was so excited deep in my spirit. It was joy unspeakable and literally overwhelming.

The next morning I awoke very early and carefully selected comfortable dress clothes. I wanted to make certain I was professionally dressed on the first day of school. It was a beautiful walk through the small village of Palatine and the school was just a total of seven blocks from our home. I had my large, leather briefcase at my side stuffed with my plans for the first day. There were over one hundred and twenty-five certified teachers at Palatine High School, one principal, three assistant principals, and ten counselors. We had a brief ten-minute meeting at 7:30 AM. There was such a large staff that we met in the auditorium. I enjoyed the professionalism of High School District 211. My career in education was really on the rise.

I truly had a dream job: twenty wonderful, motivated students, college bound and future leaders to teach and inspire each day and be inspired by them. Wasn't this assignment too good to be true? I have to admit I wondered at times was I stepping back – as we had such a dynamic reading center back at Avondale High School. Visitors (English teachers, aspiring reading specialists and several administrators from neighboring districts) came nearly every week. Oakland University's Reading professor had me lecture their Masters in Reading students once a week as my evening job. Now, this reading lab at Palatine would not draw all the attention. It would not have the room to create a center with so many learning centers, an impressive window-lined office in the center whereby I could oversee all the activities. It was creative w/student tutors from the advanced classes and three student teachers per semester assigned to our center from Oakland University.

Yet, I knew this was where God placed me at this time. He pulled me out of the spotlight to allow me to minister to these students – there would be no newspapers writing articles about the program at Palatine. I would simply take the program set up by Mr. Pethick and perhaps expand it, but I would keep my focus on these five classes of twenty students per period.

Timeout!

The educational publicity would be gone, but God
was going to do big things for the students and
Mr. Dickson. Most importantly, it would be a time
to once again have Him close to my side.

The first few weeks of school went very smoothly. We loved our little bungalow on Slade St. and I couldn't believe this district. Our English department was made up of nearly thirty teachers, a full time department head (who taught no classes – just assisted the teachers), and five teacher aides who were assigned to do all of the English teachers' typing and make copies. I felt like I was teaching at a University. And of course English teachers had no supervision duties. Could you imagine over 2,000 students and not one fight occurred that year – not even any serious incidents. Drugs and alcohol incidents seemed to be minute for the 70's and away from the school setting. God's hand was truly on Palatine High at that time. Was that why He sent me there?

Looking back at the events that occurred the first few weeks at Palatine, I realized that Satan knew what God was designing and set up a roadblock. I was severely tested and nearly blocked out of the picture. This story illustrates what happened: In the state of Illinois every new teacher had to take a TB test. I failed. Next, I was administered a chest x-ray and it showed shadows in my lungs. Surgery was scheduled for the next day: a procedure to be done in front of a class of aspiring medical students who would view from a large window overlooking the operating room. The doctor's diagnosis was that I had lymphoma, Hodgkin's, or sarcoidosis (a non-malignant condition that can cause problems with internal organs and breathing). We had no choice – I did not have TB, but surgery would tell us what was wrong. As they wheeled me out of the surgery room my sister Sharon, Uncle Bud, Chris (along with her ex-roommate during her stewardess days Sue Bullivant) were all standing in the hallway. I remember to this day that I was totally embarrassed since I was only barely covered, if at all. Oh well, the main thing is the Dr. had a smile as she reported to all of us that I had a condition, but it wasn't the worst scenario: cancer! The biopsy showed sarcoidosis.

Time Out!

God is really good! Later chest x-rays showed no evidence of any disease at all in my chest. Incurable sarcoidosis was gone completely from my body!

In order to share a wonderful side story here, I must back track a bit. During those first few weeks of school, one of the senior boys in my class told me his dad was a Pastor at Southern Baptist Church and would like to invite our family to visit. We did as we hadn't found a church yet. Even though my background was Pentecostal, we found the church very biblical and extremely warm and friendly. My student's father Dr. Schwen was a kind man who presented the scripture in a dynamic way. His wife was our son's first grade teacher at the local elementary school. When the Schwen's found out we had immediate surgery scheduled, they kindly took care of our children: Matt (first grade), Marc (Kindergarten), Melissa (three years old) and Eric (one) they barely knew us! Such a blessing that was! I had a newfound respect for the Baptist faith.

Time Out!

God's love permeates all His children. I am still continually
amazed and encouraged by this. To this day I know that I was
planted at Palatine High for purposes beyond my ambitions. I
recorded notes of some of the events that occurred during those
eleven years. Also, the spiritual battles – my failings, victories
and spiritual triumphs all need to be presented to appreciate how
God never leaves or forsakes us. We all love the victories, but
often we learn to appreciate the failings that helped mold us.

Those first couple months at Palatine were monumental in a
spiritual sense. I left that large black Bible on the corner of the desk
just as Mr. Pethick requested. He was so respected by all the staff
at Palatine that this request was honored at little risk of crossing
the public education/religious line. That reading lab was a relaxed
setting where I presented very structured reading activities that really
did produce dramatic post test results! Those students bought into
total concentration for forty minutes daily. The last ten minutes
was independent reading and book discussions of completed books
with me. What a stimulating opportunity to interact with high
functioning teenage minds. Fridays were make-up work and forty-
five minutes of independent reading, recording the pages read and
writing summaries. Points were awarded daily. The only homework
was novel reading. Two-thousand pages earned an "A" for that
portion of their grade. The students loved this class and I did also. I
should add that I gave $5.00 banana split coupons for all top readers
in each class.

Time Out!

As I look back on my teaching career, I realize that motivation was my main gift in the classroom as well as in coaching.

The guidance department strictly enforced the recommendation that developmental reading class students had to maintain a "B" or better G.P.A. and the class size never was allowed to exceed twenty. Only if I made an exception after a prospective teacher/student interview would a student not meeting the academic criteria be permitted in the class. One Senior boy was requesting his counselor to be in the class. I interviewed him and he told me that he honestly never tried and was anxious to give my class a try. Naturally, I wondered if he heard it was an easy "A", as I designed the class for everyone to exceed! I really encouraged each student daily to keep pushing for the best possible outcome! I admitted John and he ended up setting all the speed-reading and skimming techniques records for the class (his records held up when I resigned eleven years later). John became a very successful trial lawyer after a successful college career. To this day, I thank God for using me in that young man's life.

Time Out!

I firmly believe Mr. Pethick did pray for a Christian to continue the groundwork he laid in that senior reading class.

On Fridays there was a "freedom" of sharing in the reading lab. I would literally spend the entire period discussing with students as they shared their readings. They would have prepared an outline of the book's highlights before our book interview. It was during this time that some of the students and I would end up engaging in some very thought-provoking conversations regarding their readings.

David Wilkerson's <u>The Cross and the Switch Blade</u> was always a favorite of mine. I placed four or five copies on the bookracks. However, the most dynamic book that I placed on our very large display shelf in that 'den-like' reading lab was Nicky Cruz's autobiography <u>Run Baby Run.</u> I had purchased three copies at the Christian bookstore in downtown Palatine and shared them with students who couldn't find a book that could hook them to read. This book had a special anointing of its own. I never had one student in Avondale in Michigan or at Palatine High not get excited about this life story.

Basically, the book began with this ten-year-old Puerto Rican boy was put on a plane to New York City with ten bucks in his pocket to survive in America. His parents used to lock him up in a chicken coop after beating the 'devils' out of him. This went on for most of his early life. He became viciously angry and beat up kids at school and was continuously expelled. Those parents were into witchcraft and some believe the demons cast out of people ended up in Nicky's spirit. They couldn't handle him and sent him off to New York.

This book was anointed! I shared the popularity of this book with Mrs. Newberg, my department chairperson, and she gave permission to order twenty copies for the class. This was definitely God! I was very surprised that the public school district paid for these Christian books.

Back to the story of Nicky Cruz: After arriving at the airport, he was hungry and stopped at a hot dog stand. This was around 1970 and the guy charged him ten bucks for two hot dogs. He had no money left. Nicky survived on the streets by stealing, selling drugs, and alcohol. He joined The Mau Maus, a vicious Puerto Rican gang, and he was rapidly promoted to War Lord. Later, arrived David Wilkerson (the skinny preacher) from western Pennsylvania. David witnessed to the gangs and led Nicky to the Lord. Nicky later dropped out of the gangs, went to Bible school and became a worldwide evangelist. I took my son Matt to hear him speak about twenty years ago in Lynnwood, WA. Nicky's turnaround and ministry is a testament to that skinny country preacher following the voice of the Lord.

Needless to say, Palatine High was infected by the same teen problems of drugs and alcohol as most other high schools in the 70's and 80's. Yet, I firmly believe the influence of those Christian teachers and students at that school enabled Palatine High to maintain a top quality environment. That community was composed of hard working middle and upper middle class families who actively supported the schools.

Chapter 16

At this time I would like to take on the role of a storyteller and share those stories that convinced me God sent me on a "mission" to Palatine High.

Time Out!

All followers of Christ have a mission –
just ask Him to show you!

Mr. Pethick and Mike Bourbon – During the first few weeks of school in 1973 I had a very pleasant after school surprise visit from Wayne Pethick and the student he mentioned in that letter he left on the desk for the new "reading lab teacher". Mr. Pethick was a seasoned missionary of over twenty years and when he entered the lab I was in awe of his humble, soft-spoken demeanor. Yet, he was a man of seventy-two years who had the shining brightness in his eyes of a passionate teen. I was touched by his soft-spoken voice as he introduced Mike Bourbon and himself. We sat and had the most pleasant and invigorating fellowship, as they shared how God was moving at Palatine High School and the entire community of Palatine. They told me of their Friday morning Bible studies in Mr. Anderson's room. Recently, a large contingent of the football team and several of the Pirates' coaches began attending. Also, Mike told me of the Sunday morning worship services that just began at the local theater with nearly two hundred (mostly teens) attending. Mike was in a rock band and his group ministered in music. I was excited to check all this out.

Mike Bourbon then shared his personal testimony of how Mr. Pethick led him to the Lord in this very classroom. I got chills listening to this very charismatic young man share his story that apparently was still developing. Mr. Pethick ministered to Mike in this very reading lab.

Those Friday morning prayer meetings and Bible studies were fresh and anointed. It seemed to be the popular event on Fridays. Everyone was there: coaches, teachers, cheerleaders, football, lacrosse, cross country and soccer athletes, along with a wide variety of the study body all attended. It was truly uplifting to see such a youth movement outside the church. The Sunday church meetings at the Son Village Theater were even more dynamic. A young pastor, Bill Hybels, came from California and was the leader of these "on fire" young people. The third largest non-denominational church in the United States blossomed from this group of "on fire" Christians. Oh what a privilege to be a small part of this development!

Mike Bourbon, a dynamic drummer; became the worship leader for the Willow Creek Community Church in South Barrington, Illinois. It was founded on October 12, 1975 by Bill Hybels, who is currently the senior pastor. The church has three weekend services averaging 24,000 people. It was so inspiring to me to see how God so mightily used Mike Bourbon in the foundational years of that mega church. Mike a young man converted from a downward life style to a dynamic leader for Christ by the quiet, mild mannered servant of God, Mr. Wayne Pethick (former missionary and reading lab instructor). Mr. Pethick was willing to listen to the voice of God.

<u>Pam Ray and Mike McBride</u> – Of all the one hundred high achieving students in the five developmental reading classes, one girl especially stood out. Pam Ray was an attractive gal who was so poised and genuinely sweet in nature, but I could immediately

sense from day one that Pam had a mission in life. Being extremely gifted academically, Pam blossomed quickly in her reading and study skill techniques. Her intelligence was obvious, yet it was something else about her that made her shine. She was absolutely, one hundred percent given to a life that wanted to know Jesus Christ more intimately. As I previously described the end of the period each day, students had a few minutes to interact with me or others regarding their readings. Pam, on day one asked me why the Bible was on the corner of the desk. I mentioned that it was the tradition of the former reading instructor. She wanted to know all the details. Soon the days moved on that fall, I had ample opportunities to share some of my previous Christian experiences at Avondale Senior High in Michigan. In a couple months my wife Chris and I were invited to her home for dinner and to meet her parents. Pam's dad was a music and band teacher at a nearby High School. Her mother was a nurse. They were lovely genuine Christians. Pam was an only child and you certainly could tell. They were in awe of their wonderful, unusually mature, beautiful daughter. They wanted to meet this reading teacher that had impressed their daughter with his love for Christ. I had shared my testimony of healing in Michigan to Pam and how God has led my life. We did have a wonderful student-teacher relationship, bonded by our love for Christ.

Pam's parents were Lutheran and I have always had respect for all denominations, but during some of our conversations, I shared with Pam my personal beliefs in baptism and the baptism of the Holy Spirit. Pam was fascinated, studied the topics and had shared with her parents that she wanted to be baptized at Mr. Dickson's church. Those wonderful Christian folks respected Pam's wishes and she was given their blessing to do so. During classes the next four weeks Pam had been sharing her desires to be immersed like Jesus to other students and soon she had talked another student to join her.

Mike was also in Pam's reading class and he had been reading Run Baby Run and was so inspired by reading the experiences of Nicky Cruz and his dramatic transformation of his life. One Friday as Mike was sharing the events of this book to me, tears appeared in his eyes and he said:

> "Mr. Dickson, I need to change my life. I want a
> life living close to Jesus. What do I do?"

I shared with Mike that Pam was getting baptized that next Sunday and Mike was on board to join her. This entire conversation was brief and during the last five minutes of class during sharing time.

That next Sunday morning both students arrived at our Des Plaines United Pentecostal church to attend service and be baptized at the closing of service. Pastor Burns included in his message on the significance of baptism and that early Christians were all baptized in the name of Jesus. Mike asked me to accompany him to the restroom to change and when he was in his swimming suit and T-shirt we knelt down and prayed. Mike literally sobbed as he was repenting and asking God to lead him to bring others to the Lord. I was overtaken by the intensity of his commitment.

Mike was a very popular student-leader at Palatine High School. He was a starting defensive back and wide receiver in football and he was a star wrestler and captain of the wrestling team. Mike had one of the most dramatic conversions that I ever witnessed. He literally became an aggressive soul winner. God used him to convert many of his friends and classmates to believing in the Christian life as the only way to happiness. Mike was "on fire". In the final weeks of that semester Mike shared with me his desire to go to Bible college and become a preacher. One day I was approached by Mr. Pietrini, the wrestling coach. He shared his concern that Mike was considering not wrestling that season. He was so caught up in ministering and studying the Bible that he lost his passion for wrestling. Mr. Pietrini asked me to encourage Mike to stick with his commitment to the team as captain and key wrestler. I did talk to Mike and he completed that season very successfully. After graduation Mike McBride went to an Assembly of God Bible College in Wisconsin and became a full time minister.

After graduation from Palatine, Pam Ray would stop by during her college breaks and she remained as steady as a rock in her Christian life. I remember on one of her visits I gave her a copy of David Wilkerson's book <u>The Vision</u> as she was very interested in end times and the future of America. Mike and Pam both left strong imprints on my mind that you never know the impact of your words to another. My key as a teacher and coach was to follow the Holy Spirit and not my ambitions.

An interesting note – the next fall I had a young lady in one of my developmental reading classes that continually just stared at me with no smile as I lectured on reading and study skill techniques. She was an attractive blonde and I often wondered why she never seemed to smile. Then one day it came out as I walked over to her desk.

"Mr. Dickson, you're the reason Mike McBride
dropped me and became a Jesus fanatic!"

I was flabbergasted as I told her calmly that I mostly just answered his questions. I had nothing to do with his decisions. Throughout that semester I was very kind to her and she finally warmed up a bit in class. Mike was now in Bible College, a young man on a mission. He left his old world behind and followed the vision God put in front of him.

Chapter 17

Timeout!

Be prepared Christian brothers and sisters: when God's Holy Spirit is moving in your life, Satan will rise up and bring distractions and eventually discouragement. Yet, do not be dismayed – He Will Never Leave You!! God remains at your side desiring to bring you back on track!

Those books, the fruit of David Wilkerson's ministry, carried an anointing seemingly unmatched at the time. The <u>Cross and the Switchblade, Run Baby Run, The Vision, Racing Toward Judgment,</u> all had an effect on its readers. Yet, it was the strong anointing on Nicky Cruz's <u>Run Baby Run</u> that literally brought some students to tears and initiate a change in their minds and hearts. Over my eleven years as the reading lab teacher, and later the director of three reading labs at Palatine High, hundreds of students read <u>Run Baby Run.</u>

Many students read this book and recommended it to fellow students, but there were times when I, following the leading of the Holy Spirit, handed it to certain students as a good read. If a student had trouble finding a book that caught their interest, this book was always my first recommendation!

While reflecting back on those days at Palatine, I remember other students who read the book and appeared to be very interested in the life-changing story of Nicky Cruz. Kevin the six-foot seven inch center on the Palatine High basketball team, and also star golfer and baseball pitcher, read the book and seemed to enjoy the story. Kevin went on to play in the NBA for the Los Angeles Lakers. Hopefully, an imprint of God's power to change lives went with him from this book.

I also think of another student who read this story had a much darker side. Mike was a very quiet student who diligently followed the prescribed program for reading development in the lab. One day I remember noticing Mike only needed two hundred more pages to raise his total to 1,500 page and a "B" grade for the term. I suggested Run Baby Run as a fast read. Mike signed the book out as he had less than a week to complete the readings. A very pleasant young man, Mike did not interact a whole lot with other students, so I attempted a few conversations with him and I enjoyed our short conversations. He seemed to be enjoying Nicky's story in Run Baby Run. I never forgot that last day I saw Mike. It was a Friday morning and as I climbed the final flight of stairs to the third floor, Mike was sitting on the floor in the hallway right next to my door. He was reading the final chapter of Run Baby Run.

"I made it Mr. Dickson, I'm done! It was a good book, thank you for telling me about this Nicky Cruz!"

That was the most animated I had ever seen Mike. Unfortunately, that was the last time I would ever seen the young man. Over the weekend (according to reports from students) he was at a party and on cocaine; tragically Mike was playing Russian Roulette and he shot himself. When I walked up those stairs leading to the reading lab and library complex, I missed seeing Mike outside my door. A lonely feeling came over me. Mike was gone. Soon I heard the reports as students entered the lab. I was down over the loss of Mike, but I had a hope inside my spirit that Mike got to know the Lord through reading that brief but strongly anointed story of Nicky Cruz.

Timeout!

Dear believers – those aspiring to teach – nothing can
stop your ministry – pray silently, tap into the Holy
Spirit's power as you enter the classroom daily. I completed
40 years of full time teaching in the public schools.
This was my source of strength and anointing.

God's blessings continued at Palatine High: Friday morning prayer meetings grew so large they moved to a large lecture hall. The Son City church was blossoming at the local theater. Soon in 1975 this group purchased several acres in South Barrington and eventually became Willows Creek Community Church – the third largest non-denominational congregation in the United States. They grew to 24,000 attendees during the three weekend services.

Thankfully the kind, compassionate elderly gentlemen, Mr. Pethick and those Christian teachers at Palatine High followed the leadings of the Holy Spirit; thus, they became the unsung heroes in the foundational years of the Willow Creek Church.

Soon the administrators (principal, assistant principals, and our athletic director) recruited me to return to coaching. I was an easy recruit since my passion for coaching was temporarily covered over with my professional pride to get a PHD and eventually teach college.

Coach Don Crandall, a first year math teacher and coach who played basketball at Northwestern, and I teamed up to coach one of the two ninth grade squads. There were nearly fifty aspiring ninth graders and we had a draft as we divided into two squads. Our team finished the season 9-0 and I was hooked on the return to coaching. There was a bond like a family unit that was created when coaches and players are all on the same page and focused toward a goal. I loved the relationships that were created during the season and often lasted a lifetime as I later experienced.

Basketball season came and I was offered the assistant coach's job as head of the sophomore team. Don Crandall took the J.V. just like football, there were two freshmen teams (A/B), a sophomore team, and a Junior Varsity squad, and the Varsity team. Sophomores played on Friday nights right before the Varsity team. The Junior Varsity and frosh teams played on Saturday mornings.

My team raced to three lopsided wins to start the season. I had a superstar on my squad in six-four Kevin McKenna who was averaging thirty points a game. Soon he was promoted to varsity starter. Kevin ended up as a six-seven center his senior year and was one of the top players in the state. In our mid suburban league was another future collegiate and NBA star, Dave Corzine. He was the six-eleven star of Arlington Heights High School.

Dave Corzine was older than Kevin but it was really fun watching them play at the high school level and later on in college. Dave Corzine went on to De Paul University in Chicago and led that team to some strong finishes in the NCAA tourney. He was a top draft pick (18th overall). Later in his career he was a standout center for the Chicago Bulls where he played seven years.

Kevin McKenna had four outstanding years at Creighton University as a top scorer averaging over twenty points per game. After college the Los Angeles Lakers in the fourth round selected Kevin in 1981.

Kevin came to Palatine High as a highly talented basketball player his frosh year. I think my greatest contribution to his success was rebounding for him when he came in early (before school) to shoot two or three times a week. However, my most vivid memory was handing him <u>Run Baby Run</u> to read....I hope he remembers this true story, or at least the spirit of the message.

After Kevin, and a few years down the road, the coaching staff at Palatine joined the Fellowship of Christian Athletes to put on a fundraising game: Our PHS coaches versus the 1983 Chicago

Bears. This was a memorable game for me on the same court with Walter Payton and his Chicago Bears. Our Palatine High coaches' staff team had a starting team of Rod Judson (U of Illinois), Marc Denny (Ball State U), Alan Dickson (Butler University), Tom Wolz (Northern Illinois football), and Arv (a football star at a college in Wisconsin). Walter gave a very "heartfelt" talk at halftime, on saying "No to Drugs and Alcohol!" The Bears went on to win the Super Bowl in 1985! Walter gave a heartfelt message at halftime encouraging the students to stay free of drugs and alcohol. After the game my sons Matt and Marc came into the locker room and Walter signed autograph cards for each of them. When I asked Walter to sign one for Melissa she was outside in the hallway Walter said I'll go get her and he came into the locker room with Melissa on his shoulders and she was all smiles. The future Miss Washington U.S.A. had her beautiful face way back then.

Timeout!

Remember when I said beware of when God is
moving in your life – Satan will not be lying still…..
be aware of his treachery, be strong in the Lord…

As I got caught up in the world of coaching again – I remained a believer but my focus was very divided. The teachers knew I was a Christian and I did endeavor to be a light in the students' lives; yet, some of the coaches closest to me seemed to be having so much fun. They were looking for a new drinking buddy, a pal to shoot pool with, bet on NBA games, and have beers at the local pub. This was a life that I had shunned. These were great guys but the Holy Spirit wouldn't grant me the freedom to enjoy that life again.

Here's how the plot unfolded: several teachers and coaches met at 6:00 AM for staff basketball games before school every Monday, Wednesday, and Friday. It was great competition and we became a close-knit group. In fact, we formed a team that won the city men's league a few years in a row. The guys usually went to the American Legion Hall for beers after each game. Trying to maintain a good Christian example, I would always go straight home. I told the guys that I would join them sometimes, but I only would drink a glass of red wine as that was Jesus' example – fellowshipping, but with moderation. Well, we won the championship and they all talked me into celebrating at the "Legion" with the guys. I joined them for one glass of red wine. When I arrived at the Legion Hall there were ten glasses of red wine waiting for me (they) all chipped in and each bought me a glass. Needless to say, I drank each one of those glasses of wine. In a few hours we were racing down the main street of town, seeing who could get to the pub at the end of town first. One of the assistant principals was on the team and out with us that night. I remember his quote: "let's celebrate but all of you better be at school bright and early in the morning!" We were, but it was hard for me!

I will never forget the drive home that night. It was 1:00 AM and I had mostly a country drive home. We lived on beautiful spring fed lake (with only ten estate type homes on this private lake). Our house was located in the quaint village (pop. 2,000) of Sleepy Hollow, just two miles west of the town of Dundee, Illinois. As I was driving through the town of Dundee, I thought I noticed a police car following me. Therefore, for those last two miles I literally was so careful that I drove my 1972 Buick straddling the yellow line in the center of Highway 72. Then I turned down the private lane leading to our house. The moment I turned left onto Pine Cone Lane, blinking lights lit up the lane that was dark due to the evergreen trees lining our road. I was humiliated as I had to stop right in front of the first house on the lane, our good friends and neighbors that I had witnessed to several times.

As the Dundee policeman approached he calmly said: "I need your driver's license and insurance information." As I handed it to him he further stated, "I have been following you from town as you straddled the yellow line. Are you okay?" I shared the complete story of my evening and said: "Sir, I am not used to drinking and I was driving down the center to stay on the road as there were no cars coming." Believe it or not, he responded as follows: "Okay you're on your private road, you're home now. I expect to not see you driving like this again." Thank you Lord! I learned my lesson and no damages to my car or more importantly another person.

Chapter 18

The strong anointing, with which I arrived at Palatine, was beginning to fade. Several factors contributed to this demise: the drinking with the coaches was only a couple times a month, but it was too excessive. In fact, one of the coaches shared with me a confession. He was a good coach and popular teacher that at one time felt called to be a Catholic priest. He went to mass every Sunday. He shared with the priest that he had this teacher/coaching friend that was always witnessing to him. However, he admitted to the priest that his goal was to pull me away from my religious ways and get me to party with him (gambling and drinking). I really admire what the priest said to this coach: "young man, if you do not quit this foolishness, your very soul may be at stake!"

Another factor that led me off the mission that God had for me was real estate sales. When we moved to Illinois home prices were so high that we were forced to rent. However, after a year, we were looking to buy, as we had owned two homes in the Detroit area. We found a friendly realtor and purchased the lowest priced home in the MLS book, a three-bedroom ranch home in Hoffman Estates for $33,000. The house was not nearly as nice as the three-bedroom tri-level we sold in Sterling Heights, Michigan. Yet, it was a start! Soon, the real estate market in the N.W. suburbs of Chicago began to heat up. A realtor offered us a guarantee sale of $39,900 only six months after we had purchased. Of course there was a catch, we had to purchase one of their listings. We selected a large raised ranch with tall columns in front and it was only six years old. We were excited and soon we were relocated to Schaumburg.

Realizing how easy the sale for the realtor I thought I should sell houses. Then, we could purchase a really cool house down the road. Just as soon as the basketball season finished that year, I began my real estate classes. A friend of mine from the high school days was very successful as a "head hunter" in the city of Chicago. My friend loaned me the five hundred dollars to cover my classes and license fees.

I passed the exam, and looked for an active realty office. God led me to Kole Real Estate (they had ten offices serving the N.W. suburbs). This small little office was red hot in producing sales and served the modest neighborhood of Rolling Meadows. Financially desperate and being two house payments behind, I needed success soon!

That first week in real estate was unbelievable! My first week in the spring of 1975 I sold four houses. I did work harder than most of the full time agents. I would arrive at the office at three often since I came directly from Palatine High School. I would literally be the last agent to leave the office at nine-thirty P.M. each night. My first sale was at eight o'clock P.M. as a gentleman walked in the office and said, "We want to buy the house down the street!" They had been looking at buying this home for a few weeks. They told me to jump in their car and ride to the house. We were back in the office in thirty minutes and I had written the sale up and also listed their house. On Thursday I sold their house, and on Saturday I sold another house. This gave me four sales for the week. The Saturday sale was to the grandson of Ed McCaskey, president of the Chicago Bears. By the end of the month, I had sold eight houses and amassed nearly ten thousand dollars in commissions. I had made nearly one-half of my yearly teacher's salary in one month! Yet, with all this success (especially as a part time agent) I knew my true calling was teaching and coaching.

Al Folkes, the manager of that highly successful Rolling Meadows office called me into his office and asked me to sit down as he stared at me and then released a huge smile of confidence in his words:

"Alan, you are the best new agent who has worked at our company in twenty years!" "Why don't you resign from that teaching job and make some real money?" Then Mr. Folkes tossed a one hundred dollar bill across the desk to me and said, "Take this and get yourself a new jacket."

I looked at him and a boldness came over my normally humble face. "Mr. Folkes, I will make enough to buy my own jacket" Then, I tossed the bill back across the table! I then knew that this real estate sales was a blessing, but I could not depart from what in my heart I knew what God called me to do. However, distractions continued to cross my path.

Timeout!

God's Holy Spirit would continue to minister to me as I pursued both teaching and real estate sales. Yet, it seemed impractical to continue coaching as I was so productive in selling houses and making it possible to enable my family to live in a more beautiful home, and have a higher standard of living. But my prayer time became less and less and my decision was not based on God's word. "Your word is a lamp to my feet and a light to my path." (Psalms 119:105). My anointing and ministry at Palatine High seemed to wane as I now was more focused on making money after school.

That spring in 1975, I resigned from all coaching at Palatine High School. We had a great athletic director, Chic Anderson, and he seemed understanding. However, he kept me involved by asking me to run the clock at all the home games. This I was glad to do as I still maintained a strong love for basketball.

With more time freed after school my real estate sales continued to flourish. We made a move to a custom home in Schaumburg situated on a half-acre lot. Land was at a premium in the Chicago suburbs – so this yard was very desirable. We liked it there, but soon we found another place, a community, that seemed to be a perfect place to raise the family – Sleepy Hollow, Illinois.

Part of my success in real estate was that I would search daily the classified ads for "homes for sale by owner". I was really good at listing these houses. In my searching one day, I came across a by owner ad that had a house on one and one-half acres on a private lake. Chris and I made an appointment to tour the house. It was marvelous to me, but a bit overwhelming to my wife. As we passed through this quaint town of Dundee, Illinois, the village of Sleepy Hollow was one mile west and contained 2,000 residents.

Turning off the highway (Route 72), we entered this private land leading to the ten homes nestled around this private lake, Pine Lake. Driving down Pine Cone Lane was so enchanting. Three of the homes were built on the large creek that led out to this beautiful spring fed lake surrounded by evergreens. It was like you were in the northern woods of Wisconsin and we were just eighteen miles from my teaching job at Palatine High. "What a blessing this could be", I thought.

The Sleepy Hollow home was a family paradise, so to speak. The Pine Lake was surrounded by ten custom built homes. Ours was the original home on the lake. It was built by the founder of Bell & Howell estate, Mr. McNabb. Clients were entertained at the home. It was a lodge type building with a dramatic living room with hand crafted cedar walls and a dome ceiling lined with cedar. The floors in the living room and the two adjoining master bedrooms were beautiful cedar tiles. On the far wall was a field stone fireplace built by stones from the nearly two-acre lot. The front porch was also built by field stonewalls with screens open to the panoramic lake view as the house was built on a hill. In the front yard was a field stone waterfall and garden and built underneath was ten cement steps leading to a cellar and spring that was the water source for the home. Wild life abounded on the property with ducks, large turtles in the lake, a variety of birds, and of course deer.

We enjoyed family Christmas times at the "lodge" as well as

entertaining friends from real estate and teachers at Palatine High. In the winter the lake would freeze over and our neighbor (a builder) would take his bulldozer and plow the snow off the lake and put lights up on posts, which gave us a huge ice skating rink right in our front yard. Our sons, Matt and Marc would also spend hours ice fishing on the lake. With our long rambler house set on a hill Matt, Marc, and Missy designed a slide that led down to the lake for sledding. Much family fun year round at this house with a sports court for basketball, an in ground pool in the back just above the fifty foot patio surrounded by a field stone wall with a huge stove outdoor grill. The pool was located above the patio. Beyond the pool was an evergreen lined playing field where the Dickson kids and the neighbors held numerous football and baseball games. I must not close this section without describing the huge large mouth bass that filled our clear spring fed lake. It was truly a family paradise. And, I was making enough money in real estate to have Matt, Marc, Melissa, and Eric attend the excellent private school in downtown Dundee (Immanuel Lutheran).

Timeout!

I could not close this section without describing how God was always with us. One wintry morning Eric and Marc were sledding down the hill before school and Eric's sled shot out into the lake and slipped through the ice. By the time we arrived Marc had dragged Eric and the sled to shore. Thank you Jesus for Marc's alertness and bravery to save my youngest son!

While at Kole Realty, I had numerous successes; one of my early sales was the grandson of that owner of the Chicago Bears, Ed McCaskey. I really enjoyed young couples like Ed and his wife and guide them to the perfect starter home. They were quality people and very humble, not wanting to boast of their famous family. After closing thirty plus real estate sales my first year, as a part timer with a full time teaching job, I became a hot recruit for other agencies.

Soon some associates talked me into interviewing with Condo Realty, as condos were becoming a hot item in the Chicago suburban area. I joined and became a trained condo specialist, selling a home a week by just working a couple afternoons and evenings per week lining up prospects and getting a sale nearly every Saturday. We were trained in a high-pressured technique of showing three condos and selling one of them. It was a great plan and the market was red hot.

Condo Realty was like a family and the agents were treated like royalty (gourmet coffee in the office, lunches and treats served to agents). Life was good. I loved my teaching job, my home on the lake was fantastic and all was good. I even was blessed to sell Greg Latta of the Bears his town house. Greg was the starting tight end for the Chicago Bears that year. I will never forget Greg Latta exclaiming as I drove him out to our Sleepy Hollow home: "Dickson, I thought you were a school teacher – you are a millionaire!" So I thought! After nearly eight successful months at Condo Realty, averaging nearly one thousand dollars a week part time, a strange event happened to force me to make a big decision.

The owner of Condo Realty whom I saw several times meeting with our manager of the office, was featured on the evening news. He was running several illegal abortion clinics in the Chicago area. *"Oh great!", I thought to myself. "Was Condo Realty a front for these illegal businesses?" My mind was in a dilemma.*

I loved this job, and the people were all really wonderful. Yet, I soon realized that the sale income would not make me happy if I compromised. When I gave my life to live for Christ back in School Craft, Michigan, and was healed and renewed at the Troy Christian Apostolic Church in Troy, Michigan, God instilled His Spirit in me and it suddenly came to life. I had to leave. The next evening I went to the office and after all the agents were gone home for the evening, I cleaned out my desk and left a lengthy letter to JoAnn explaining my beliefs. I locked the door and put my key in an envelope and deposited in the night slot. Of course I had remorse in leaving such a "cash cow" for our family, but I knew in my mind that I had no choice but to leave.

In a few months I hooked up with a growing realty firm in Carpentersville near Sleepy Hollow. Before long I was generating good real estate income again and life was still good. I stayed involved with the coaches at Palatine High by scouting for the basketball coach and assisting at games by running the clock. This gave me a prime seat to view the coaching strategies employed by some of the great coaches in the Northwest Suburban League. Needless to say, I was starting to really miss coaching at the high school level. I satisfied this desire by playing ball three times a week with the coaches and teachers at Palatine High before school and one night a week our staff team competed in the City League. In addition I spent two nights per week coaching Matt and Marc in the Dundee Parks Recreation League. We played games on Saturday mornings.

Timeout!

With all apparent happy outward events, there was a growing unhappiness in my soul. My ministry as a teacher/coach was practically non-existent. We struggled to find a church that inspired us to live strong for Christ. Probably I should have maintained my ties with Willow Creek Church, but I was looking for a church more like Troy Christian Apostolic.

The disillusionment continued and I was losing my zeal for my teaching job even though we were extremely well paid – my problem was spiritual. I was out of balance. No longer was I "on fire" for God, but I was rooted and did not lose faith, thank God! I still ministered to students but not with the same anointing. To be honest, I think I was living more for myself than for the Lord.

Daily I became more and more dissatisfied with my life. Something must change. To this day I remember teaching in my second floor reading center and God started talking to me. I was so overwhelmed that I walked out in the hall and leaned against the wall. I was overwhelmed with depression and frustration with my life. Then out of the corner of my eye I saw a poster placed on the wall. I read as follows:

"A ship in a harbor is safe, but that is not what a ship was made for."

"God," I thought. I know what you are saying to me. "Remember that vacation to Seattle in 1975 when you took Chris and the four children you had then to visit your in-laws, the Fassnachts?"

It was an exciting two-week trip funded by my newly earned riches in my real estate sales job. During that time there we sailed in the Puget Sound, dined at a couple seafood restaurants on the Seattle waterfront. We concluded the visit with a fantastic road trip – the Cascade Loop. My father-in-law, George Fassnacht, rented a leisure van and we traveled the northern route through the Cascade Mountains, along the semi-arid Columbia River valley, past glacier fed Lake Chelan, through the scenic Methow Valley and North Cascades National Park and back to the Puget Sound area and their home in Bellevue, Washington. In Eastern Washington we stayed in cabins for a couple nights and Matt and Marc fished the local river for trout (caught several) and we had fried fish for dinner. Matt was nine years old, Marc eight, Melissa five and Eric just two and one-half. They really enjoyed this trip through the majestic mountains of the Cascades. Without a doubt Seattle was an ideal area to raise our family. However, I contemplated how sorely we missed not having a church where we felt planted, like our Troy Christian Apostolic Church in Michigan.

This thought monopolized my mind as I boarded the large (747) jet to return to Chicago and my summer real estate job. The rest of the family was staying for an extra week with their grandparents. The plane was huge. As I settled into my window seat near the middle of the plane, I noticed a tall very striking young lady hurry on the plane and she was one of the last to board. She had a big smile and sat near the front just behind the business section. This didn't mean much to me at the time, but what happened soon after was startling to me.

121

The plane took off and we began cruising. My mind was reflecting on the beauty and majesty of the great Northwest. It truly seemed like a natural paradise compared to the flatness and smog of the Midwest. I remember the battle in my mind: "This Seattle area is awesome, but family and natural beauty is not enough of a lure without a church that we were excited about. We need a church like the one in Troy, Michigan, I thought.

Just then, about one and one-half hours into the flight that beautiful lady that I happened to notice upon boarding walked back to my seat and handed me a letter. All she said to me was "God told me to write this letter and give it to you."

"Yikes!" chills ran down my spine as I opened it, hesitantly.

In the meantime this "angel" lady disappeared back to the front of the plane, I assumed. As I opened the letter and began reading the eight pages, tears rolled down my cheeks. I felt a warm sensation all over my body. "God was talking to me through the words of this total stranger," I thought. The letter started that God told her that there was a man on the plane who was called to her Community Chapel church in South Seattle. She mentioned in several pages that the church began as a home fellowship and developed into a mega church. People were coming there from all over the country. And the letter closed with the statement that "God wants you to be a part of this fellowship of believers!"

What an amazing experience for me! Here I was desiring to move to Seattle and the only thing keeping me from it was a great church of my religious preference (apostolic, spirit filled), and this person (perhaps an angel) hands me a letter from God that tells me about a church fitting my preference.

Well, I returned to Chicago and my summer job in realty sales, but lingering in my mind was this really supernatural experience on a large United Airlines Jet. I really did not feel comfortable sharing this with my teacher friends or people in the realty office. Only my wife, Chris, and my sisters in Indiana (Sharon, Joan, Pat, and Barbara) did I mention this unusual event. I didn't want people to think that I was whacky.

Time passed on and I kept very busy enjoying our lake home in Sleepy Hollow teaching at Palatine High and now coaching my sons Matt and Marc in the Dundee Park's League. Also, I really enjoyed watching them play at Immanuel Lutheran and later on Dundee Middle School. My sales success slipped somewhat and we got behind in the tuition payments at Immanuel Lutheran. Matt, Marc, Melissa and Eric were all really prospering there. One of the elementary teachers at Immanuel (Mrs. Ness) lived across the lake from us. She kindly made a home visit and advised us to join the church and we would not have to pay tuition. We considered it for a while but my insistence that I would stay with my own church and God would provide the extra funds needed through real estate.

Timeout!

Maybe God was trying to help our situation by presenting
the offer to join the church? Did I reject His assistance by
spiritual pride? We could have maintained our fundamental
beliefs, and enjoyed the Lutherans fellowship.

We met many wonderful people at the Lutheran Church School. Melissa and Marc were good friends with the Besinger girls whose father was a successful developer and owner of the huge shopping center in Carpentersville, Illinois. One year he housed a Super Bowl party that included a majority of the Chicago Bears. In addition, Marc played on the highly talented school basketball team and Melissa was a cheerleader with the Besinger girls. On Saturday mornings the parents and coaches of the team would meet for pick up games. Mr. Besinger often brought the all-pro linebacker of the Bears with him. Somehow I always was matched up guarding Otis. I'll never forget this incident that occurred one Saturday morning: Otis brought the ball up court and I pressured him and he stepped back over the half-court line, so I called over-and-back. He glared at me and blurted: "Dickson, this isn't the N.B.A.!" Then, I said: "Otis they call over and back in seventh grade." He fired the ball at me and didn't say another word. Yet, as my team was running down the court on offense, he slammed his powerful elbow into my ribs. I paused but never let out a grimace.

Surrounded by so many physical blessings for an ordinary guy, I knew I was blessed maybe even favored of the Lord. Yet, unhappiness crept into my spirit and spread throughout my body, penetrating to the very center of my bones. Depression continued to swell throughout my mind and body. I missed coaching at the high school, I longed for the strong anointing that I had once had as reading teacher director at Palatine High School. The real estate earnings were not enough to satisfy my soul. I needed a spiritual transfusion (like back at Troy Christian Apostolic). Was God leading me to a spiritual awakening in Seattle?

Months passed and soon I became seriously ill. The colitis returned and my body was inflamed. My doctor recommended a two-week rest with daily cortisone injections. After a few days of rest I felt so much better. With life slowed down immensely. I now had time to enjoy the children and get to know my wife, Christine, in a new way. We had many talks out on our screened porch (stone) overlooking beautiful Pine Lake. I never fully realized how blessed we were to live in this estate like setting.

Most of my days during that two-week rest were spent lying on our king-size bed in the beautiful knotty pine master bedroom. The doctors had me taking cortisone treatments twice daily. I had plenty of time to lie there and think. One morning while I was lying there and trying to seek God for healing and clarity for my life, Chris came bounding into the room all excited. "Alan, I found the letter that was given you eight years ago on the plane from Seattle!"

We read it together and hope swelled up in both of us, "God was directing our paths again", we thought. Chris suggested I call the number of the church mentioned in the letter and I did.

"Hello, this is Cindy at Community Chapel Bible
& Training Center, how may I help you?"

I really did not expect anyone to answer as I wrongly assumed it was one of those charismatic groups that sprouted up in the 80's and quickly disappeared. Well, I soon learned how wrong I was!

"My name is Alan Dickson, and I am calling from the
Chicago area. Actually, I am about eight years late in
making this call. You see I was on an airplane and…..you
will probably think I'm nuts but this is what happened."

"I was on an airplane returning to Chicago from Seattle and this lady on the plane handed me an eight page letter. The letter was very specific telling me that I was called to this church in Burien and how God was moving mightily at this church!"

Cindy interrupted in her natural, sweet tone:

"Alan, this has happened time and time again. We
have people led to this congregation from all over the
country. They drop everything and just follow God."

We talked for a lengthy time, as I was mesmerized that God was leading me to Seattle and had a church there for me that held my personal beliefs. In addition, they had a five hundred-student Christian School and a 1,200-member bible college, all this nested on a ninety-acre campus right near Puget Sound. During my agonizing over God's will for me at Palatine High, I often felt called to work at a Christian school. This would be a true, untarnished ministry, I believed.

Timeout!

God definitely was able to use my teaching/coaching career for ministry, but only when I was full of His Spirit. It seemed that my spiritual tank was in dire need of a filling of the Holy Spirit.

My health improved after Don Locrem, one of the pastors at Community Chapel, prayed for me during that phone call. Soon I was back at work at school and real estate sales. Yet, my excitement grew over that church in Seattle, especially being called of the Lord to be relocated and be a part of His work there.

My Indiana brother-in-law Bud Weldy offered to pay for a flight to Seattle to attend the New Year's Eve service at this mega church in Burien. We flew out to Seattle and my father-in-law met us at Sea-Tac Airport and drove us directly to Community Chapel. I had talked numerous times to Ron Lowrie, the chief pastor's number one assistant and he seemed to believe God was calling me there to take the helm of their athletic program at the Christian School. I was excited and finally believed this was my true calling (so I thought).

Chapter 19

Seattle or Bust

Upon returning from the Seattle visit to this mega church, Bible College and comprehensive K-12 Christian School, I was in total awe of God seemingly directing this school teacher/coach. I flat out was lit up in my spirit with the possibilities of full time administration at the Christian School utilizing my broad scope of experience the past sixteen years of high school teaching and coaching in large high schools in Michigan and Illinois. God had equipped me for this new ministry (so I thought). The bonus of taking Bible college courses and having my kids full time at the Christian school campus seemed like a bit of "Heaven on Earth".

Time Out!

Since I was a young boy around eight years of age, I felt a calling and I know my ministry was now just around the corner. All I had to do was follow God: Step out in FAITH!

Spring came quickly and Chris and I made plans for the venture to the Northwest. We sold our picturesque lake front estate on a "contract for deed" netting us about five hundred dollars a month and a lump sum due in two years. This was not the fortune I thought we would gain when we eventually sold this special property, but we were more concerned about following God. Our treasures were going to be stored up in Heaven we mutually decided.

Our oldest son Matthew was a very talented drummer (triple tenor) in the nationally acclaimed Dundee Scots Marching Band. He would be willing to stay with the family of another drummer when we headed for Seattle in June when school was dismissed for the summer. Chris' dad had a vacant rental house in Redmond, WA and we would be able to move directly into that house for $500 per month. Things were settling nicely for us. The other five kids were excited about the venture to the beautiful Northwest, and being closer to their grandparents (George and Pat Fassnacht).

June 15th came and we were packed and ready to roll onward to the majestic Northwest (God's country). In all honesty we looked like the Beverly Hillbillies heading to the Northwest. All the worldly belongings, including our family cat and dog, of now a family of eight were stuffed into the largest U-Haul and the old Buick Sedan towed by the U-Haul. In addition, we had our Chevy Day Cruiser van which was towing our 16' fishing boat and trailer stuffed with bicycles and yard tools. Definitely we looked like hicks from the Midwest. (Well mom grew up in French Lick, Indiana – maybe we were hillbillies).

Full of anticipation and optimism for our new life, the Dickson family headed north to Wisconsin. Two hours later as we were passing through Wisconsin a loud noise came from the boat trailing the van with Chris driving. The boat tire blew and I had no spare! I pulled the U-Haul behind the trailer and Chris got out of the van shaking. My immediate response was one of despair. This brave, bold, Christian man led by a humongous faith to venture away from such earthly security and prosperity to pursue His will, was ready to fold.

I staggered over to a rock by the side of the highway and sat there staring as the kids read and played games in the van.

"God, I'm done! We didn't even get through Wisconsin and the boat tire blew and I never got a spare. Jesus are you telling us to go back to Illinois?" Remember I was not led to resign my job. We could rent and not close in a year on our house. We could return back to our old life.

Within minutes Chris came boldly out of the van and said:
"Alan, this is nothing, just a flat tire on the trailer!"

Her faith in our mission gave me strength. I unhooked the van from the boat trailer, took the back trailer wheel off and drove to the nearest service station. Fortunately, a service station was a few miles down the road and they happened to have the perfect replacement size boat tire. I knew we were being taken care of. "Only 2,000 more miles and we will be in Seattle", I thought.

The rest of the journey was uneventful, except for the fact that we met a homeless man at a truck stop in Montana and he talked me into riding in the Buick being towed behind our van. He said he would love to keep the cat company. We dropped him off at another truck stop three hundred miles down Interstate 90. I was probably not thinking clearly, but I felt God's presence on this very bold venture.

Well, four days later we crossed into the state of Washington. I was on a high, like never before. Being called by God and my spirit was radiating – like the time when I came back to the Lord at the U.P.C. church in Schoolcraft, WA when I un-mistakenly had this awesome vision of the heavenlies open up and Jesus smiling down at me. This vision has later strengthened me during some of my later trials.

We settled into our Redmond, WA rambler on Education Hill and were very comfortable. We were so impressed with the strong anointing of God at the Community Chapel services at the mega church in Burien (nearly 3,000 members). Soon we learned that the leader, the chief pastor and founder had a policy that all new school district employees must establish themselves in the church as a member for one year. Then, they would be considered for a position. Apparently, the Christian School Superintendent wasn't fully aware of this rule. Neither did the assistant pastor who recruited me. I was literally shocked. Yet, through this major setback, I still believed this church was meant for us. There was a spirit of love among the members that was a great treasure. After we realized that the church had a branch in our town of Redmond we visited it. We absolutely loved this branch church. The pastor was a great Bible teacher and the worship service was equal to the main church. This was going to be our home church – after all I was told to wait a year to serve as a teacher and athletic director at the main campus. The Kirkland church had nearly two hundred members and their own small Christian School with a gym and classrooms attached to the church. We loved the people in this Kirkland Community Chapel. And I was a person who believed he could build a great athletic program with emphasis on hoops. To me it was such a sweet spirit at every service. So much love was spread among the pastor, Fred, and the congregation. Once again the music ministry was uplifting and the passion of the congregation was contagious.

Timeout!

This church experience was everything we could ever want in a spiritual sense; yet, was it worth giving up the security of a fantastic teaching position at one of the top school districts in the Midwest? I was getting doubts.

Toward the end of the summer, my "Northwest Ho" spirit was shrinking and as I was sharing my doubts with my brother-in-law and mentor back in Indiana; we came up with a plan. Since I had not resigned at Palatine High, I would fly back to Chicago and be on time for my first teacher meeting of the year. Our house was leased out, so I would stay with a dear realtor friend, Mary Osterman and she would drive me to the first day to Palatine. I would find housing and two weeks later, Bud and I would fly out to retrieve my family.

School District 211 kindly Okayed the venture and we were on our way.

That first day of teacher meetings as I walked into the auditorium five minutes before the required time; all my teacher friends and coaches stood and cheered! I felt at home again. The staff at Palatine had no idea whether or not I was returning, but they seemed excited to see me walk in – I remember giving them a big wave like the politicians do.

During the next two weeks I drove out to see my real estate broker and he was a master at creative financing. He sold millions of dollars of real estate when homes in his market area averaged fifty thousand dollars at the time. Russ found a beautiful custom build rambler on a half-acre in an exclusive neighborhood for ninety-nine thousand. Since I had no cash until my lease option on the Pine Lake house was paid off, I literally had no down payment! We structured the deal where I paid $109,000, and would receive $10,000 back from sellers at closing plus my commission. The sellers agreed to give me a second mortgage of $20,000 as a down payment. Since the sellers owed nothing on the house the bank Okayed the deal.

My broker Russ, had a rental house in Elgin, Illinois that we could rent for the few weeks until this Carpentersville house closed. All was set; now the Seattle retrieval must be planned.

That next Monday Bud and I flew to Seattle to pack the family and complete the five-day drive back to Illinois. I felt terrible as Matthew and Marc had already begun the school year at Redmond High and Melissa and Eric were at the Junior High and Elementary schools. This was tough on the family but our kids knew that we loved them and dad was not ready to give up his tenured and high paying teaching profession. Allison and Brittany were so young and trusting. God seemed to be with us through dad's search for His (God's) will, and now dad was more concerned about financial stability. At least I sold that one house during our summer in Washington and the commission was enough to pay the expenses for the return trip.

One problem loomed, the commission would not be awarded until after the closing in late September. God bless Uncle Bud, he stepped up voluntarily and paid the costs of the return trip. And I love to share how this masterful negotiator blessed our travels back to Illinois (actually God just seemed to bless everything in a business sense that he did, supernatural wisdom). We stayed in luxury suites and hotels for the entire return trip with Uncle Bud negotiating the cost of three rooms that was about the same price as someone would pay for one room at motel 6. Including the cost of professional movers to load, the U-Haul, all the gas, and the towering platform for the Buick, and all the rooms the total bill was $1,850. And I made sure that when I got that commission check, I paid back every penny, even my airfare. Uncle Bud truly looked out for us – he was my best friend and spiritual mentor all the way back to junior high days. He said I was one of the few people who ever paid him back. That made me feel good. And bless Aunt Sharon for letting her husband leave for a week.

Chapter 20

Northwestward Ho #2

Back at my teaching situation at Palatine High, the family comfortably settled into our newest home on Maple St. in Carpentersville, Illinois. A return to my secure teaching position and real estate sales job – it all felt good. Soon, I would be financially set and I would return to coaching at the high school. Perhaps working with Eddie Molitor, the dynamic varsity boys coach at the high school. Having been offered the position previously of head girls' basketball coach, I really thought working with Eddie Molitor would be more stimulating. After all, the mid suburban league was known to be a "hot bed" of Division 1 ballers! Then, I would return to a Christian ministry in sports like Fellowship of Christian Athletes, or whatever God led me to do.

As the months passed and spring was once again approaching… the cloud of depression having missed God's will was strongly wrapping around my mind. And it continued and became more severe! "I missed God's will", I thought. Even though the blessings of real estate commissions started flowing again and I really liked my teaching job (especially the pay) the passion was decreasing and the satisfaction just wasn't there. I really was caught up in the American Dream of wealth and security and material blessings, and of course, still being a good person. A quality-reading teacher was important to me, but the security of the job, allowed me to focus on real estate sales.

"We seek relationships but God gives us divine
connections, ones that last forever..."

As I look back part of my loss of passion was related to the
lack of a passionate leader. Both the department chairperson
and the principal were more focused on "following the revered
curriculum," rather than new ideas and innovative learning. It was
so different from Principal Joe Coe at Avondale Senior High and the
environment there, for me anyway. What I am saying is that Palatine
at the time was overall a great school and district but sometimes
tradition can only carry you so far. It had highly motivated students
and phenomenal parent support, highly paid teachers, but passion
seemed to wane for some administrators and staff. However, it was
loaded with quality people.

Timeout!

I really believe I was there for a season. I believe
I did some good, but with more anointing, more
passion – I really know God could have used me in
a greater way. Perhaps it was a lack of an anointed
fellowship of believers like I had in Troy, Michigan. True
ministers of God cannot walk in this world alone!

I am not blaming anyone for my loss of passion for the ministry
God blessed me with at Palatine, for sure! I just let the world creep
in – a close bond of saints would have helped. I really loved my
friends at the school: students, teachers, and coaches. Yet my light
was dim, and that was not what God called me for: remember the
poster in the guidance hallway on the second floor of P.H.S? "A ship
in a harbor is safe, but that is not what a ship is made for." Also, I
remembered that day during my prep period when I called out for
a confirmation and I desperately opened the Bible and my finger
pointed to Deuteronomy 11:11.

One day that spring I walked out of my study hall and just leaned against that sign as I was overwhelmed with frustration I felt like banging my head against it – why didn't I stay in Seattle where His anointing was flowing? As I continued to lean my entire body against that metal wall in the new Palatine High School on the second floor, I wasn't returning back inside the room (of nearly seventy hard working study hall students) until I got a peace. It never came and of course it was only seconds later that I returned to my duty to oversee these highly motivated juniors and seniors who signed up because they wanted to study. I must say I could see inside the room, but I needed to be more visible.

One memory of our short time in Redmond and our fellowship at Community Chapel was the seemingly wonderful youth group headed up by a quality young leader named Corey (he also left the church later as the church doctrines became dangerously awry). Corey asked me to use our light passenger custom van (Chevy "Day Cruiser") to haul some of the youth to Ocean Shores for a day trip. Normally I would say no to such a request; however, they were such responsible teens that I without a pause gave permission. The van returned that evening without any blemish and the entire group custom detailed the van. And, it was full of gas. A very special group they were. They roller-skated, went to a movie, and hiked as a group. Nothing but group dates we allowed until you began courting like pre-engagement.

Now, I must share both sides of the picture. The assistant pastor did not seem to have the same sweet spirit as the head pastor, Fred. I remember him sending my oldest son, Matt home from youth group because he wore flashy red "parachute" pants. This was poor judgment I believed then, and now really know it was. Yet, I was not going to allow one incident deter me from the "Lord's calling" for me. As Matt demonstrated a strong calling as a young boy when we were locked in on a snowstorm and not able to go to church, Matt prepared a message in the cathedral type living room of our lodge home. He was only twelve. As a teen having a strong calling himself, he had his own battles. I remember in Illinois, Pastor Huerta of the local Pentecostal Church recognized his tremendous talent as a drummer. He had him very involved in playing the drums worship service – and immediately Matt would sneak outside of the building after worship and have a cigarette with his buddy from Dundee High who was a negative influence. I found out later this young man also smoked pot. I was worried about Matt.

Timeout!

Matt, was a charismatic personality and he drew all types of friends – I always felt that I needed to guide him at times, he seemed drawn to the down and out. But, as the spiritual leader of the family, I recognized a strong calling on his life. You will hear more later about that!

---

30 Second Timeout!

Looking back again I should have cut back on real estate, and focused on fishing on our lake, etc. with my boys. I did some ice-skating with them. But, more father involvement and less dependence on the youth group to raise my kids, spiritually.
"What if you gain the whole world and lose your soul?" – certainly could be applied here.

Needless to say, when God penetrates your mind with a calling – it never backs off. As the school year was winding down I knew we were returning to Seattle. This time to stay. A great church was there and I believed that I was called to oversee the development of the most comprehensive and wholesome athletic program in the northwest.

Timeout!

I did help coach Matt and Marc in basketball and baseball, which they both had some fine moments…and Chris got Melissa and Matt involved in ice skating lessons. They both had awesome talent here (rhythm and grace and super coordinated) much like their mom, Chris, who was a talented ballerina at Butler for her two years there.

My regrets were that I thought providing a beautiful house and even a private school was my main mission. Thus, I missed a lot of those special dad/child moments working all the time. However, that was the 70's and 80's and moms stayed home and dads often-worked two jobs. Yet, my teaching pay was pretty decent then with nearly fifteen years of seniority. Our life style demanded two jobs for me. Coaching was on a second burner to real estate sales as the commissions were unfortunately so enticing and I loved competing to win the monthly sales awards – even though I was part time. When I left school for the day I grabbled a coffee and a donut or two at Dunkin Donuts and just transitioned my mind to real estate sales. I read lots of "how to be successful" books and learned a lot of techniques from Uncle Bud. However, I always gave God the glory for sales. When I didn't the sales dwindled.

Timeout!

God was always there: blessing me in realty sales, teaching, and being a strong witness at school. Like a loving Father, He never left me alone!

We needed to heed the call and make the trek again to Seattle. I remember calling the lady who witnessed to me about Community

Chapel (she gave me the eight-page letter telling me I was called to Seattle and that church. Chris and I had met her a couple times during that summer in Seattle at church, and on a picnic with her husband). She described how Satan would work to discourage me again, so I needed to completely trust God and resign from the teaching job before we left this time. And I did! Looking back at all of this it seems crazy for a man with a great job (retirement was one of the best in the nation, 70% of your final years salary after only thirty years). Medical benefits, sick leave, one hundred and eighty days for serious illness all were fantastic benefits. Nevertheless, I was following God's call, as spiritual benefits would be there for our family and me. Chris was on board completely as she had confidence in me and also her entire Fassnacht family now resided in the Seattle area.

I just couldn't tell Uncle Bud until after I moved. He was so great at helping us in our return trip that I wanted to give it some time before I called. We leased out the new rambler in Carpentersville with an option to purchase and made quick plans. I cashed in my eleven years pension in Illinois and paid a penalty for early withdraw, but we were starting a new life in Seattle. I did not pursue a teaching/coaching position as my desire was to fulfill the call to minister at the Christian School and have the kids attend there. Our only income would be the four hundred and fifty dollars from the Sleepy Hollow contract sale (after we paid the payment there was $450.00 leftover). The Carpentersville house was a break-even rental.

Two weeks prior to leaving for Seattle, I purchased a red Volks Wagon Rabbit (hard top convertible and I left as soon as school was out for the summer) my plan was to drive Melissa, Eric and myself to the Grandparents house and leave them when I would return for the rest of the family. One big challenge was I needed to learn to drive a stick shift, as I was one of the few 41 year olds who did not know how to shift gears.

The caravan was again packed and when I flew back to move the rest of family and all our furniture and stuff, we returned to

Seattle. My in-laws were on a sailboat cruise through the San Juan Island and we were able to land at their Bellevue home and occupy the basement until they returned.

It was a fun trip the little rabbit got forty plus miles a gallon and the only problem was sleeping in the rest areas. My six foot three frame had to sleep on the passenger's seat, totally reclined, with Melissa behind the wheel and Eric stretched across the back seat. They were young at the time, so it worked fine. Missy was the lookout while I slept a few hours. I was a pretty trusting guy back then, as I didn't really like guns – even for protection. God had us covered. My kids sure learned to be flexible – I hope it helped them in some way.

Timeout!

Writing this story did show me how God prepared all of my children for "Battles of their Faith" in later years. If I didn't mature enough in my Faith to understand God's ways, I would think I was a horrible father. I hope this book shows how God has plans, sometimes contrary to the world's ways.

We made the trip in two nights and three days – and all went well. We arrived late on a Saturday and on Sunday we went to the Kirkland Community Chapel Church. It was a blessed service and the Spirit of the Lord was so sweet that day. After church I searched the Seattle Times classified ads for housing and found a tiny ad for a one hundred and thirty-nine acres home on the Snohomish River. I called the owner and she gave me directions to drive out there. "Oh my goodness! It was beautiful!"

The next day we met at their lovely Capitol Hill home in Seattle to discuss the renting of this beautiful home – a paradise on the picturesque mountain river. The house was a four bedroom Georgian style two stories, yet one of the bedrooms could have all three boys, as it was twenty-four by eighteen feet! This farm home was located on a quarter of mile Snohomish riverfront and on the backside was Lords Hill, with a logging road that took you to the top of the property, which elevated to five hundred feet. I was in awe coming from Chicago where an acre and a half lot was huge. Our Pine Lake home was awesome, but this farm was quite majestic.

I shared my vision for a Christian ministry and why I followed God out here to the Seattle area – Community Chapel Church, the letter, and it seemed to make sense to these people. They rented us the house with all the amenities for seven hundred a month. We would be like pioneers with the entire wilderness surrounding us. Mrs. Miller mentioned the sightings of bears, cougars, eagles, and all sorts of wildlife; not withstanding all the salmon that migrated in the river. I rented it and couldn't wait to show Chris this gem and the antique town just 1 mile down the river. At this point, no job, no income but a wonderful place for my family to live to enjoy the true beauty of the mountains, streams, rivers, and the Puget Sound, but most importantly to grow spiritually.

With the paradise on the Snohomish River secured, I flew back to Chicago and packed our U-Haul for the final trip to the Northwest. Although we had my wife's family in the area, it took a strong call from God to even make the venture. Unless you've ever been led by God's Holy Spirit to fulfill a calling, you could never relate to this venture. I was leaving a teaching position at High School District 211 that most teachers would "die for". I was risking the financial security of my family of eight for a "call" that I did not fully understand but all I honestly knew is that it was powerful!

Timeout!

I recently researched the average salary of High School District 211 teachers and in a recent survey the highest paid teacher received an incredible salary of $160,135. And he was a driver's education teacher. My district was the largest High School district in the state. In 2010 a P.E. instructor made $150,000 where districts elsewhere in state made $58,000. No research shows the instruction was any different.

In the back of my mind, I knew that I was starting over out in the great northwest. I had to go. It was totally a blind trust that everything would fall in place – God would never leave me alone! He would bless our family! The search for His calling would be completed!

Timeout!

Whenever I got doubts I reflected on that day in my reading lab when I desperately sought guidance by repeatedly opening Mr. Pethick's large black Bible and ten straight times it opened to Deut. 11:11. God used my simple trust to guide me. Not sure I recommend this but He was there in my foolishness.

Chapter 21

Settling into the farm home was such an adventurous feeling. We were modern day pioneers in a sense – moving from the fast paced Chicago area to an entire new life. I led my family here with only $2,000 dollars in savings after the costs of the move. Imagine six children, my wife, a dog, a cat, all trusting me as I trusted God. I had sent a request to the state of Illinois Teachers to cash in my retirement benefits – with all the penalties I would receive $17,000 in a couple months. I certainly was not following the advice from any credible financial advisor. I was forty-one and would be completely starting over. Yet, I knew He was there; He was guiding my life. I had a peace.

Timeout!

We made this second and final move to the great northwest with $2,000 cash. Six children, no job, and insurance through the summer, yet, I had an unbelievable peace.

The farm stretched along the Snohomish River for nearly one-quarter of a mile. The backdrop of the home was the picturesque, majestic Lords Hill. The property extended up the logging road for nearly five hundred feet then it leveled off, and along that trail was a beautiful waterfall. A fishing pond was situated just south of the house about three hundred feet. Cougars had been spotted lurking around that pond in early morning. We saw at least one. Bears were known to habitate the woods up on Lords Hill. It was truly a natural paradise with the river full of salmon and trout.

Our youngest son Eric (10 yrs. old) was able to raise chickens in the cute old-fashioned chicken coop. He also purchased a couple goats that used to jump up on the hood of our Ford wagon. Tragically, coyotes killed them; I felt so sorry for Eric as he loved his animals. We were like the TV family "The Waltons". Since I had to be a member of the church for one year before teaching and ministering in athletics, I resumed my real estate career. In addition, I worked for a private, non-profit alternative school in Seattle part time. My salary was a mere $7.50 an hour and I worked 5 straight hours with only a twenty-minute lunch break. We sold our custom van for $4,500 to pay expenses until my pension check arrived. Our sister-in-law, Lynn was a manager at Tunturi so she got Chris her first job since having six children. She worked in the mailroom and enjoyed it, but had to travel to Bellevue each day. Things were tough, but we really never got down about our move. Our needs were always met.

The Benjamin's lived just down the "Short School Road" from the farm; they were good Christian people and Mrs. Benjamin offered to take care of Allison and Brittany – before and after school. We put Missy and Eric in the Chapel Christian School in Kirkland and it was a great experience; however, the cost ate up most of my Illinois retirement funds. Melissa was in ninth grade and she would watch the children until Chris and I got home. I purchased a Ford Wagon for $1,500 for Chris to drive and I drove the Rabbit. The Volkswagen Rabbit kept breaking down – try selling real estate without an auto. Things were very difficult, yet somehow we always had enough. The owner of the farm gave us permission to chop down alder trees for firewood. Since the farm had about one hundred and forty acres there was an abundance of Alder trees. Marc and I purchased a chain saw together and we cut enough firewood to pay the rent.

At an early age Marc was an entrepreneur. He idolized Uncle Bud's ability to create a business and make it go. Marc gathered and sold earthworms and night crawlers to the local bait shop when we lived in Dundee, Illinois. At age fifteen, he worked at Gosley's Farm raising catfish in his ponds about eight miles from our Sleepy Hollow house.

We did quite a little business selling firewood. Once the rent was paid Marc got to keep all profits. (I believe he got the better of the deal). He also worked at Van Batavios dairy farm down the road. Early on I financed Marc's antique truck for our business. I purchased it for seven hundred dollars - it had a good engine and was previously used to haul cement blocks. I wasn't too sure how Marc liked it by the "look" on his face when I brought it home. He was kind and didn't say anything to me, but quickly named it "The Grey Lady".

Marc came up with another business plan to sell steelhead passes on the river as our property was private and on the best fishing part of the river. Originally, he was going to sell thirty a year; however, I am convinced he far exceeded that. Once again he shared the profits with me as I paid the rent, and we were still struggling.

My teaching job was the most difficult one I could ever imagine. I taught four classes (U.S. History, English, Math, and P.E.) with no prep period. It was a challenge each day and I began to wonder what had I done, but spiritually I was so happy (with our church) that we were able to forge ahead.

At the end of that first year, a cloud came over the church we had given up so much to become part of. The main pastor in Seattle came up with a doctrine that was called "spiritual connections". Men and women were becoming connected to another – like in a spiritual bond. It began by paring up during worship songs, in the service and dancing unto the Lord as spiritual partners. Nothing of it seemed right to me and my oldest son Matt, who was then a senior at Snohomish High School. I called Uncle Bud and some seasoned Christians back in Indiana and I remember Bud's words:

"Alan Satan has no new tricks, he had the same
thing back in Elkhart, Indiana in the 1950's. Many
marriages were destroyed and it left an ugly mess!"

We had to leave the church, I thought as I prayed in a corner of the barn on the farm. I was down there feeding the three horses we boarded for extra funds. Soon depression set in as I often substituted prayer for drinking a few glasses of wine in the barn, reliving my dire mental state.

Soon I arranged a meeting with Pastor Fred of the Kirkland church for his explanation of this new spiritual move. Walking up the steps of that beautiful quaint church in Kirkland that was our spiritual home, I thought to myself: "Fred better have an explanation that exceeds any of my arguments against this seemingly false teaching". I loved the pastor and so many of the people. It was the church I sought – reminiscent of that wonderful church in Troy, Michigan and my home church in South Bend, Indiana. Not too far into the meeting with Pastor Fred and the assistant pastor, I realized that they were totally deceived – the church I gave everything up for was becoming so cultish in that everyone seemed to think so much alike. They were captivated by the founding Pastor who had a spiritual control over the satellite churches, like the Kirkland church.

"Pastor Fred", I said with a great emotion. "My family will be leaving the church! This doctrine is not right and I hope you are able to see it real soon!"

We were the first family to leave that church over the changing doctrine. Unfortunately, many marriages were destroyed over the spiritual dancing, and connections. The deceptions grew as married people were becoming "prayer partners' with others – not their spouses.

The main church in Burien had three thousand members and in the years to come it became just a couple hundred. The Bible College of twelve hundred and the Christian School all failed shortly after this false teaching began.

My heart was broken. "Lord, what did I do?" I gave up so

much leaving High School Dist. 211 in Palatine, Illinois. My realty business was so blessed! We had an estate home on a private lake. Yet, I was depressed there.

God quickly spoke to me one morning as I was once again down at the barn. "Alan, that church blessed you and Chris so much, you learned about me in a way like never before. You grew spiritually so much in that year. Satan came and destroyed a good thing, but I have new plans to return you to your original calling: teaching and coaching in the public school."

Timeout!

God had never spoken to me like that before. Never so detailed. It was awesome and such a peace came over me. I found the spiritual peace that I had been searching for and now I was ready for the next phase of His calling for me.

During the days following that spiritual encounter in the barn, I prepared an updated resume and dropped it off to both Snohomish and Monroe Public School Districts. Within days I was given interviews at both districts. Snohomish offered me a position as an English teacher in the fall with a possibility of coaching the boys Varsity basketball squad. Monroe had an opening in a few weeks as a teacher was taking a pregnancy leave. It was an L.A.P. teaching position (remedial reading) at Salem Woods Elementary School. I remembered back to my previous sixteen years of high school teaching and coaching in Michigan and Illinois when I said: "I would never teach elementary!" Right then it seemed so wonderful. It was so wonderful! I felt so blessed that God covered my blunders and had me back on track.

Timeout!

God was there again leading me back to my true calling. At both Avondale Sr. High in Michigan and Palatine High in Illinois I was an idealist. I saw through those years how there could only be a great education for students if God was included throughout the curriculum and the teacher's hearts and minds. Now, after giving up everything to be a part of such a school district, I realized that this was not my real calling. God molded me for the public school children. Christian schools can be a wonderful experience, but educators and coaches are needed for those who were in the public schools of America. And as I look back, God placed me in districts that were "friendly" to my beliefs.

My interview at Monroe went super well! They were ultimately looking for a reading specialist to run the LAP program at the Monroe Middle School, but they would place me as the LAP teacher at Salem Woods for the second semester. They seemed excited to have me and I was so thankful to save my career.

Timeout!

Once again the peace of the Holy Spirit came over me, as I knew I was back in God's will.

I began at Salem Woods on January 5, 1985 right after winter break. Our Christmas vacation was so blessed as I could relax knowing that my financial blunder of moving without a job was salvaged at Monroe. The Superintendent (who was anxious to get me into coaching at the high school) said they would find a spot for me the next year. I was willing to do anything!

At Salem Woods I was so blessed to have a lady as the educational assistant that was so bright and full of experience to help me learn the ropes of the program on a daily basis. It was well organized and I seemed to be a perfect fit! Rather than take the teacher breaks, I offered to do her playground duties, as I couldn't believe that I got paid to play tag football with the older kids (5th and 6th) during breaks. I would quarterback one team, as the six graders would load up the other team. It was competitive and so fun. The principal, Mr. Straub, loved how I organized the games at lunch and recess.

When the winter set in and lunch recess was held in the gym I joined the kids for basketball games. Soon I organized an intermural basketball program for the older kids as they had the same lunch as me. I met with the principal and he was very excited that I was willing to set one up. This really was when I realized the strength of my organizational skills. Mrs. Nelson, the teacher aide in our LAP Reading program was extremely creative and made colorful charts for the teams. I had a desire to make it coed and we got nearly seventy players from the lunchtime. Teams were fairly matched up and at the end of the year we held a few tournaments with awards for all!

Timeout!

After coaching in the high school leagues in Detroit and Chicago suburbs, my heart went out to so many kids left out. And now I was able to organize an all-encompassing program with boys and girls. Maybe my vision for coaching girls was blossoming.

On a side note that first year in Washington we had enrolled Melissa and Eric at the Kirkland Christian School, but when I was hired at Monroe, one of the ladies from the church who lived in Snohomish drove them each day. As I previously said, Allison and

Brittany were dropped off at a neighbor's house on Short School Road and picked up the bus there.

The next year, we left the church and attended the Monroe Faith Center Church. A wonderful pastor, Bill Davis, had just employed a principal to start a Christian School at their facility. I thought to myself, "I now know that I was called to serve in the public schools; however, I would be willing to help Pastor Bill develop an athletic program.

That same year, we had a basketball squad that was quite intimidating for a first year school in sports. The Christian league that was formed was extremely flexible and I used it to our advantage with the tremendous support from Pastor Bill who was also the Principal. Our squad included Eric Dickson, a smooth shooting lefty who was in seventh grade at the time. As the league was Co-Ed since the Christian schools were considerably smaller than the public schools. Melissa Dickson, my long legged daughter in ninth grade who was very aggressive with an amazing shooting touch from the corners. There was Kyle Davis in eighth grade and his sister Julie. That gave us five. Bill and I talked and he conferred with the league director and we were permitted to pick up two or three older recent high school grads as long as they had not played high school basketball for four years and were not yet twenty years of age. I jumped on it! Marc Dickson, and two of his high school close friends, who loved hoops and played nearly every evening after school were recruited. There was one catch; they needed to take one class at the Christian School to be eligible. Bill and I rejoiced, as they were all three immediately enrolled in the Bible class. What an evangelistic tool!

That hoops season was so much fun. We opened against a Skykomish team that combined their school team with a few ringers. One guy was at least six-four, bearded and looked like a lumberman. I was convinced that he exceeded the age limit of twenty, as he looked closer to thirty. We opened the season against them at Faith Center as we had a beautiful gym then which also served as the church meeting place with the baskets raised. I loved the atmosphere. That first game was loaded with parents and fans and we did not disappoint. We led after one-quarter ten to eight. My daughter Melissa hit four jumpers from the wing – all bank shots like I taught her from that spot. I was beginning to notice just how coachable girls were. We won that game and six in a row before we lost. I must admit that having Marc and his buddies strengthened our team. Marc was varsity material in high school at Snohomish, but since we moved out here his junior year, somehow he was convinced (by returning varsity players) that his playing time would be limited. Deep down I think Marc was anxious to spend his time learning how to build log homes under Creasy Log Homes.

Eric Dickson had a break out game at Bellingham as we played a very competitive team up there. When he entered the game in the second quarter, he hit three straight jumpers and grabbed three rebounds against a squad that had four players over six feet tall. Bill Davis' niece, Dana Davis, grabbed five rebounds and played extremely tough defense. She also made a driving lay up to tie the score right before half time. It was another team victory as the older guys really worked to move the ball to the open person. A very fun season was had by all!

The school year winded down and I was technically a long-term substitute. What was coming for me next year? Mr. Straub informed me that I would be receiving a formal observation the second to last week of school and I had no major concerns as the LAP program seemed to be moving along very effectively, kids were highly motivated, and my TA kept telling me that she couldn't believe how the students loved coming to class. I was not flattered, as I knew God was in charge; I had a great peace. He gave me the anointing to be effective. Honestly, I loved helping those students who struggled and labored in school – I had been well trained and I grew to love them. Our little LAP room was a center of love and solid teaching.

During that observation, I noticed a smile come over Mr.

Straub's face as he enjoyed seeing the students so involved and happy. Cathie told me that I actually allowed her to be an active part of the teaching, and not just grade papers. Everyone was much happier with my teaching style she said.

When I was called into the office during that last week of school, Mr. Straub went over the six page typed evaluation. It was glowing! Thank God! He told me that the LAP teacher would be returning next fall, but the superintendent definitely wanted me at the Middle School or High School. Right in front of me, he called the superintendent.

"Ralph, if you don't give this guy a written teaching contract, we are going to lose him!" I was stunned as he winked at me. "He will be signing at a nearby district by next week!"

I never told him that, but I guess he believed in my abilities enough to say it. The superintendent said he would do everything to keep me. The principal assured me I was secure in having a contract.

By the end of the week I was asked to meet at the administration building and meet with the staff. I was told that I was getting a contract when technically a job was not open for certain at that time.

Timeout!

Thank you Mr. Straub and thank you Holy Spirit
for leading and guiding the situation. I was not
sure how this all works, but God was in it.

The contract included my eleven years of teaching in Illinois and my previous five years in Michigan. Whoopee! I would be starting with sixteen years of experience. Nothing had been wasted!

The family had a wonderful time living on the beautiful farm God provided on the Snohomish River. No more struggling. We could relax and enjoy this wonderful Northwest paradise.

Timeout!

The LAP program was organized into centers of learning and I had learned back in Michigan and Illinois that this was the way to develop a true reading center. Variety of learning and keeping everyone involved was much easier managed. The children had more responsibility and they loved that aspect. My coaching background played an important role in this thinking.

Timeout!

I wanted to include that short time at Faith Center as I believe it showed my desire to build great teams, be competitive, and have fun. Yet, ministering was always at the foremost in my thinking. Leaving good memories and lasting relationships were always so important to me. Now, we need to get back to that description of my first years at Monroe Schools.

Chapter 22

Monroe Middle School

The fall in the Northwest was unbelievably beautiful. Chris and I looked out over the 140 acres with the majestic Lords Hill behind us and the pond and river in front of us. God's glory shined down upon us, we were in his paradise. The kids were happy – and I was extremely glad for my second chance. I would not disappoint my new district. They would be getting a teacher/coach who was going to leave it all on the court, the football field and most importantly, the classroom.

Timeout!

Please understand I had received flawless evaluations in my prior sixteen years in Michigan (5) and Illinois (11). Yet, I saw my anointing fade and God brought me to a new land and gave me a fresh anointing. I would not disappoint anyone.

The school year began and I could not wait to work in the reading lab that was housed with commodore 80's (20 stations of learning). The school had received a grant to purchase the program, but had not had a secondary reading specialist to manage the program. My goal was to add to the lab approach with some enrichment centers to keep the interest of the students at a high level.

Mrs. Bosse, the teacher aide, was fantastic. She had basically run the program prior to my arrival. The reason was they had six different English teachers – each were working one class period in the lab. Mrs. Bosse held it together. Fearful that I might offend this kind lady, I slowly added learning groups, along with the computer skills training. It went really well and Mrs. Bosse became like a sister to me. She loved the Lord and what a blessing to spend most of my teaching day in the lab with her.

Our principal was Mike Weatherbie. I had never worked for such an outgoing and positive educational leader. Principal Straub had told Mr. Weatherbie that I had a lot of charisma and would be a great Leadership teacher as the person who taught that class had left to become an administrator. Mike Weatherbie assigned me the class along with the four hours in the reading lab. He said, "Alan, this will give you a great balance as you will be working with the most motivated kids as well as those who need some motivation".

It was a great combo. I loved my lab students. We became close as the classroom was like a family (Mrs. Bosse and I were like parents). She shared my love for those students. The emphasis that I wanted was to restore confidence in kids who basically were tuned out to school and their skills waned. Others needed very little motivation as they were in the class knowing they needed an improvement in reading skills and language skills in order to have the skills for high school and college. It was a good mix many of the students were highly motivated by the one on one learning program that the computers offered. Remember this was 1985 and computer learning in schools was new. It was all new to me and I humbly learned right along with those students.

"Mr. Dickson it's easy, just follow this sign in procedure," one boy eagerly informed me. I asked him not to be so loud as I didn't want the class to know their lab instructor had zero computer knowledge. Teaching can be very humbling.

Timeout!

I remember back at Palatine Dist. 211 where all of the
staff were given some computer introduction on an in
service day. I was in a group with the Palatine coaching
staff and we all, being a seasoned group of teachers/
coaches didn't take it seriously as we thought that we'd all
be retired before these computers were part of education.
God had other plans for me and some of those guys.

It was fall and football was in full swing. My coaching assignment
that first year of Monroe was ninth grade football and ninth grade
girls basketball. Previously at Avondale Sr. High in Michigan and
Palatine High in Illinois, I had great success at coaching this age
group. The enthusiasm and hopes usually were high and this football
squad at Monroe Junior High was no exception. My assistant and I
felt we were dealt a promising group of players. A great line anchored
by the powerful Brady Scott, and a backfield that was explosive with
the powerful running of Mike Fierke. These two young men were
two of the most focused and determined athletes that I ever coached
in football. I only coached them for two years as I soon turned my
personal goals toward developing into a top head basketball coach.
Well our offense was so impressive that the head coach asked me
to move up to the Varsity staff as the offensive coordinator. After a
season of that I enjoyed it, but the required Sunday morning coaches
meetings kept me from attending church with the family. I resigned
at the end of that season. I would wait for my future as a head coach
in basketball.

Timeout!

I had been an assistant to two exceptional coaches
in Chicago suburbs and the Detroit area. I was
content being under dynamic coaches, but I knew
my time would come. God gave me a peace.

Basketball season was soon approaching and it seemed refreshing to walk into the gym after school that first year as basketballs were bouncing and both the girls teams warmed up at opposite ends of the court. Well, this was not how I expected to make a reputation as a top basketball coach. I remembered back at Palatine High where I turned down coaching the Varsity girls (I stayed with the boys program as an assistant). Here I was - and I had to make a splash in this district coaching ninth grade girls. The coach who had them as eighth graders told me that they had some talent; their record for him was five wins and five losses.

The first two weeks of the season we went up to the high school and ran drills with the junior varsity and varsity team. Watching my ninth graders perform with those girls, I saw a very promising season for my squad. Leah, a lanky post about five-eleven with a smile as wide as Magic Johnson's really impressed me. Then, I had a pair of very athletic twins who were soccer stars but eager to learn the game of basketball. They were both strong enough to compete on my ninth grade team and were aggressive and fast. Next, I saw a very solid power forward in a girl, who was also a twin to a boy who was a standout on my ninth grade football team. These four girls along with a heady and very sweet guard named Kerry impressed me as well as the high school staff. This girl would be able to play the point guard as well as the two guard. Another guard really impressed me – her name was Darcy. My attention was drawn to her in a special way because the other coaches warned me that she could be a challenge. I smiled to myself and saw an abundance of talent in this very skilled player.

Timeout!

Attending services at the Kirkland Church at the time, gave me so much love from God's anointing there. I was full spiritually and had a strong desire to love all of these players and just give them faith in their ability on the court and in their lives. It really was almost magical. It was so hard to explain, but I could feel it and knew it was genuine. Life was exciting. God gave me passion for coaching girls basketball.

We steamrolled through the ninth grade league and won every game for the first month of the season. As the leadership teacher, I had assigned one of the students in the class to interview the players and do write ups for the school paper. This girl was named Stephanie. She got so caught up in the wave of excitement that she asked to be the manager. Her skills were such a blessing and soon I turned over the position of stats to her. The students and staff at Monroe Jr. High started attending our home games and it was refreshing to a district that had limited success in athletics in several years. The boys ninth grade basketball squad that year was struggling and managed only one win. The high school football and basketball teams were also having a rough road at the time. Along with the ninth grade football team, these girls were the future.

As we neared the end of the season and were getting ready to play the Shorecrest ninth graders who were also undefeated, I really started pushing the girls. We added a full court "run and jump" press that I thought might be helpful in a close game. It was as we utilized this press I learned from Dean Smith of North Carolina while I attended a coaching conference when coaching in the Chicago area.

The press seemed to shock Shorecrest's talented young guards.

The twins and Darcy were all standout soccer players and understood the concept of trapping and releasing. Karen, the power forward and Leah our center were excellent at the zone concepts needed to protect the middle and the basket. Shorecrest fought back and made the game close. I called timeout and Darcy walked slowly to the huddle grimacing as she whispered: "Coach, I need to rest for a minute." All I could muster up to say was, "Please hurry back, Darcy!"

The game continued and we held on to our slim lead of three points until Darcy returned. "Darcy, are you OK? Do you feel good enough to play?" I spoke quietly to her. "I am good to go, coach," she answered. Darcy returned for the final three minutes and was a key in our press break offense along with our heady captain. We won by six points in our only close game of the season. Previously, we had average sixty-three points to the opponents mere twenty-eight. I really grew fond of coaching these young ladies, and Darcy's determined spirit really helped create a bond with me. I knew that coaching girls was way beyond what I ever expected, but this first experience really impressed me in so many ways.

Our season was so successful that the athletic director arranged for a game with a top A.A.U. team from Canada. They were touring the U.S. and the game was scheduled in our gym on a Saturday morning. Our regular season had ended undefeated and now we had one more challenge. I loved the excitement this team was bringing to our school and especially a coach reviving his career that had been dormant. Yet, it was only ninth grade girls basketball.

Timeout!

As I looked back, God had blessed me with coaching
under a great coach at Avondale High in Michigan (Barry
Davis). And my other mentor Eddie Molitor at Palatine
High in the N.W. Chicago suburbs. Those mentors as
well as Coach Tony Hinkle, the Hall of Fame coach at
Butler, that I was so blessed to learn from in my three
years there – really prepared me. Now, I could bless
these young athletes as my passion was really lighting
up to serve in Hoops and as a testimony of God's grace.
The cool thing was God renewed my coaching passion
and it was in Girls Hoops – remember I turned down a
varsity coaching position at Palatine High years before.
Now, I was thrilled to be the ninth grade coach.

<u>A sign that God was in it!</u>
At the same time our family was increased by one, my nephew
Alan Forrest from Mishawaka, Indiana. He was a sports nut and
he was named after me. Alan was knowledgeable and skilled in
all sports in high school, but it was baseball where he excelled. He
headed our way on his way back from a Los Angeles Dodgers farm
team as his career was shortened by ankle and knee injuries. He
fit right in as he helped with Allison and Brittany after school and
actually became our house cleaner. He was a neat boy and Chris was
thrilled to have a clean house to come home to from her mailroom
job in Bellevue. He attended a few of my ninth grade football squad's
games and the guys referred to him as Miami Vice man with his
trench coat, collar up, and large black sunglasses. I considered him
a son.

The basketball season with the girls seemed to interest Alan and
he was a big help with stats as he also had the Hoosier passion for

hoops. It was a great time of my life with the entire family involved in my girls team. My youngest son Eric served as the manager and had the opportunity to get in a lot of shooting practice when not getting the cones and balls ready for our drills. I noticed he had a sweet jumper as a lefty and showed great promise. He quietly listened to all my shooting skills instruction and just practiced on his own.

We defeated that Canadian squad and finished our season 13-0! What a season! Needless to say, all the girls had a great season, but Darcy's skills really intrigued me and I felt successful in helping her gain the confidence to realize her potential. No longer was she easily discouraged, but vibrant and eager to use her skills for a full game.

My wife, Chris and I hosted an overnight at the farm (at the players request) to celebrate the season. We watched some movies, had popcorn, pizza and shared funny stories of the season. My oldest daughter, Melissa helped supervise; yet when we fell asleep around 1:00 AM we heard screaming and joyful yelling from the pasture. Marc was giving the girls joy rides in his jeep through the cow fields. I sent Matt and Missy out there to haul all the kids and we finally got them to sleep. At least they were quiet. We really bonded as a team in such a short season.

Timeout!

Darcy needed rides occasionally during that season and we
would talk about basketball and I brought up God. We had
the same beliefs. I soon learned. Today, I would not drive alone
with a player, boy or especially girl, but I did call her mother for
permission. A week after the season I invited her mother and
her to my Kirkland Church – I felt close to Darcy. Then, they
invited me to Cornerstone Church in Woodinville where they
used to go. I believe that I helped get them back into attending
church again. It was rewarding to me. And I later became an
active member of their church; however, they had moved to
Wichita, Kansas. Her dad was transferred there by Boeing.

The rest of that 1985-86 school year was perhaps my best ever. I
gave every ounce of my energy to the Monroe School District because
I was so thankful to be back in God's plan for me. And I received
much encouragement from Mr. Weatherbie, our principal and the
parents of my Leadership class as we really did accomplish a lot. I
had those students the entire year and they were the "cream of the
crop". We set up six committees and literally were the teachers and
principals helping hands. In addition to organizing all the assemblies,
some field trips, recycling for the entire school; the students reached
out to the community and served the retirement center in many ways
as well as served as apprentices in local businesses. This class helped
connect the community and the school. It took a lot of energy, but
my passion to develop leaders and a creative nature that came out of
me made me a perfect fit to be their leader.

Timeout!

I guess I showed leadership skills last spring semester as I taught at Salem Woods. Mr. Straub had told me that he recommended me to Mr. Weatherbie as the new Leadership teacher for the Junior High. In addition, he recommended me to a parent group as a leader and mentor for their Christian club that was just getting off the ground (Young Life). I knew that I was where God wanted me. God always orchestrated my life. Looking back, that previous move to the Northwest at the end of the summer, I sent out a few applications when the leaders of the Community Chapel Christian School were asking me to wait a year before employment to get to know me. Immediately, I received an invitation for an interview at a new high school in Issaquah. The assignment was teaching English and coaching girls basketball. I thought I would be the perfect fit as the interview went well, and they told me I was one of the two selected from the field of sixty-six. When they called me three days later with the report that they hired the other candidate I was totally devastated as that meant we were moving back to Chicago. I flopped on our king-size bed in the Redmond home, face down and cried. They selected a first year teacher, which made me more understanding as I recovered from my sadness. We moved back but just for that one year.

Timeout!

Reflecting back I realized that God had the perfect school
for me and that was at Monroe. There were a number of
fundamental Christians in administration and the staff. I was
never alone as He led me there. Perhaps the road to Monroe
could have been smoother if I had listened to the Holy Spirit
more clearly, but I ended up there and it all was good.

Chapter 23

It would be nearly five years before I moved up to coach high school basketball. In the meantime, I coached both eighth grade boys and girls at Monroe Middle School. I took both jobs seriously as I pushed the girls as hard as I did the boys. Constantly studying, attending coaching classes and creating new offenses and defenses became a fun way to spend my evenings and weekends. I loved to be original and I always wanted to take the best from the books and videos including; Bob Knight (Indiana), John Wooden (U.C.L.A.) Dean Smith (North Carolina), and of course my college mentor Tony Hinkle of Butler University.

Soon I found time to return to selling real estate again as I had both my teaching well organized and my coaching at the middle school was also set up with both defensive and offensive plans completed. I joined the staff at the Century 21 office in the spring of 1988 and soon became one of their top salesmen. My wife, Chris, had just been hired as their office secretary and she bragged about my sales awards in Illinois. It wasn't long before the office manager called me in for an interview. Three jobs was a bit much and does wear on you, but it seemed as though all blended smoothly. My main emphasis was teaching, next coaching, and real estate was third. However, in the summers I was free to be extremely effective in the field of real estate.

Timeout!

My connections in teaching, coaching as well as contracts
that I acquired when sitting floor time and open house
enabled me to make a very profitable part time income
in real estate. Yet, looking back I think that I would just
teach and coach. Sure, we were able to soon purchase some
beautiful homes, but I am not convinced it was worth it.

There were many wonderful teachable moments in my classroom
at Monroe Middle School. I poured myself into teaching the
Leadership students – as all the classroom lessons were creatively
developed. There was no textbook as I literally created twelve units
of emphasis (topics) for each trimester class. Several students chose
to take the class for two or three trimesters as their elective. They
became strong leaders as they were able to mentor the new students.
No principal could have been more supportive than Mr. Weatherbie;
he gave his full confidence in my running both the reading center
and the Leadership class. This was vital to my motivation. All
teachers and coaches need strong support and continual motivation
to do their best. It sure moved me to strive for excellence in the
classroom and the gym.

The eighth grade girls basketball squads became very competitive
during those years. I enjoyed the girls competitive spirit and desire
to learn. My boys eighth grade basketball squads won two league
championships. Coaching the boys' teams was my first priority –
even though the girls' were certainly fun to coach. My personality
was a bit lighter with the girls, but I got tough if I needed to as
winning was always foremost in my competitive spirit. I was a true
Hoosier.

Soon the high school varsity boys position became available
and I updated my resume and applied. I was a finalist, came in

second and was offered the junior varsity job. I felt my experience in coaching at large high schools in Michigan and Chicago certainly prepared me for the job at Monroe, which was only a 2-A school at the time. In addition, how many middle school coaches attended coaching conferences like I did? Disappointed but not defeated, I continued my coaching at Monroe Middle School.

Then, some of the more passionate basketball fans of my middle school parent group talked to me about assisting at the high school in either the boys or girls programs. I accepted the C-team position for the high school boys team and soon realized that it was very limiting. The coach wanted very little input from the assistants and I really didn't agree with his overall philosophy as well as offensive and defensive schemes. My experience under (great) coaches back East taught me otherwise. I returned to Monroe Middle School and Mr. Weatherbie put me in charge of both boys and girls programs. Once again we were quite successful. I think my fondest memory of that period of time was coaching with Kelly Baughman. He was a highly spirited great skills coach. I let him run a lot of the ball handling and conditioning part of practice. And Kelly made me feel so talented as a coach as he kept referring to me as the master of team offense and defenses. I needed that encouragement at the time. He headed up the seventh grade team at game time and I assisted. Then, he sat on the bench to support me during the eighth grade game. This was the girls basketball season and to me Kelly was invaluable. His experiences when he served at NBC Basketball Camps for five years taught him so much. In addition, he was successful as a head varsity coach at a school in Toledo, WA prior to coming to Monroe. He kept insisting that I belonged as the Varsity coach at the high school. I soon needed that push.

In the fall of 1992 a very involved person, who was assisting the varsity girls coach approached me to consider coaching as an assistant at Monroe High School. I held tremendous respect for this dad as he was the father of a very skilled point guard/shooting guard that I coached his eighth grade year at Monroe Middle. He was a coach's dream; high basketball IQ and the skills to match. It was obvious his father had taught him a lot of this. In addition, this dad had observed my coaching style during the years his oldest daughter played for Kelly on the seventh grade team. He felt that the high school girls program needed my influence.

After a few weeks of thinking it over, I told the high school athletic director that I would move up to the girls J.V. position. My thinking was that I had two daughters (Allison and Brittany) coming up and maybe it would be a great experience to be their basketball coach. I envisioned it would be a tremendous family bonding – and later this vision became real!

Allison was in sixth grade and Brittany in fourth at the time and both were very girly with dolls and dresses and "Little House on the Prairie" movies. Their weekends were often filled up video taping each other, not playing hoops, but dancing, singing and acting out skits. That was all really good, but my passion for hoops would add basketball drills on our sports court Marc had built on the seven acre ranch we now enjoyed on Florence Acres Road, across from the Blue Boy Golf Course.

I should digress back a few years and explain how real estate sales blessed our family. When I worked at Century 21 in Snohomish we attended a Christian fellowship at Snohomish High School under the leadership of Pastor Gary Allard, a wonderful young man who also loved basketball. Soon we were able to purchase St. Michaels church on Ave. B in downtown Snohomish. It was a dynamic church and a good fit for our family. Yet, it failed to continue when several members of the congregation opposed Gary starting a part time business so that he could keep his children in (Kings Christian School) near his modest home in Edmonds. Gary decided to step down as pastor and the church soon dwindled.

One evening while sitting floor time, Gary walked into the office and showing a surprised look to see me there. I asked him how I could help him and he answered what I feared was the answer;

"Alan, we are selling the church as the numbers had dwindled to financially make sense to continue."

Immediately, I replied with the question: "How much will you need to sell it for?" The young pastor looked at me and said in his honest and sincere way, "we just need enough to pay back the members who donated to the down payment."

My immediate reply was "Gary, how much would that be?" "About $129,000", he replied. "Can you wait a few weeks and let me purchase it as I have cash coming from the sale of my Sleepy Hollow house in Illinois", I told him.

We made arrangement with a handshake and the church was never listed. Within a month the deal was closed and we left the farm on the river for this new in town mansion. The parsonage was 4,400 square feet and the church held over two hundred people. Our kids loved this new adventure.

All six of our children were still at home and the parsonage held us all very comfortably. Matthew had returned a while back from his two year stint as an honor guard representing the navy at the White House during President Reagan's presidency. It was his marching band experience and tremendous skill as a drummer that really helped him get that opportunity. Being tall and handsome certainly helped also. God blessed us in many ways. I felt like I should have forced him to finish college, but joining the navy gave him a rare opportunity to experience life in Washington D.C. College could come later.

That year living at the Saint Michael's Church was memorable. I loved walking through the corridor that connected the parsonage to the church, and walking around the auditorium just meditating, praying, and feeling God's blessings. Sometimes, I would climb the stairs that led to the balcony and look out the corridors overlooking the beauty of downtown Snohomish. That view was wonderful, yet the most phenomenal view was from the den in the parsonage where Chris and I had our bedroom surrounded by windows that had spectacular views of Mt. Rainier and the entire Snohomish River and downtown area. The upper windows in this sleeping paradise were all stained glass. With six bedrooms and four baths the Dickson's were quite comfortable.

On a side note, when we were getting close to closing the deal on the church, Gary asked me if he could join me on the ownership. He felt the church would be more comfortable letting us assume the note if he was also on the note. Chris and I prayed about it and a few days later agreed to it. Sharing the liability might be a good thing. We would live in the parsonage, assume the responsibility of paying the very small payment of around eight hundred dollars and he would help with all improvements. He was a professional painter and he agreed to paint the entire building with Matt's assistance as he also had some experience in that from summer jobs.

Some other notes on Saint Michael's "Twice in a Lifetime" with Gene Hackman was filmed there a few years before we purchased it. It was a true Victorian Style church with a tall bell tower and a cross at the top. The fact that the cross had been unpainted really bothered me. Marc and a friend offered to climb up there and paint it for us. I prayed heavily as Marc climbed up that steep roof of the church with a ladder nailed to the roof. His friend was up there to secure the ladder, but I did not allow him to climb up to where it was extremely dangerous. The mission was successful and now I look back at how I trusted God, perhaps immaturely.

The year at the church was 1990 and our daughter, Melissa was just named Miss Washington, U.S.A. It was an amazing feat since she had very little training, but she seemed to have that fresh look and open personality that endeared her to the judges. For some reason, I really felt God was in control here and had a purpose for this accomplishment. Melissa was only nineteen and the youngest ever Miss Washington. Ambitious and thankfully well rounded in her goals, Melissa attended Edmonds Community College, and also had a role in giving speeches to the local schools. Having always been compassionate she was very active in supporting the Big Sisters program in our state. My leadership class at Monroe Middle School organized an assembly and Melissa was the key speaker, and her theme was basically "treat others as you wanted to be treated". It was a big hit and her younger sisters Allison and Brittany were proud to have their sister speak so confidently and poised in front of the nearly eight hundred students in attendance.

That year the Leadership class in the spring had one of the best groups of young teens ever assembled. There were about ten students who were especially dynamite, all wholesome, well-rounded leaders. They stepped forth with great ideas for the class. It was no secret that I was a strong believer in Jesus Christ and so were these ten students. When I shared stories to some of them in response to questions about my previous experiences teaching, they were most captivated by my sharing about the dynamic youth group back at Willow Creek Church in Illinois where many of my Palatine High students attended.

Caylin Lee, one of the sweetest young girls I ever taught, asked me directly. "Mr. Dickson why don't we organize a "Son City" youth group at your church in Snohomish. Soon she had others in the class pushing this idea. "What was I to do? I thought. The Holy Spirit was clearly moving here and I went with the flow. I shared the idea with my principal and he seemed favorable as long as it was not school related in any way.

Within two weeks we had nearly fifty students involved every Thursday evening, as I did not want to conflict with the many churches who held Wednesday evening youth services. Basically, Chris and I provided the church sanctuary, and in our kitchen my wife provided treats for all the kids after the message. The students met at the church and we walked over to the nearby elementary school grounds to play kickball and sometimes basketball of course. We were able to get almost all involved in the outside games. After about one-half hour we would return to the church and Caylin, Andi-Kay, and several others would lead worship songs. After about fifteen to twenty minutes, one or two of the students would share a testimony or give a talk from the Bible. I was in seventh heaven just to be able to help facilitate this experience for these students, some of whom were not church attendees.

It was just simply beautiful to hear these kids speak so sincerely. One of the early meetings Melissa shared her testimony and the boys seemed especially proud to have a picture with Miss Washington, U.S.A.

For these skeptics who might think that I crossed the line between church and school, I had not one complaint from a parent. These were eighth graders and were driven to the youth meetings by parents and some would observe or go downtown and return later. They seemed to have smiles on their faces. I know that I sure did!

There was one "scare" toward the end of the meetings as school was drawing to a close for the summer. One of the most distinguished mothers, a very prominent doctor in Seattle, asked to speak to me during the end of our second to last meeting. We walked through the corridor and I asked the Holy Spirit to give me the right words to whatever she had to say.

She looked intently into my eyes and said, "Alan, this is the most wonderful experience for our children. Thank you so much." I should have hugged her, but I just replied, "Thank you for your support."

Timeout!

At this point of my career, I had taught and coached for twenty-three years; and never had one complaint or nothing but glowing evaluations in teaching and coaching. Put your whole heart into serving others and He will watch over you!

Chapter 24

As mentioned my teaching position consisted of four reading lab classes and one leadership class; it was a wonderful blend, as I loved to motivate and both programs needed that as well as enthusiasm. The passion to help my reading students and guide both those classes as well as the Leadership students was genuine and it came from the Lord and it's hard to explain other than: deep down I wanted to change lives and the Holy Spirit gave me the power to do so.

My vast experience and education in reading skills instruction sure prepared me for all the years of assisting students who struggled in reading. Just like good coaching the instructor should be able to pinpoint weakness and strengthen them. However, the key always was praise their efforts and look for their strengths. Most always struggling readers would improve rapidly if you were very diagnostic in your technique just like coaching basketball or any other sport. The reading labs that I developed and supervised at Avondale Senior High, Palatine High and Monroe Middle School all were great tools of instruction, but really blossomed if the instructor was trained and passionate to assist the students.

My contentment with this combination of teaching positions at Monroe Middle and coaching the boys and girls basketball teams was soon to be disrupted. I accepted the offer to assist the high school girls varsity coach and I really was content with just that! Instead of just playing dolls and watching "Little House on the Prairie", I noticed Ally and Brittany shooting hoops after school on our sports court. It was time to activate my true passion to a higher level and return to high school coaching, and the opportunity to bond with Ally and Brittany down the road through the round ball would be invaluable.

After completing her tour and duties as Miss Washington, U.S.A., Melissa had expressed a strong desire to relocate near my family in Indiana and continue her studies at Indiana University, South Bend campus. I was very comfortable with that as she expressed an interest to attend our family church 'Apostolic Temple', in South Bend. Energetic and all around talented, Melissa was soon on the cheer team. I learned never to doubt her determination.

After two years at Indiana University, she returned home being engaged to the star of the I.U.S.B. basketball squad, Todd Vaught! Before Todd completed his studies and had a few games left for I.U.S.B., Chris and I visited family and attended a holiday tournament at Bethel University. Todd scored thirty points and grabbed eighteen rebounds in the championship game vs. my old school Bethel. That summer they were married and relocated to Seattle to live with us on our farm on Florence Acres Rd., Monroe.

Now with Todd on board, and my son Marc recently married and living in a cute custom cabin he remodeled completely from a garage located on a bluff on this gorgeous property, we had a basketball family. Once again God had blessed us with a beautiful family home. Situated on seven private acres across from a golf course, and it was just twelve minutes from my teaching job at Monroe. It was a huge three level home with four bedrooms, an office, and nearly 3,000 square feet. It was only about eight years old, and guess what? There was a fantastic indoor pool attached to the family room through a sliding glass door. We had room for all with three bathrooms. Marc built his first barn on our property to house our horse and two beef cattle that Eric bought at an auction. In addition, he made part of the barn into a unique wood shop as he began building log furniture as a part time job. With seven acres, a sports court, a large family home, and an indoor Olympic size poolroom complete with a diving board, our family felt blessed again by the Lord.

The path to purchase this property and home was surely led by the Lord. I had purchased the church for about $125,000 and sold it in ten months for $275,000. My share was $100,000, and the balance was given to Gary Allard as per our agreement. It felt good to allow Pastor Gary benefit and enable him to continue his ministry. It was just a verbal agreement with Pastor Allard and it was great pleasure to honor a fellow Christian who had sacrificed much to be in the ministry. After the closing, I carefully put my check for one hundred thousand dollars in my briefcase and that afternoon I remember showing it to my children as a validation of God keeping His word that He would take care of us.

We then purchased a ten-acre farm on Westwick Rd. The property was beautiful horse property with a small, but very cute farmhouse. However, since it needed many repairs and did not have a solid foundation to expand, I sold it for a modest profit to a local pastor who loved horses and the property. He and his wife were horse people and the property was ideal for them as he also had been a builder before going into the ministry. All of this led up to our Florence Acres home.

Working in realty at the time, I sold the Florence Acres property to clients who called me six months later as they wanted to move back to the city. They offered me a fantastic price and terms that were quite enticing. It was all in God's plan as we were now part of the Monroe community that became my ministry. The owners of the property shared my belief that this property would be ideal for my involvement in youth ministry.

We certainly used the indoor pool to house some of the youth activities and later church activities. In addition, the sports court designed and built by my son Marc, and assisted by Melissa's new husband Todd, was used nearly every evening as we all lived on the Florence Acres ranch property. Day and night memories were made on that court, as we installed pole lights my father-in-law got from the demolition of the The Kingdome. Todd Vaught was fresh off a two-year stint as the leading scorer and rebounder at I.U.S.B. in Indiana and he gave Marc and I some challenging games. Even though a couple of Marc's friends would show up, I always got paired against Todd. It reminded me of my days at Butler always competing against a taller and more skilled baller. My competitiveness was always there; it's amazing how far that can take you!

Later, as Allison and Brittany grew older, I was able to train them on this court. Chris and my sister Pat purchased a sign with the phrase "Hoosier Court" at a flea market back in Indiana, as we all came from 'Hoosierland'. The girls loved working on ball handling skills with the music blaring. I heard it was good for rhythm and though it was all right except when I was teaching – I turned it down. This time spent with the girls was the perfect opportunity to practice on drills to teach my J.V. high school girls during the season. My appetite for coaching was peaking and my love for basketball was really blooming again. Yet, I was content at the J.V. level and helping out with the Varsity. When the next season got underway, the varsity coach felt he had the squad that would really make an impact in the playoffs. He was content with just letting me have the "other end of the court" and stay out of their way. Allison was now our J.V. manager and got great experience being at the practices with me. I was happy and I liked the squad I was given for the junior varsity. Three or four of the players returned from the solid year we had the previous successful season, and we picked up four or five frosh not quite ready for the varsity.

This year was so special to me; we were becoming a team and this is what I always wanted "team ball". They eagerly learned the motion offense that I had been studying from Bobby Knight (Indiana University Hall of Fame Coach). In addition, I ran the Butler shuffle offense at various times as it had some great quick hitters. Both offenses blended well as they were based on the passing game with good movement. I continued my study of the game through books and tapes that I pulled out of boxes in the garage. In addition, I attended basketball clinics on weekends at Washington State University and a couple Seattle area clinics. My passion was becoming "red-hot".

The junior varsity squad won its first eight games and became even stronger when Brandy was sent down to the J.V. as the varsity coach seemed to be frustrated with his squad. I loved this girl's spirit and competitiveness. She had been in my eighth grade leadership class and I learned how strong she was when she challenged all the boys to arm wrestling. A few attempted, but she beat all of them and with a smile on her face. Of course, she was always smiling when competing. This girl had potential. She was a goalie in soccer and varsity shot putter. We finished the season with seventeen wins and three losses. The highlight of that season was a pool party at Coach Dickson's during winter break after practice – organized by Brandy.

The varsity team went into playoffs with Brandy added back to the roster. They suffered a tough loss to Lynnwood, one of the top teams in the state. This loss devastated the coach and he kept us all in the locker room as he went over how tough it was on him. He resigned within weeks and Monroe was looking for a coach.

Soon I was called into the High School office and the personnel director said "Alan, we would like to offer the job to you before it was posted on the W.I.A.A. website." Later I found out that most of the girls on my squad and several of the returning varsity girls were behind my selection. I asked for the weekend to think about it as I knew from my previous coaching as a boys assistant at the high school level in Michigan, and Illinois, it could be a big commitment. During that weekend I reflected on the tremendous work ethic and "fire" that most of my J.V. squad showed that year. Trisha Keating came to mind; she played two years with me on the junior varsity squad. She was a tenacious defender; probably attributed to her soccer skills and she knew the offense as a guard for me. Of course there was Brandy, a tough five-ten post who would continue to develop. Along with those returning from last year's varsity squad, I knew we could compete even in the tough Wesco League, which always had two, or three of the top teams in the state. Maybe we would become the fourth top team? I decided to take the job.

Monday came and I met the principal and athletic director Denny Coates after school at the high school office. They seemed excited and there was just a peace for me that this was God's will.

Chapter 25

Season No. 1

It was late spring when I was officially the Monroe Varsity Girls basketball coach. No big fanfare was given to the appointment, but I was taking this assignment more seriously than any coaching assignments that I had previously done. Having served under great head coaches in the boys basketball programs at Avondale High in Michigan and Palatine High in the Chicago area, I was ready for this assignment to coach girls.

Timeout!

Once again our Heavenly Father had His divine plan for me, and I knew that I was in His will coaching girls hoops. Little did I know it would become "big time" in the then small town of Monroe. My first head-coaching job was coaching girls basketball – a position I turned down at a 5-A school (Palatine High).

The Monroe girls basketball team had already begun their spring tournaments headed up by some dedicated parents. The girls were taught sound fundamentals, and the parents had the entire summer schedule worked out.

Spring sports ended and I was able to lead my new team. The parents handed the reigns over to me that first weekend tournament at Mt. Si High in Issaquah. All I had to do was show up and take over. Feeling relaxed and totally in God's will, I couldn't wait to finish my coffee and early breakfast to drive the forty minutes to meet my team. Of course, since I was the J.V. coach for two years, I was very familiar with their skills. My excitement to lead my own team was swelling before this summer contest. To be honest that excited feeling to compete continued for the rest of my career. It was my calling, which quickly became my passion. Monroe was going to compete like never before. I was given the opportunity to make it happen.

Our team had one returning senior who the previous year was elected captain. However, the young lady was now very successful in modeling and we weren't sure if she was even playing her senior year. When she decided to join the team in the try-outs, I honored her election as captain, but I added Brandy and Allison as captains with her as they were with us all spring and summer and provided great leadership during that time.

Timeout!

I was learning to make tough calls, but God was giving me wisdom to also be fair as this was to be a fun experience for all – yet, I needed to be as fair as possible and be in charge.

After that first tourney I needed to assemble my coaching staff. We won three straight games to win the tourney and I did not want to "miss a beat" into developing Monroe into a state contender.

I really liked and valued those parents who had been running the off-season with these Monroe girls, but with the previous coach the administration felt the parents were too involved. Trying to show respect and gratitude for all their work in training these girls through the traveling leagues in middle school, and high school summer leagues, I enjoyed working with them during that first summer. Yet, when the summer concluded and we won every game in the City of Everett League, and several summer tourneys, the fall it was important to put together a really competent and loyal staff. I did not want to coach three years and out; my goal was a solid foundation where the love of hoops matched my passion – from the staff all the way down to the grade school program. It would be a comprehensive program, one built to last through the years. Monroe School District had been good to me and this was where I knew I could enhance the overall image of the school. I wanted to make this community love our program.

Our goal was state after that exciting and very successful summer program! When I agreed to take the position as head varsity girls coach, the administration's mandate was that it was my program: parents could volunteer at open gyms, and fall league, etc., but I was to select the ones involved and let them know that they would not be on the bench or coaching in any way during the season. Of course, this was what I wanted anyway. In my years coaching in Michigan and Illinois under some top boys varsity coaches, it was always that way. Apparently, the previous coach had let the parents be too involved and I noticed that, but it was his program.

The roster handed to me had great potential, even though they were a .500 team the previous season talent was there. Allison Kirk was a 5-11 gal who could play the post, wing, or even bring the ball up the court if needed. Brandy Meier (who spent some time on my J.V.) was a tough low post with a powerful drop step to the basket. Joni Carter was a quick soccer player who was "cat-like" guarding the ball. All three were my top juniors. The sophomore class was loaded: Kristin Stringer, talented and could literally play post, forward or guard. At 5-10 and left-handed, I saw great potential in her. Alyssa was one of the most determined girls that I ever coached, and she worked hard every second on the court. Her father had fine-tuned her skills through the years growing up and she was ready to roll.

Amy Skillen, a sweet natured post player that I definitely was moving to shooting guard, as she had the "prettiest" shot on the team, and was our designated zone buster. Another top sophomore was Anna Kloeck, I loved her attitude and desire to compete. I saw her as a great utility player as she could handle the ball and even defend the post. She had great fundamentals. Quinn Olson, another sophomore was pegged as the starting two guard with Alyssa running the point guard. Quinn was extremely smart and was a great off guard who could also beat the press. The varsity was blessed with a very talented frosh center at six feet-one, Emily Shultz. Like Magic Johnson she was always smiling as she loved the game and had fun while going 'all out'!

The 94-95 season began with a lot of excitement! The Lady Cats raced to seven straight victories and were ranked number six in the *Seattle Times* early rankings. The high school students and the entire community of Monroe seemed to be behind these girls. Coach Dickson was given a group of girls who were totally committed to the commitment and focus it took to put Monroe on the "Girls Basketball Map" in the state of Washington. After spending most of the previous summer studying video tapes recorded from college coaches that I most respected at the time (Indiana's Bobby Knight, Dean Smith – North Carolina, and John Woods – U.C.L.A.), I was well prepared to take these girls to the highest level that we could achieve. The pieces seemed to be in place to have a "state-bound team" in Monroe.

Offensively, we ran a high post motion offense that I simplified from what Coach Tony Hinkle taught us at Butler. The practices were structured to incorporate the following daily plan: (1.) dynamic stretching (2.) ball handling warm ups (3.) fundamental drills: passing, shooting techniques, guard moves, post moves (4.) defensive techniques and team defense (5.) offensive break down drills (6.) team offense (7.) team defense (8.) conditioning (9.) 30 minutes of shooting drills.

The firsthand experience of learning under two very successful high school coaches (Eddie Molitor – Palatine High School, Illinois, and Barry Davis – Avondale High in Michigan) sure paid off when I took this job as the pilot of Monroe Girls Basketball. In addition, I studied every basketball training video that I could get my hands on and every college game that I watched on television. I also had a notebook on my lap. I was totally focused. This was my second chance.

Timeout!

I was fully aware how I turned down the varsity girls basketball position at Palatine High nearly twenty years earlier. The lure of real estate commissions, and my being too prideful to coach girls at the time kept me from serving in a very rewarding position. Now, I was ready for His will. My passion was full and the love of the game of hoops was on fire in my spirit again. Just like my younger days. It must be stated that my dear wife Christine (my gift from God) worked as a real estate secretary and got her realty license to free me up and we were an effective team. I was able to pursue my dream, my God given passion.

Coaching at Monroe soon became a true family event: greater than I ever imagined. Our family was labeled "Hooked on Hoops" and "The First Family of Basketball in Monroe". I was the head coach. Son Marc was an assistant coach. Daughter Allison (Ally), a former Monroe and college player, coached the Monroe seventh grade select team. Daughter Brittany was a guard on the varsity basketball squad. Also, my son-in-law, Todd Vaught was a volunteer coach after two years on staff. He kept getting promoted at work; therefore, we were only able to utilize him as a special assistant. He was a highly talented college player at I.U.S.B. and had much to offer the post players. His spin move to the baseline was nearly as good as Shawn Kemp's move (minus the thundering dunk).

A representative from the *Seattle Times* spent a day trailing me at school and later at practice and wrote an award-winning article in the year 2000 "Hooked on Hoops – Dickson's are First Family of Basketball in Monroe". He wrote that we are 'united in faith and an orange ball' and our coming out West from the hoop-crazy state of Indiana had a big impact on the sleepy town of Monroe, WA.

The Dickson's may have been the lead family for Monroe Girls Basketball, but so many other families stepped up and played key roles. Dads and Moms coached our feeder program (originally called "Cyclones" for our fast break mentality – and later named the Lady Bearcats).

Another key factor of the community wide buzz toward the Lady Cats program was our team's annual involvement with the elementary schools. Our players traveled once a week to the five elementary schools to mentor boys and girls in academics and become like big sisters to them. I remember going to state the first time in 1996 and seeing many of those elementary kids wearing black and orange and cheering loudly with their parents joining in.

Another key factor in the community growth of Monroe girls hoops was the fact that each of our players had a buddy on the eighth grade select team. These players bonded strongly and attended most of the games donning the number of their high school buddy.

Teaching a leadership class at the Monroe Middle School prepared me to come up with several ideas to build unity for our team and the community. The "Buddy Program" was one of the best! Often times the parents of the players and the younger A.A.U. players became close friends. Having been raised in a very close knit family in Indiana and raising my children to be very close, I strongly desired this for the basketball community of Monroe!

Chapter 26

Optimism and excitement rained down on the 1994-1995 Lady Bearcats of Monroe and it was certainly overdue. The girls varsity team had never qualified for the state playoffs and the basketball community finally had something to satisfy their thirst. After a summer full of training sessions, practices and several tourneys and summer league, we were ready to roll!

After coming out strong the girls won five in a row and started gaining statewide recognition. The early rankings placed the Monroe team in the top ten AP polls and the Seattle Times rankings. In mid season the team lost a couple of overtime thrillers, one to Meadowdale by one point and another to Lynnwood by two points. I honestly felt these losses helped us to prepare for the tough District Tournament that would soon be upon us.

As the regular season winded down the Monroe Bearcats won their 10th straight game with a 41-34 victory over Meadowdale in a Wesco AA girls tiebreaker game at Monroe. Monroe was now 17-4 and advanced to the Northwest AA District tournament as the second seed, and Meadowdale received the third seed. The spirit of "Hoosier Hysteria" was upon us here in the Northwest! The small but growing town of Monroe got caught up in following this girls basketball squad.

The *Seattle Times* and the *Everett Herald* were beginning to showcase the squad with some very favorable coverage. Attendance at home games was increasing weekly as we were fun to watch. These girls played the game of basketball the "right way". Our pressing defense played "all out" and full of energy. Our stats person (asst. coach Marc Dickson) recorded the team stats with extra attention to the "hustle" points. Deflections, rebounds, steals and blocking out all were key stats and Marc encouraged all the girls in these areas. Talking on defense was one of Marc's favorite aspects and he continually stressed that with the girls.

The coaching staff that first year was very family oriented. Marc was a volunteer coach who was in charge of videotaping, scouting, and stats. Todd Vaught, my son-in-law was the junior varsity coach. Todd was a great asset as he played college ball in Indiana (I.U.S.B.) and in the state of Kentucky. Kathleen Potthast was the "C" team coach and also the head coach of Monroe Girls Soccer. I recruited her after a round of golf at the annual coaches outing at the Blue Boy Golf Course. I knew her personality (a blend of toughness and humor) would fit perfectly. These coaches all stuck with the program in some way during my thirteen-year reign at Monroe.

Motion offense soon became our trademark and these coaches learned quickly the basics and the additional "wrinkles" that I added to fit our personnel. Our goal was to teach the girls how to really play basketball and not how to just "run plays". Each year I did incorporate ten to twelve plays that fit certain situations when we were struggling in our motion offense. Yet, when a play broke down – no problem, we just evolved into our motion game.

At Butler under "Hall of Famer" Coach Hinkle, I learned a high post, motion offense. He taught us to think continually and not just run through the sets. I even took "Theory of Basketball" courses for my P.E. minor under this mastermind of basketball. Little did I know that eventually I would share the same passion as this legend.

Timeout!

As described in my Butler days chapters, I was just "floating through those college days". I wish I had maintained the determination and intentional life that I had my frosh year at Butler and my senior year in high school at Mishawaka! Yet, again God guided me back on track and He planted me at Monroe to do His will and I was not going to fail this time!

I have to admit that a lot of my energy and mental focus was given to the task of building a powerhouse program at Monroe. All the hard work was really never work because I was "in love" with my task. Those games became so exciting and it was gratifying to see the crowd at home and key away games swell to overflowing at times.

I loved watching the girls showcase their skills, yet always playing "team first". Having always been a Celtics fan (especially during the Larry Bird era) I loved great passing and team ball! The games to me were like a ballet performance, or a musical with the performers totally ready to entertain. The game became a beautiful dance and was music to the true hoops fans' ears.

Most fans appreciate great fundamental skills and our players drilled on the fundamentals to incorporate into a true motion offense. We were always a "fast break first" squad, but if there was not an easy shot we moved directly into our free flowing motion game. And the players moved the ball quickly side to side – looking for any mismatch. All the players were very good ball handlers and passers; in addition, all could post up strongly when needed. I loved watching these Lady Bearcats perform on the hardwood.

That year the district playoffs were composed of the top four teams from Wesco and the top four teams from the Northwest league. Stanwood, Meadowdale, Monroe, Lynnwood, Lynden all were ranked in the top ten in the State. This district was loaded with talent in 1995. The Lady Bearcats could have easily been satisfied with a good showing at districts my first year, but we felt we were destined to make it all the way to state: a feat no Monroe girls basketball team had ever accomplished. We blasted Sedro Woolley in the first round and then faced Stanwood – a team that was ranked No. 1 in the state going into districts. It was a closely fought game, but we fell short in the final quarter. This dropped us into the losers bracket, but we fought our way back with two resounding wins that elevated us into the winner to state-loser out battle with Lynden.

It was a game to remember for our girls: we exchanged leads several times before Lynden took over late in the game. Determined and gritty, the Bearcats fought into a tie to end the fourth quarter. The overtime was a period of five minutes that most of our twelve girls remember to this date. Lynden made fifteen of sixteen free-throws in the overtime period. Their talented 6-2 center made nine of ten! Four of our starters fouled out and we suffered an extremely disheartening loss. Our dreams of state – a first ever – vanished in those heart breaking five minutes of overtime. We huddled up briefly, tears streaming down the cheeks of several players, and my words were brief and forceful: "Ladies, line up and congratulate Lynden and then jog directly to the locker room. No exceptions!"

The coaches and I walked to the locker room directly behind the squad. That long walk from the huge Marysville gym to our locker room took about five minutes. I needed every second to think what I was going to say. My son Marc could be heard behind me chirping to the other coaches that those refs took us out of the game in overtime. I kept focusing on the girls and my message to them.

"This needs to be a tremendous learning experience," I thought. I asked God for wisdom and He came through.

"Girls we just completed the best ever season for Monroe Girls basketball!" I am so proud to be your coach and I am so excited for our future – we started a tradition that will continue to grow and the entire state will know that Monroe High School will always be a contender!"

The players continued to hold their head between their hands, no one looked up. Yet, the tears and crying began to diminish. Next, I asked them to look up and they did.

"I love you girls, we are like family. If you join with me to dedicate next year to get all the way to state, I guarantee that we will do just that next season. We will have a plan – I just need your total dedication and I know by your focus that you will do just that!"

We only lose two players. We will make them proud of us."

Timeout!

We concluded our post game meeting with a prayer of thanks – led by Quinn (our spiritual leader). I am not certain how it started but we prayed before every game – and the players were always leading it. I was a passive spectator; yet, I must admit it always blessed me.

Timeout!

Coaches have a tough job, and mine was never easy. We had our program ready to produce top quality teams for the present and for the future. It's like life – you have everything set in order and something comes up that can break your plans down. In August I received news that Alyssa was transferring to Blanchet (one of the top prep schools in the Seattle area). At first I was devastated as she was such a fine athlete and always gave 100%. Yet, the parents wanted her to receive a top quality education at a private school to prepare for a Stanford education.

Late in the summer I met with our returning players and we all made a commitment to not let this be a roadblock to our success. We decided to turn it to our advantage. The already loaded defending state champions just got one of our best players, but we were going to overcome this roadblock. Our goals were set and we had prepared our team to function with eight or nine key players. Now we would have eight, and develop a couple frosh for key minutes in the playoffs and the future.

Chapter 27

Key Player: Mike Weatherbie, former Monroe Middle School principal and Monroe High School principal.

Looking back my principal at Monroe Middle School, Mike Weatherbie, was certainly a key player in my success in the classroom and coaching. Mike was a strong believer in my coaching ability as he watched several of my games when I coached a number of league champions at the middle school. The excitement on his face at the games was inspiring to the team. He was like an enthusiastic general manager of an NBA team.

My first year at the Middle School Mr. Weatherbie placed me in charge of the leadership classes and I appreciated the break from teaching reading/language arts skills all morning. Those classes became very popular and I took my position very seriously. I researched great leaders from all walks of life and also had the students research and share with the class. Teaching to me was just like coaching: (1) Get the students to work together (2) Diagnose their weakness and applaud their strengths (3) Have fun and watch them grow as individuals and a class.

Teaching three leadership classes certainly enhanced my coaching effectiveness. It prepared me to perform at a higher level than before. My favorite saying came from Vince Lombardi, the famous football coach of the NFL champions Green Bay Packers: "Leaders are made not born, they are developed by hard work!"

Well, I took those words seriously myself and I hit the books, attended clinics, and studied videos relentlessly in that next off-season to be prepared to lead my team. Today my garage shelves are stuffed with instructional videos, coaching books and clinic notebooks. I was totally dedicated, but to this day I am convinced it was a God-given passion: To teach life lessons through competitive girls basketball. My desire was to reach an entire community! However, to accomplish this we had to be successful!

Timeout!

Once again, God was always preparing my path. Those years
at Avondale H.S. and Palatine High helped prepare me as
I served under great coaches. This is the best way to learn
coaching – find a great coach and work directly under him/her.

My plan for preparation was to begin slowly (many of our players were two or more sport athletes and I respected that) Yet, I wanted a plan for the entire team, and the year round basketball players needed many opportunities. Therefore, in the spring we had open gym twice a week, and several girls shot in the gym after school – when track ad softball went outside. Four or five of the players played in A.A.U. ball for the Seattle Magic and Flight programs. The ball was rolling toward our success in 1996!

Many of the players would visit me in my classroom after school. We usually finished our discussion with a walk to the gym, as I would chaperone for middle school students and of course my players who wanted to come down to the middle school to "shoot around". My players knew which shots to work on and what drills to perfect: it was fun to watch them work out on their own. I was always aware and respected the W.I.A.A. rules toward off-season coaching. I was only a spectator.

Summer came and we had team practices and joined the Everett Summer League. We competed very well in three summery tourneys (The Lake Washington tourney was the most challenging back then!). Our free flowing motion offense was becoming more fluid as we trained four players to play the point guard – our perimeter play vastly improved when I adopted this concept. Alyssa had always handled the point, but I thought with Joni, Quinn, and Stringer we had several ball handlers.

Coach Marc Dickson spent so many hours studying tapes of our games; he taped everything from practices to summer games. He came up with an excellent idea to consider looking at Kristin Stringer as point guard. Marc pointed out that she was a point forward, who saw the court like an NFL quarterback.

Timeout!

My philosophy was to respect and honor all assistants and volunteers. Their contributions were of great value to me. Our program was not a dictatorship and it paid off. I learned this from delegating and developing students to participate whole-heartedly in my leadership program at Monroe Middle School! Times were changing and young people were eager at an early age to lead – in the classroom and sports. I was in support of the change.

In all my coaching years perhaps the most effective (venture) that I ever did was to run our own team camp at Monroe. I had heard great comments regarding a point guard camp run by Dick DeVenzio, a former Duke point guard. In addition, he developed a comprehensive Team Camp program. After checking it out I was totally sold on this program. It included the following: coaches manual, players' workbooks, instructional tapes and daily lesson plans.

We ordered the program and I charged each of the twelve players selected $150.00. $75.00 would be refunded at the end of camp if they missed no days and completed the workbook exercise. I charged nothing for my time. All twelve girls completed the program and I must say it laid a strong foundation for our program. It was a six-day camp and we spent equal time in the classroom at Monroe High as well as the gym. All aspects of the game of basketball were covered mentally first and then rehearsed in the gym. It was a tremendous experience for a high school team. I felt like we all went to basketball college for a week, three hours daily in the classroom and four hours in the gym. We even ate lunch together just like one big family. The final day the girls parents served us a tremendous lunch in celebration of a group of girls and a coach willing to give up a week of summer to meet in an un-air-conditioned classroom and a hot gym to develop a team that would set the tone for Monroe Girls Basketball.

Timeout!

DeVenzio's team camp taught me to develop all aspects of the game – and his program laid out a solid plan for that preparation. To this day, I still refer to those tapes and the coach's manual.

Fall came to the Northwest and I was ready to return to the classroom. My classes were Language Arts and Reading Skills. A large percentage of my students were boys and there was a golden opportunity there to help students at the middle school level to get prepared for high school (and possibly college) and life in general. My vast experience in reading instruction really enabled me to utilize the teaching materials in a structured learning experience that really helped the students. Of course, the leadership class was equally challenging and really balanced my day.

The game of basketball was a passion for me that I even utilized in my classroom motivation. If the students really worked hard and completed their individual goals for that day (and worked right up to five minutes before passing time), they would get a ten to fifteen minute playtime in the small gym where there was basketball games and four square every Friday. This worked great and I never had one discipline problem in the classroom or the gym. I went out on a limb for the kids, but they really appreciated it. Educational research shows that such breaks are very worthwhile for middle school students.

Fall sports at the high school were in full swing and as the varsity girls coach I felt it was wise to attend volleyball and soccer games to support the members of my squad who played those sports. Also, I watched some of the practices of our feeder teams "The Monroe Cyclones". Often I caught a game or two on the weekends.

I was getting anxious for the season to start as I was expecting something good was going to happen. Some of the players were getting that way also. I was delighted one day to see that Brandy rode her bike over to our house on Florence Acres Rd. She was out on my sports court working on her post moves. I knew the 1995-1996 season was going to be special for us!

In 1996 the state of Washington was organized into five levels of competition: 1B, 2B, 1A, 2A and 3A. In my opinion the top girls basketball squads were at the 2A level. Monroe was growing rapidly but we were still in the 2A division. Meadowdale, Lynnwood, Monroe, Blanchet, Mount SI, Arlington, Chief Sealth, and Kennedy were some of the strongest programs in girls basketball! We were new to this list of premier programs and we strongly waited to make a big splash in the 1996 playoffs!

Once again our season began with the Lady Cats of Monroe winning its first seven games. We were soon ranked number five in the state. Blanchet, the defending state champions, were also red hot! They won their first six games by extremely lopsided scores. On our next contest we would be traveling to Blanchet in an effort to derail the defending state champions.

Blanchet was loaded with talent as they had two posts who were 6-2, and 6-0 and were extremely skilled D-1 prospects. Perhaps their biggest weapon was a 5-9 wing who was strong, quick, and could shoot the eyes out of the basket and was also a D-1 signee. In addition they had two experienced guards to run their offense. They were like a smooth running machine that did not break down easily. Our job was to disrupt them and make that fine-tuned machine break down.

For you with basketball minds out there, our plan was to hold them under forty points. Imagine that we were going to hold them to ten or less points each quarter. This was the plan; and offensively we were going to move the ball to fluid open shots, and ten or less turnovers.

We were ready.......then disaster struck on game day morning. Our extremely versatile and talented 6-2 sophomore center woke up with the flu. I received the phone call at nine in the morning from Mrs. Shultz giving me the doctor's report.

"Mary, I agree with you. Let Emily rest tonight, we need her down the stretch. Tell her the team will be fine, but she will surely be missed," I responded in a concerned but still confident tone.

As the Monroe bus pulled into the Blanchet High School parking lot, the late December evening was chilly and snowflakes began to cover our bus windows. Our team filed into the gym in a single line led by Brandy and Allison. There wasn't a smile on the faces of any of our girls. We were there for a thirty-two minute battle. The gym was nearly packed before the junior varsity tip off, and by the varsity game it was standing room only. This was an early season match-up of the state's best team challenged by an upstart team from Monroe. Some college coaches were in attendance as Blanchet had three D-1 prospects and the blossoming team from Monroe had a couple of their own: only one of ours would be cheering on the sidelines as she was battling a tough bout of a cold/

flu. Against my wishes and probably her parents Emily showed up all dressed warmly and sat close to the team. We were one – and she wanted to be there with us.

Our defensive scheme was a triangle and two. Joni Carter had cat-like quickness and we had her chase and pester their all-state wing, Monique. Stringer face guarded Nadia, their 6-2 post who was heavily recruited on the west coast. Allison Kirk and Anna (who replaced Emily in the starting lineup) manned the blocks with Quinn at the point of our triangle defense. The key was to talk, pester and block out!

The plan worked perfectly as Monroe led at halftime 20-17. It was a classic high school battle of two powerful, and talented squads. We played eight players who performed extremely well against the best in the state, but remember Monroe was missing its top two rebounders: Emily and Brandy (who suffered a season ending knee injury). Yet, all of our bench players loved basketball and we were a determined bunch of girls – not afraid of any challenge! It continued to be a see-saw game with the Blanchet Braves taking the lead in the fourth quarter and holding on for a 45-41 victory. Almost! But, we knew with our full team we could beat them at State!

As the season continued on there was only one team that beat us twice – Meadowdale! A rivalry with the Chiefs was definitely in the making. Arlington stole a game from us up there but we clobbered them in the playoffs 57-28! And that was the victory that got us into the district championship game and a rematch with Meadowdale. This time we lost a close game with them, but we now made it to state! It would be Monroe's first ever trip to state in girls basketball.

Full Timeout!

As I mentioned before, I never desired to be the varsity girls basketball coach. When they approached me about the junior varsity position, I accepted with thoughts that I might be able to steer daughters Allison and Brittany into being serious about Hoops! It worked as Ally was now on the J.V. and Brittany was playing on the eighth grade squad. When the varsity coach stepped down – I was asked again to now take over the entire program. I was content teaching, being assistant coach and free to sell real estate. That routine would be interrupted. My dear wife (Chris) got her real estate license and helped me with clients (she already was the office secretary). Chris told me that she knew all along that I wanted my own team – and since the boys varsity coaching position never opened up for me, I took this opportunity as the Monroe Girls Varsity coach. Friends, when the principal at Monroe High called me into her office, I didn't agree to take the job at that moment. I asked for the weekend to think about it. I knew that the weekend would be spent praying about this new venture. By Saturday evening, there was such a peace and confidence in my spirit that there was no doubt what I would be telling Ms. Nancy Martin (principal) on Monday. I was internally excited that I knew that I was totally in God's will for me and my family.

Right from day one this coaching assignment became a family affair. In 1990-91 when our daughter, Melissa was selected to be Miss Washington, U.S.A. she decided to continue her education in Indiana at I.U.S.B., near my hometown. She returned home two years later with a wonderful husband. Todd Vaught was a very skilled post player at I.U.S.B. and Melissa was a cheerleader there.

The young couple moved back to Washington after college which added another member of the Dickson family of basketball to help the cause. It was my vision to make Monroe a top contender and I wanted my family to share this dream which most of them did!

The ranch home in the hills outside of Monroe soon had a sports court built by Marc and Todd. Soon the family games became very competitive with Todd, Ally and Melissa vs. Marc, Coach, and Brittany. Afterwards, we swam in the indoor pool (This beautiful home was the fruit of my real estate efforts). The evening often included watching the Celtics on TV or any team that was playing. Indiana was also a top choice at the college level.

My vision began to unfold as the Lady Bearcats finished the 1995-96 season 19-5 (3 losses to Meadowdale, including the close district loss and one loss to Arlington and then the Blanchet loss). Our second straight successful season, but being a Hoosier I wanted to make noise in the state playoffs.

I still remember my hometown of Mishawaka High School making it to the sweet sixteen back in 1955! I was eleven and I still could feel the excitement of our town of 40,000 celebrating the success of that team. Most of the city still remembers the players on that squad and the coach. We still talk about them – 60 years later! I wanted the same for my new town of Monroe. I watched the same excitement for these girls as LeRoy Johnson, John Ronchetti, Dan Hixenbaugh, Jimmy Carnes and those guys back then. The team of 1996 could be just the group to do it!

Brandy Maier attempted a comeback, but we lost her in the Lake Stevens game in late January. It was devastating as she was a tower of strength (at only 5-9 1/2). Her quick feet and strength intimidated our opponent. Her leadership on defense was going to be missed. Once again our squad would pull together as we had eleven other girls who believed in the concept "next girl up".

District playoffs went smoothly as the Lady Cats blew by Bellingham and Arlington as our high-powered fast break led to two easy nearly thirty point wins! We roared into the championship game with Meadowdale and we now qualified for state!

The Mavericks were led by four powerful post players – and Kellie O'Neill (a future U.W. recruit) was the toughest of the four. Without Brandy we became more of a finesse team against their power-motion offense. We lost, but it was sure closer than the 54-47 score. Words cannot adequately describe the exhilaration and rejoicing the Monroe team felt after qualifying for State: First time ever! After the Saturday night District Championship game I insisted that the players get home early – be out only with family and rest for our first ever journey to state. Monroe Girls Basketball had arrived.

---

30 second Timeout!

Thank you God for giving me the vision back then "that winning isn't an end in itself but the journey is what has the real value!" I strongly sensed this, as no one wanted to win more than me for our town, our school, our families, and our team. But, depression never engulfed my mind after a defeat. We were always to look ahead to the future and better days! I am so glad that God gave me that philosophy in my first year of coaching.

Denny Coates, the Monroe athletic director and our biggest fan reserved a school van to drive myself and coaches Potthast, and Marc Dickson to the state parings for the sixteen teams that qualified for state. We were in the "Sweet Sixteen" just like Mishawaka High back in 1955! My dream as a little boy came true (but not for me as a player – for a girls team – way out in Seattle, Washington.

30 second Timeout!

Interesting how God gives us the desires of our
hearts, but in His time and His place.

The drawing at the W.I.A.A. headquarters began at 10:00 AM
with the head coaches and athletic directors sitting around this
huge conference table. The other assistants and the press were all
hovering behind us and into the lobby out front. It was an extremely
long and dragged out affair, but it finally concluded, Monroe had
drawn the hottest team in the state – Chief Sealth. Last Friday night
Marc and I scouted them against Blanchet and Chief Sealth upset
them 70-50! We knew how good Blanchet was and Chief Sealth
completely dominated them. A flashy point guard, Sheila Lambert
who averaged twenty-eight points per game, led the Seahawks. She
was the leading scorer in the state as a sophomore. In addition, they
had a D1 post who was athletic, strong, and had the potential to
score thirty herself.

Driving back to Monroe that Sunday afternoon, I told my staff
that our work was cut out for us. We would need a "perfect" game
plan and an all out effort to beat the Chief Sealth Seahawks who
were now ranked No. 1 in the state of Washington.

Needless to say, the Monroe girls were really focused at Monday
and Tuesday's practices. Since our game began at 10:30 AM the
administration was very supportive and booked us rooms at the
Ramada Inn adjacent to the Tacoma Dome. State here we come!
Coach Potthast was given the assignment to get the funds for each
person's food money as well as line up the vans and gas cards. Our
state contingent consisted of managers Chris Bengston, Rebekkah
Carrol, Justin Moore, and Liz Kinsella. Those four were in charge
of all the equipment. Coach Marc was to take care of video taping
equipment.

Denny Coates, our AD, organized a very energetic pep assembly for the team and my speech was not full of promise, but I was just thankful for this opportunity and I guaranteed that our effort at the Dome would make Monroe proud!

Our practice was really a "walk thru" of our game plan. We covered every detail of our defensive scheme, the plan was a "Box and 1". Joni Carter would face guard Sheila and drive her nuts. Stringer would be the top of the box helping with Sheila if she broke free. One of my favorite defenders, Trish Keating would relieve Joni and chatter like a crow in Sheila's ears – just talking and communicating with other defenders. All the girls were to talk without ceasing on defense. We were going all out!

On offense we would, as always, push the ball but not force anything – just keep moving.

One of the girls led us in a prayer after practice – the girls all held hands – I loved seeing this as I stood outside the circle. Thank you God for always being there. It was joy to my heart to see different girl step up to lead prayer. This all just happened, as I made certain that I was not orchestrating it.

Marc and Coach Potthast had the vans ready to go and all I needed to organize was my coaching materials. We were a well-organized team from top to bottom. My wife was following the vans along with Jen Dickson, Marc's wife in their car. This gave us the look of a small caravan with the vans and our cars all decorated in orange and black with the players' names and numbers.

After arriving at the Ramada Inn in the late afternoon, Coach Potthast assigned the rooms and everyone unpacked. After dinner I had the team walk over to the Tacoma Dome as we had some time to walk out on the court and just get a feel for the dome. This reminded me of the Hickory (Milton H.S.) team in "Hoosiers".

Marc woke up at 6:00 AM his excitement was really contagious. This was a special moment in time for our family – the basketball crazed folks from the Midwest and Hoosiers at heart. Our family was closely bonded by our mutual love for God, but a close second sure was our love for basketball.

Marc and I went down to the restaurant at the motel and were surprised to see our 6-2 center already eating with one of the managers. We sat at a table in the corner and carefully went over the game plan. Soon Coach Potthast had all the girls up and ready for breakfast at 7:30 AM our players seemed focused and ready to go to battle. We sure didn't seem like a team that was just excited to be at state for our first time ever in Monroe's history. We were prepared for battle.

I left Marc with the girls and went upstairs to get ready and send Chris and our girls Ally and Brittany down to eat. This state experience would certainly plant seeds into my daughters' mind as a great experience – and also all those young Monroe girls to follow.

When we walked into the Dome we watched the Arlington game vs. Cheney (20-4). Arlington was led by their super twins who relocated to Arlington this season. The Eagles of Arlington clawed their way to a solid win and advanced to play the winner of our game vs. No. 1 Chief Sealth (19-1). All we had to do was beat Arlington to advance to the Elite Eight! But our focus was on the game ahead. Chief Sealth just roared into state with that 70-50 win over defending champions Blanchet.

Our game plan was set and the Lady Bearcats all bought into our strategies. It was important in such a high profile game to all be on the same page.

Kristin Stringer was rapidly blossoming as a star point guard for the Bearcats in her transition from playing post. As a lefty point guard she was quite deceptive. Her "hesitate and go" move devastated most high school defenses. Her 5-11 frame and being extremely athletic made her a top D1 recruit in only on year. Marc made a good call talking me into switching "String" to point guard (for her and our team!).

It was time to take the court; fans from Monroe had streamed into the Dome during the Arlington game. It was so awesome to see all the orange and black in the stands. I was so fired up – I wanted to lead cheers, but I had a very big job to lead our team to make the community of Monroe proud and unified.

Everything possible fell into place for us during the first quarter. Chief Sealth's star guard was held scoreless for the first eight minutes. The defense was talking, communicating and Joni and Trish were making "Squawking" noises as they took turns face-guarding Sheila. Monroe's shots were falling – even Quinn Olson's bank shot from the top of the key for three points. Our motion offense wore them out as our players passed, cut, screened away and just kept moving, and the ball moved around the outskirts of their defense like a cannon ball. Needless to say, our bench was so strong that we were able to keep everyone fresh with frequent substitutions. We were up 33-16 at halftime and the top pick to win state looked really frustrated. One of our girls shouted at halftime "The Cowgirls from Monroe came ready to play!" The final score was a nine point Monroe victory, and better yet I was able to play everyone on our bench.

One more win and we are in the "final four" at state! Our opponent was a familiar foe and league rival Arlington. Our 57-28 victory in districts over them can be thrown out the window. This was state and nothing else matters but to play each possession as a singular battle.

The game was close right from the start with Monroe hanging onto a three point lead, Kristin Stringer tumbled to the Tacoma Dome floor, the pain shooting through her right knee showing on her face.

Stringer after reinjuring her knee, hobbled to the Monroe bench early in the second quarter. Stringer was reunited with her constant companion of late, an ice pack. After a few minutes of ice therapy we got the OK from our trainer to let her go back in.

Stringer who bruised her knee in practice the week before really wanted to play as Arlington pulled ahead. We got some quality minutes out of her, but as our gals pulled back into the lead I pulled her out as Trish Keating and Anna Kloeck were playing fabulous defense as her subs. Stringer, who was on crutches Monday and Tuesday because of her knee, canned a 16-foot jumper before I pulled her out. Monroe led the rest of the way and garnered a 41-33 win over Arlington. Stringer had 10 points, a game high 11 rebounds, three assists, two steals and two blocked shots. A complete game in such short playing time. This game demonstrated why over 200 colleges and universities were recruiting our 5-11 point guard.

Chapter 28

Full Timeout!

I took great pride in being a professional well-respected coach as a representative of the Monroe community. Yet, there were a couple instances that few know about that may alter that view, or at least show that I was still a basketball junkie from the Hoosier state: In some ways, these could be considered humorous.

1. After our thrilling upset of the No. 1 team at state, Marc forgot the video player so he talked the bartender at the inn into letting us go in the bar after hours and watch the game tape. We did not drink anything, but it probably would look bad if anyone saw us in there – especially when Marc was standing on the bar putting the tape in the video player hanging high above the bar. Since we were there 'till 2:00 in the morning, the bartender left and trusted us to not drink the alcohol in the bar. Mission accomplished and we were ready for the next game vs. Arlington: (Jen Dickson drove home and retrieved our recorder the next day).

2. When Meadowdale was upset in the first round, some of
    my staff and family were too exuberant way up in the top
    of the bleachers. They were excited to have one of the top
    teams eliminated. Apparently, we upset their coaches as
    they noticed it and one of them made a comment to the
    paper. "That Wesco teams should root for each other."
    But to me, we were there to place as high as possible. And
    the Meadowdale/Monroe rival was intense. I still wonder
    how they noticed us way up at the top. I also was excited
    to get such a great team eliminated. I kept my composure
    though. I talked to the staff and players about us always
    being a "class act". Constant learning experiences in sports.

Monroe (21-5 overall) would play Kennedy, a 41-40 winner over
Ellensburg in the semi-finals Friday evening. Walking out onto the
championship round court, it was an awesome feeling looking up
at the thousands in the stands and the bright lights added to the
presence of the moment. I grabbed Marc by the arm and told him
to look up at the Monroe fans – once again decked in orange and
black; this was becoming a normal sight at the games. A win would
place us in the championship game on Saturday. Kennedy was a lot
like Monroe with an attacking full court defense; they reminded
me of a soccer team (in fact, most of their squad played on a state
qualifying soccer team. They had one key player, a point guard who
had signed with Gonzaga.

I felt we were stronger on the boards and that could be the
difference maker. We played a very strong game for three quarters.
Kennedy had a slim two point lead at halftime, but at the end of
the third quarter we held an eight-point lead. Kennedy's offense lit
up and thanks to a few of our turnovers they pulled to within two
points with thirty seconds to go. Against my game plan, one of our
guards took a quick jumper and it bounced off the right side of the

rim. The Lancers had new life and scored on a running baseline bank shot as the buzzer sounded…OVERTIME!!!!

The Bearcats had eased out to a 41-38 lead with about two minutes to go in overtime. Then, Kennedy's Robyn Perkins, who had missed four previous free throws, went to the line and sank two free throws to make it 41-40 with about a minute left. Monroe missed a layup on the other end. Their star pint guard went coast to coast for a bucket that gave Kennedy its first lead since halftime at 42-41. Their Gonzaga bound guard penetrated again for a 44-41 Kennedy advantage. We fouled, and they hit one free throw with 12 seconds remaining. Stinger pushed the ball up court to a wide-open Trish Keating for a Monroe three pointer. The final score was Kennedy winning 45-44, and the Bearcats fell short in OT.

Full Timeout!

The thrill of the playing in the semi-finals of state was deflated a bit by our close loss. One more stop on defense, or one more basket and we would have been in the championship game. Once again, after congratulating Kennedy, I asked the girls to jog directly to the locker-room. We had one more game to play and here was my message to the team. "Ladies, you played your hearts out; a basket here or a stop there and you would have won. Now, we have a chance to make Monroe proud by winning the game tomorrow morning at 10:30 AM and talking home the third place trophy. This game will be a test of our character after tonight's disappointing loss" We left the locker room and the players went directly to their rooms. Coach Potthast once again roamed the halls to insure all were sleeping. They were. Marc and Banger (one of the mangers who also did stats) and I returned to my room and studied film of Mt. SI – one of the top teams at state that year.

Once again the number of Monroe fans who packed the stands this game for third and sixth place trophies overwhelmed me. Being our first ever state tournament at Monroe, we wanted to leave with a victory.

The Bearcats did earn third place in its first-ever trip to state. While the Bearcats 50-42 win over Mount SI was exciting at courtside, the celebration didn't stop there. As the Lady Bearcats traveled home, they were met at Highway 522 and Highway 2 by six or seven police cars, each decorated with balloons in the school colors, black and orange. And the 40-50 car parade continued along Highway 2 to the east end of town before turning right and traveling along Main Street to end with a pep rally in the high school parking lot. It was historic to say the least!

This team was my first group of players as the varsity coach and in this second year we created such an exciting atmosphere for the girls basketball program. My goal was to continue this dynamic tradition. Our foundation was laid with the Cyclones A.A.U. feeder program, and our varsity and junior varsity girls reaching out to the young girls in the elementary schools through our "Buddies Program". In addition, our staff and varsity players made plans to email nearly one hundred young hoopsters into our summer camps at Monroe High School. Through the years we averaged 70-100 annually.

As the leadership teacher, I learned that "Let the players organize and run this camp – Coach Dickson would always be the overseer. Some key volunteers form our players parents also contributed greatly. It became a community event!

Camp T-shirts were totally designed by the players and some year they were quite amazing. In the later years our middle school coaches joined as camp volunteers and even some of the boys staff joined as volunteer coaches. It was thrilling to me to see such unity at Monroe schools and especially the excitement that now surrounded our program.

The 1996-97 school year began with lots of optimism surrounding

Monroe High School girls sports. The senior class was loaded with athletes and they played volleyball, soccer and hoops. Since several of my ballers were top athletes for their fall teams, I made it a point to attend several of their volleyball and soccer games. Plus my longtime assistant, Coach Potthast, was the head varsity soccer coach. High school sports are a great opportunity for the multi-sport athlete. We always had a few year round basketball players and I made certain that they were scheduled open gyms and training opportunities for these girls. And every Saturday morning many of our varsity and J.V. girls played together in the Kirkland Boys and Girls Club League. In the late fall we began a 6:00 AM weight lifting program for the girls to increase strength and quickness. We kept busy. Nothing was required but the participation rate was quite high!

Late in the summer we had a new player move in from Texas. Her dad was the new pastor of Community Chapel in Monroe. They asked to meet the coach and I was excited to add another gem to our bag of precious stones that returned to our squad.

With all the promise that surrounded our 1996-1997 team, the Monroe girls basketball team was poised to make another run to the state title game in 1997 at the Tacoma Dome. Of course, we were focused on making the championship round that so narrowly slipped through our grips last year. We would be missing Joni, Alison K., Jamie and Trish, but we had a strong nucleolus headed by Stringer, Olson, Skillen and Shultz.

By the end of the summer, Stringer was one of the top recruits in the state of Washington. She had nearly two hundred colleges and universities pursuing her to attend their schools. My job now became more comprehensive as I now became an active part of the recruiting process. Here was a great, loyal competitor for the Monroe basketball program and I wanted to represent her to the best of my abilities as an advisor. She trusted me as we developed a close, but very healthy coach/player bond. I loved all my players and when I could help them to play at the next level I was honored and determined to find them the best opportunity. String's parents trusted the two of us to select the six schools for home visits. Gonzaga, Santa Clara, University of San Francisco, Pepperdine, and the University of Portland were all high on the list! Our state schools of Washington and W.S.U. were too large for Stringer as she liked the smaller campus. She knew what she wanted and was able to select just that. Kristin was enamored with Kelly Graves (the recruiting coach at the University of Portland). Also, their head coach, Jim Sollers, reminded her of me in his personality. She selected Portland.

Mrs. Stringer provided home cooked meals for all the home visits, and I enjoyed meeting and discussing hoops with some excellent West Coast coaches. I was committed to becoming a top high school coach and this was another avenue to help me reach that goal.

Monroe now had its first D1 signee in basketball and I was determined to have many more. I loved building a program that offered so much to those athletes who loved hoops like I did. Alison K from the 1996 team played four years of college ball and played at D2 level. During my thirteen years at Monroe I was able to help thirty-four girls play at the college level (community college, NAIA, D2, D3, and D1).

Chapter 29

Yes, the Monroe girls basketball program was poised for greatness. Yet, as much as I endeavored to control the destiny of this program, it became a test of my faith and dedication to the real journey I was on.

Timeout!

My desire to coach always sprung forth from my purpose in life: To positively influence the youth of America. Most of my teams joined hands in prayer before or after games. This went back to my days as a football and basketball player at Mishawaka High in Indiana. I always followed the guidelines for these prayers, and I am glad I followed the leading of the Holy Spirit. Winning was great, but giving our best was paramount. Team was paramount over individual accomplishments. My coaching philosophy did not waver much from my initial coaching assignment of that 9th grade football team at Avondale High in Michigan. I loved challenges of rebuilding.

The 1996-97 season was to be another final four team. We had a great season with twenty-one wins, but had a tough draw at state vs. W. Valley and the Borkland sisters. Stringer got hurt and our fire seamed to diminish as we went on to win one at state, but lost again to a Seattle team and our season ended quietly at 21-6.

We definitely missed the all around play of Alison as she continued her career at the college level. Brandy's tough rebounding and relentless defense was also missed. Joni Carter and Trish Keating our cat like quick guard defenders were sorely missed. Yet, we all felt there was enough to even advance further the year of 1997. It was nice to see our 6-1 forward, Karen Elmgren really step up at state as she made the all-state team as a sophomore. We were a smooth, very efficient offensive squad with 6-2 Emily Shultz, and 6-1 Karen Elmgren providing solid rebounding to elevate our heralded fast break machine. We won a lot of games, but deep down I knew we missed the toughness of those above-mentioned gals from 1996.

Back to back trips to state sure wasn't anything to cry over. Stringer, Olson, Anna, and Amy all were getting attention from local colleges and D1 schools. Monroe was building a tradition of developing top hoop talent.

The 1997 season was the end of my first three years at the helm of the Monroe Girls program. Our record was 60-18 during that span. With two trips to state, and a league championship, the program was built on a strong foundation. We had the full support of the athletic director (Denny Coates) and the school administration and the school board. Teachers and students were a big support and we sure felt it. The cheerleaders organized tremendous "spirit nights" in cooperation with the Monroe elementary schools. On the night of a major battle between Monroe vs. Meadowdale or Monroe vs. Arlington we were packed – nearly 2,000 fans! I will never forget June Daugherty was at one of our home games (scouting a couple of our players and the opponents), and she exclaimed; "Coach Dickson your team draws as many fans as the Huskies."

Timeout!

As many other times in my life when God is working in my life, voices of distraction would try to distract me. I remember considering moving on from Monroe as I was starting to get inquiries for new opportunities. After prayer, I knew this was not of God. He planted me here and my mission was not completed. He gave me a love for girls hoops and it was a great outlet for my passion for basketball! The relationships that I was forming with these players became so genuine – it was like family. Little did I know then that they would be everlasting relationships.

The following year we would be rebuilding as we had seven seniors graduating. One player decided to play year round volleyball, so that left us with four returners. Still, I felt our program was strong enough to endure and we did. Emily Shultz and Karen Elmgren gave us two very talented big girls (our version of the "Twin Towers"). They were tall 6'1 and 6'2, athletic and could run the court. In addition we had Allison "Ally" Dickson and Annette Gaeth – both experienced wing players. Annette was a great defender with her quick feet and Ally could play both guard positions and small forward at 5'9 and blessed with long arms. In addition, being the coach's daughter she was like having a coach on the court.

As the head and chief helmsman of this blossoming Monroe program, I made certain that I was involved in the middle school girls basketball programs as well as the youth and A.A.U. programs. And of course each summer nearly every prospective Monroe girls basketball player attended our summer camp (grades 1-8). Having watched these younger players develop the past few years, I knew we had a couple really talented frosh joining our 1998 squad. Our junior varsity team was 19-1 last season so overall we were pretty well set to rebuild and maintain a very competitive team. Perhaps a year or two from a top five team, but we'd be a contender in the District 1 tournament at Marysville.

One of our top incoming frosh was Fauziya Muhammad. I always knew the value of a floor leader – and with the graduation of our All State point guard, Kristin Stringer, I had to jump start Fauziya's career by playing her with the varsity squad in several summer tourneys. We needed her to be ready and I saw the talent in this athletic and highly skilled young point guard.

It was a lot of fun for me to meet the challenge of rebuilding after the graduation of those seniors who led us to sixty wins over the past three years. These new aspiring hoopsters were really a joy to develop. They loved to work and were eager to learn the game of hoops from this old Hoosier coach. Since I had followed most of them since their middle school days, we quickly became family – one unit with one goal to compete at a high level representing Monroe, ourselves, and our families. There's so much to gain from participation in high school sports.

At the beginning of summer, I was visited by an old real estate mortgage loan friend who had done several loans for my clients at my summer real estate sales job. Denny Pewitt wanted to tell me that he was moving to Monroe and that he always wanted his daughter Nikki to play for Coach Dickson! I was overwhelmed and honored. I had watched this 6'2 post score eighteen points against the Monroe eighth grade team in a middle school game. Nikki had great hands and a soft touch as a shooter (unusual for a post at that level).

Nikki loved to shoot the three ball, and I never chose to discourage my players from a part of the game that excited them; yet, from what I saw early on we needed to refine her post moves and the outside shooting would come later.

Our defense and rebounding helped us get going early that year. We were quite physical and with the speed of our young point guard, and the ability of Allison "Ally" and Annette to run the outside lanes, the fast beak was always there after a quick outlet from our "bigs". Karen Elmgren also ran the break real well as a forward. We brought Mel Shultz, Emily's little sister up to strengthen the defense and she was a big plus with her team play and enthusiasm. Her big game was a fourteen point and ten rebound effort against Roosevelt – a top team in state.

Timeout!

Every couple of years a high school varsity coach needs to evaluate the passion and purpose that motivated him. My passion was simple – it was the same as a young boy growing up on the basketball courts of Indiana. I felt called to the mission of creating a basketball atmosphere like I experienced at Mishawaka High and later Butler University. I loved hoops.

Yet, a deeper purpose was growing inside me – one that I always experienced when coaching my own team. I wanted to build unity and relationships that would continue through life. The same kind of relationships I desired from the students that became close to me. When you are working with a group of students or athletes on a daily basis, you simply become like family. At least that was the way it was for me. I must say I really enjoyed the relationships with parents – especially down the road as we all look back on those years. Life is short! Live it to the fullest and become involved in your life's work.

That basketball season began well and we battled fiercely to remain a contender for the playoffs. Perhaps our most significant win was a twenty point blowout at Arlington with Emily, Annette, Ally and Karen all having outstanding games! Ally who was right handed hit three straight left handed jumpers as she penetrated the point. Emily scored her usual twenty points and gathered in twelve rebounds. Annette scored ten points in the first quarter. Fauziya had her usual game as the general of our offense. It was a fun night to see the offense and defense jell so perfectly. A coach's delight!

As the season wound down it was a rematch between Arlington and Monroe with playoff implications. Two days before the battle, Fauziya reinjured her ankle and Karen Elmgren was also injured. Two key players, but it was next girls up. My daughter Allison moved into the point guard position and Mel replaced Karen as the starting forward. I was so proud of the girls, we lost in overtime, but Monroe walked off that court with their heads high.

Chapter 30

Our J.V. and frosh teams were well coached and year after year they came up with winning teams. At any level (high school, college, and pro) I believe one of the keys to a consistently successful program is to maintain a consistency in staff. I was blessed to have my son Marc and Coach Potthast, for my entire thirteen years. They were loyal and agreed totally with the goals that I had laid down for the program. We were always on the same page.

The 1998-1999 season would be built around our post Nikki and our flashy point guard Fauziya. Both were basketball fanatics and they loved the game, just as I did. My daughter, Brittany, and Mel Shultz, a couple solid players that would be moved up from last year's strong junior varsity squad. Mel had played quite a bit last season and showed her toughness. Brittany had a wonderful three point shot and was also solid as a defender. Tristin Curtis, an all-around athlete who played multiple sports, seemed to have a fresh fire for the game of basketball. This excited me because at 5'10 she could jump, run the court, and had a nice jumper. Needless to say, she was very aggressive on the boards. As a top quality outside hitter in volleyball – she loved battling for rebounds. Another girl that I knew would really help us was Jenn Johnson. She was a solid inside player, but with her high arching three point shot, we used her often as a wing and especially against zone defenses. Our final piece to this team was a tall, long armed gal who was about six feet and showed great progress last season on Marc's "C" team. We had high hopes that she would progress rapidly and she did.

Timeout!

As the varsity coach you are the overseer of your program. Pay attention to those undeveloped players who seem to improve rapidly. Usually they have smiles on their faces as they are enjoying their progress. Then, feed them positive thoughts.

I still remember watching Erin play her first game on the frosh squad for Marc. He had charted her shots and rebounds. She was 1-20 shooting and had 15 boards. I walked up to her after the game and told her "Erin, you really impressed me with fifteen rebounds!" She responded with a huge smile, "Coach I missed almost all my shots!" "Erin", I said, "after another couple weeks of post shots practice drills, you will be making those shots!"

By the end of January Erin was now 6'1 and was called up to replace Nikki for a key game vs. Lake Stevens. Nikki was out for at least a week. Erin responded with twelve points and eleven rebounds. We won the game, and our team was now deeper than ever. Yet, I knew we would have a really good season, but we were one year away from these kids returning and giving us another memorable year.

This 1999 team was a bunch of fighters – they loved to compete and played together. I will never forget playing Marysville at home in the middle of the season. We were leading in a close battle with the Tomahawks, and then disaster struck. Brittany, my daughter, was having a great game and was playing her usual "all out effort – then she collapsed after completing a steal and a driving layin to give us a ten point lead. The medics were called and she was rushed to the hospital. My wife Chris rode with her in the ambulance. I stayed to finish the game. The medics said she was stabilized, but they would need to take her to complete some tests.

After the game continued I looked down the bench and only two girls remained plus the five on the court. Five of Britt's teammates insisted on rushing to the hospital to be with Brittany. We held on to get our fifth consecutive win and secure second place in Wesco. I have to admit that team sure stuck together like family; my kind of players!

We finished the season at thirteen wins and seven losses. We went deep into the District playoffs, but lost to Shorewood (the defending state champs) on a "charge/block" call by the ref in the last seconds. It was a very satisfying season and our girls showed much promise as we looked forward to the team of 1999-2000!

During the past five seasons, I really felt blessed to have been in a coaching position where I could be effective. My goal was to take our Monroe teams as far in to the playoffs as possible and leave a legacy for other teams to follow. The relationships with the players and their families were always important to me as a high school coach. We needed to be on the same page and at times this took a lot of effort. Yet, as I discovered later it paid off.

In addition to the relationships with the players and their families – I loved meeting fans who became our teams' extended families. Two of those were Larry Roberson and Mark Alexander Zaremba. In both cases I took the initiation to create these relationships. I will share both stories.

During the 1994-95 season (my first as varsity coach) my son Marc was our video man. He always sat high up the bleachers and also had the "eye of an eagle". He noticed everything and everyone in the gym. In fact, he even noticed during the "C" team and junior varsity games that there was a dead spot on the court, where the ball seemed to lose its bounce. After checking it out in practice, he seemed to have had a correct observation. Needless to say, we often set our traps on the dribbler at that precise spot to the right of the top of the key!

Another perhaps more significant observation by Marc was this elderly gentlemen who always stood up on the top bleacher directly across from him; leaned against the back wall cheering for the Lady Cats. He was at every game in his blue jacket and hat. At Marc's prodding I walked up to him and introduced myself to him at the next home game. Then I realized it was Larry "the gum man" from the church we attended frequently in Monroe. He was an usher who always passed out gum to the children after Sunday School. We hugged and Larry said he attended every game since I became the coach. Larry became perhaps our top supporter and the players invited him to team parties and our awards assemblies. Later he often went to our team camps and rented a room just to watch the girls play. He did not miss a game until he died.

Another of our teams' extended family was Mark Zaremba. While attending a boys game at Monroe High, I noticed an older man who sat up towards the top of the stands, all alone, as I soon learned why. At every referee's whistle that went against Monroe, his cheeks would puff up and he would bellow out a complaint to the ref. Then he would remain silent. I thought "wow, that would be great to have him yell at the refs in our games – so I wouldn't have to!"

A few days later while observing the boys' team practice, I recognized this same man perched on top of the wire basket, which contains their practice balls. I went up to him and invited him to attend some girls' games. He was at the next game and never missed a game until he later died. The boys coach had told me that Mark was fondly referred to as "the Heckler". I later found out that Mark was on the 1960 Monroe team that won state. He served as the manager since his heart condition disqualified him from playing that year.

Larry and Mark became close friends and when our teams played in the state tournament, they would share a room at the Ramada Inn where our team usually stayed. It was a great place, as we just had to walk across the parking lot to the Tacoma Dome.

Larry and Mark continued to be loyal supporters of the Lady Bearcats even after I needed to step down in 2008. They both died a few years after my retirement from Monroe, and I was called by both sets of family to organize speakers and pallbearers from the Monroe teams to serve at the services. It was my pleasure to speak as well, and to tell the stories of both men, as they were truly loyal supporters.

Chapter 31

Even though the other coaches and I thought very highly of our 1999-2000 squad, many of our opponents did not rate us as high. Nevertheless, by the end of the season, we started to turn heads.

All the attention given to the Monroe girls basketball program continued to fuel my passion for the sport. Yet, I never let my love and concern for the education of my students falter. I have to think God was in the whole thing – my energy level was equal to Pete Carroll back then. It was a God thing for me; He was blessing me in my calling – right where He directed me to work.

Timeout!

Throughout the Bible and my reading of books by
Christian leaders, there was a constant theme: Satan
will do all he can to discourage you. Be ready and wear
the armor of Faith. Let God's angels fight the battle.
And just keep moving forward in your calling!
I loved my reading/language development classes, the ELL class,
and my leadership training class. It was all so fulfilling and
rewarding to know you have the opportunity daily to impact
into young people's lives. My day was full, fast paced and during
the four months of hoops season – it was amazingly exciting.

If I had a routine that invigorated me it was the following: On the way to school I meditated on the days work at school and whom I needed to nourish and motivate. God directed me so precisely in this area. Then, after a day of teaching and making the transition to hoops, I reviewed the days practice plan during my prep and then dressed for practice. During the drive to practice, I always played praise and worship songs to strengthen me for the task of molding my players into champions. It was invigorating for me and I stepped out onto the court full of God's strength! Perhaps a touch of what David felt when facing the giant. After my heart attack and cancer battle this worship music before practice was extremely vital to my energy and faith levels.

You know what? Teaching and coaching to me were so alike. Diagnose the strengths and weaknesses of the student/athlete. Then strengthen the weaknesses through drills and practice, and give opportunity to learn new skills and advanced techniques. Next, be pure to continually applaud successes and motivate for higher goals. Encourage continually and always be there for the student/athlete. Instill value and passion toward the subject matter or the team goals. Continually support each student/athlete on their journey. Teachers/coaches respect and honor your calling! Make this world a better place – touch the lives of these students/athletes.

After defeating Arlington twice during the season, we were surprised by them in districts. In fact, so was everyone else! They blazed through districts knocking off Monroe (20-4) and Meadowdale (20-3) to win it all. Meadowdale and Monroe battled to second and third place finishes and both going to state again.

At state we defeated Centralia in the first round in a convincing fashion. Next, we drew Meadowdale whom we split with during the season. Right from the start I liked our hustle and defense on Kristen O'Neill; yet, we were caught by surprise as Jane Ireland had the shooting game of her life. Normally a tough defender and rebounder, she ended up with nineteen points on 70% shooting! We lost the game to take us to the final four.

> **Timeout:** As a coach you cannot live or die by how
> the ball bounces in or out of the hoop. You can guide
> and encourage hustle, determination and efforts, but
> shots dropping are another thing. That's what makes
> basketball a fascinating game and I loved it!

Meadowdale won their next game against a White River team that just lost their top scorer (18 ppg) to a knee injury. Meadowdale won that game and made it to the championship where they defeated Blanchet 40-33.

Monroe battled back to beat Eastmont at the buzzer 51-50. We called our special last second play that cleared the paint for our dazzling point guard, Fauziya Muhammad, to go one on one to the hoop. The 'Fuz' came through and we were now in the trophy round playing perhaps the original favorite of the tourney West Valley of Yakima. We finished seventh as West Valley pulled away in the fourth quarter. Their premier center, Theresa Borton, had a spectacular game with 28 points.

I was really proud of this 2000 squad. We had an eight-player rotation with Mel Shultz, Nikki Pewitt, Fauziya Muhammad, Tristen Curtis, Brittany Dickson, Jenn Johnson, Erin Keck and Che Oh. Other girls that contributed off the bench were Kaylee Kolrud, Heidi Gaeth, Ashley Nelson, and Kara Ewing. It was good to be back at state and take home a trophy again. Thank you girls for the effort and hard work you gave and kept the Monroe tradition in girls basketball alive.

And a big part of that tradition was show casing our premier point guard, Fauziya Muhammad, and solid post players Nikki and Erin, and great outside shooting ("The Swisher sisters") Brittany and Jenn, along with tough defenders, Mel and Tristen.

Feeling satisfied for the most part after the season, I needed time to reflect on my future. The years 1994 to 2000 had been chocked full of successes, fun and excitement. I felt I had made an impact on the sports program at Monroe High. Yet, I needed to reflect and think; "Is this worth all the effort?" I wasn't doing it for the pay or the prestige. There were far more headaches, and even heartaches at times to not ignore. "However, I thought, isn't this my calling?" The relationships that I made were priceless. You can only mold strong relationships by walking through the battles with people. Sharing our lives together was part of my coaching. I became emotionally attached to all my players and their families. It was always worth any of the battles that surrounded any coaching.

It was really special coaching Allison and now Brittany. We have memories that could never have been experienced otherwise. Both went on to receive scholarships to play at the community colleges of Edmonds and Everett. Their love for the game continued to grow and I was proud to be their coach. It was satisfying to see them progress each year.

Having coached my daughters was definitely invaluable for me as a girls coach. They constantly reminded me if I was slighting a player or too hard on others. It was at times humbling for me, but I certainly benefitted from their input.

Often spending a week after the season reflecting and seeking God's will, I knew what I should do. "Continue on," I thought. "God has more for you to do as Monroe's basketball coach." My decision was made; I am going for at least another six years!

Chapter 32

After finishing strong in the 2000 state tourney, Monroe was excited for the next season. We only lost Mel and Brittany from our group of starters (8) and top substitutes. With the six experienced players we also added a super frosh in Che Oh (Cia's little sister at six foot and very advanced for her grade). The future was bright.

Snohomish (a 4-A powerhouse) came to Monroe's gym to open the season with us. That year we were still 3A and this would be a challenge. When the final buzzer sounded, Monroe won the game 65-60 as fans poured from the packed gym to congratulate the girls. I gathered them together as we gave a quick thanks to God for no injuries and a fun game. (The girls led these prayers and I stayed close by as it blessed me also).

Che, our super frosh, had eighteen points and eight boards! However, it was totally a team game as our veterans all scored rebounded and played great team defense – especially when we closed out the game.

We struggled a bit on our next two away games as we lost to tough foes: Kamiak and Burlington-Edison. They were very close games, but we had some weaknesses that needed to be remedied.

After a full week of practice we felt ready to make a run. We had six great practices after those two losses and it paid off dramatically. The Lady Cats went on a ten game winning streak! After beating the defending state champs, Meadowdale at home by three points, our only loss was to the Mavericks in a return match at Meadowdale 65-61. We were now 20-3 after winning our last three games.

After defeating Arlington (who featured one of the nation's best players in Kayla Burt a 6-0 left handed, sure shooting point guard. We were ready for playoffs. However, Arlington reared up its engine for districts and defeated both Monroe (20-4) and Meadowdale (20-3) in districts. I was upset at the outcome, but once again I needed to reset my mind and get this team to win out and make a second consecutive trip to Tacoma and the state tournament. And I must say: "Hats off to Kayla Burt for a fantastic display of outside shooting vs. Monroe and Meadowdale!"

Monroe was ready for their fourth trip to state in seven years. This is no light undertaking as coming out of the Wesco League and making districts was always a challenge back then. Often three or four of the Wesco teams were ranked in the "top ten".

Driving down to Renton for the state drawing was always a special event on the Sunday morning following the district championship game Saturday night. Coaches Potthast, Marc Dickson and I usually drove a school van and quite often our captains went with us. The entire floor of the W.I.A.A. office building was buzzing with excitement. Fresh donuts, coffee, etc.; top coaches from around the state; and so many reporters all filled the room. This was my kind of an atmosphere. A lot of really talented teams were in the year's tourney and we drew one of the best: the Lakeside Lions of Seattle.

We would be prepared as Marc got some scouting tapes on Lakeside and we felt we would match up well! My only concern was the 8:30pm game, which often runs way later.

Our game plan was beautifully laid out: soft pressing to slow down their offense and then tighten up and go into our matchup zone. We closely guarded their top two scorers inside the zone. The score was Monroe 32 and Lakeside 8 with three minutes until halftime. Then, I saw the wind come out of our girls and we went flat.

I couldn't figure it out. Our just over 6' 2" star center, Nikki

Pewitt, seemingly was totally exhausted. She played extremely hard as always and had nothing left.

Nikki was a true warrior and she played her senior year after having given birth less than a year earlier. I wish I had rested her earlier in the game as she had only one speed "all out!" In that beautifully designed and executed first thirteen minutes of the first half Nikki had 13 points and nine boards. Unfortunately, she never got her second wind. A couple other players seemed to be suffering from exhaustion and Lakeside closed the gap before half – our lead was cut in half.

After halftime the Lakeside girls continued their hot streak and eventually pulled ahead at the end of the game.

Not wanting to go home the next day, we regrouped and came back to battle Arlington in a rematch of the district championships. This time a new story was written. Coach Marc Dickson talked me into playing a diamond and one with our frosh point guards starting and chasing Kayla. I had designed the diamond concepts, but Marc picked the right defender to harass Arlington's star.

It worked and we were alive again in the tourney! Thanks Chelsea Zimmerman for sparking the defense that night. Unfortunately, our season ended the next morning with a close loss to Seattle Prep: no trophy that year but "all out" effort was given by all.

The 2002 season opened with a definite rebuilding project. Yet, challenges are always an adventure for me. I felt we could compete! We had a fearless leader and talented point guard in Chelsey Zimmerman. She had an exceptionally positive attitude and this seemed to spread throughout the team.

During the summer Che transferred to Seattle Prep and I was very saddened to say the least. However, it was a great opportunity for her to experience academically. I seriously was depressed to lose a player of her caliber; I thought that I had developed one of the top basketball programs in the state, and Che was in our youth program for several years. Since I put so much into coaching girls basketball, I really weighed stepping down at that moment.

After a day or so of sulking, the courage to meet the coming challenge swelled up in my spirit. Thank you Lord as I had twelve girls who I knew would step up and be competitive. They did too! Kacey Kolrud (Kaylee's younger sister) was as tough a defensive player as I have ever coached.

In the preseason polls we were picked to finish next to last in the Wesco League. Our girls loved the challenge ahead as much as I did. Marysville that season was the preseason favorite with their tall and experienced squad returning. In our first league game we blew them out by twenty-five points. Halfway thru the season we were tied for second with a respectable 5-2 record in league. In the end we didn't make state that season, but it was a fun and rewarding experience coaching these girls and watching them develop into a competitive and cohesive squad. Furthermore, watching Kaylee, Chelsey and the other players step up to help be the architects of another strong Monroe team.

Chapter 33

Sometimes coaches need to learn to just hang on and continue to work the field of ministry God had directed you. Seven years as head coach of the girls basketball program at Monroe had passed quickly. Many successes, some failures and a few disappointments were all part of the journey.

There was a very strong wave of excitement that spread through the air as summer approached and preseason plans were laid for the 2002-2003 season. A lot of community support helped in the building of the Monroe program to the level it was now performing. So many dads and moms spent hours investing their time and skills into our feeder program, and fundraising for the high school program. It is a fine line, but I always felt I should get the parents involved, yet not let them run the program. Our parents were super in this area and continued that way for my entire career at Monroe.

We built it together and "they would begin to come!" That summer we had four outstanding student/athletes move to the Monroe community and soon became key contributors to an already strong team. Remember, I lost two star ballers a few years back, well now I gained four all in one year! As soon as these girls relocated, we included them into our summer program and I needed to prepare to coach like never before!

Reflecting back on the previous season, it was a rewarding year as the players were unified and really played strong, as it was a true rebuilding season. This season was going to be an opportunity to take those key players from last season and blend them with the transfers. Hopefully, it would lead to more state tournaments!

Wesco was a tough league again that season (2002-2003). Marysville, Lake Stevens, Snohomish, Cascade, Oak Harbor and Monroe were all capable of making the state tournament. These six teams were all ranked in the state polls. It would be a rough road to just make districts – let alone all the way to state! Our optimism was not tainted by the presence of these giants in our path.

Once again we began the season with a strong start by winning our first six games. A close defeat by Marysville gave us our first loss. However, we won eight of our next nine games and finished the season at nineteen wins and five losses. Blending the transfers into our rotation was a bit sensitive as a number of our upper classmen were solid players and worked hard. Nevertheless, the new additions were year round ballers and had set very high goals for themselves. I did my best to keep everyone involved and happy. It was perhaps the biggest challenge that I had faced in coaching girls basketball. I had six girls who were now seniors and faithfully worked their way up the ladder, all now were hoping to have a rewarding final season for Monroe. These girls all stepped up and contributed – the team made it to state and a couple of these seniors had outstanding games at state. Unfortunately, we drew Kennewick who was No. 1 for most of the season.

Arriving at the Dome on Tuesday evening after practice since we played early morning, we checked into our rooms and then reported to the Tacoma Dome to complete a walk thru. Not all of the teams did this but I always enjoyed walking the lines of the court endeavoring to get my squad familiar with the playing court (I guess this goes back to my "Hoosier" roots). We met our sponsors there and that year our hosts were the Teamsters Union.

Waking up early Wednesday morning I had breakfast with the coaches and a couple dads who were my off-season coaches. We talked some basketball but my mind was already engaged on the 9:00AM battle with Kennewick (one of the tournament favorites).

Our young squad (four sophomores who played a lot of minutes) was ready for this early morning contest. It was full court pressure for thirty-two minutes by Kennewick and our young guards for three quarters met the challenge. I expected this defensive pressure as they were quick and had no answer to guard Kirsten in the post. It was a classic state tournament battle but our inexperience in the fourth quarter showed along with some critical misses at the charity stripe. Final score was Kennewick 38 and our Lady Cats 32. One very pleasant surprise was senior Kirsten Dunseth-Orth came off the bench and was a key defender and rebounder the entire second half. She sure showed that she would be an asset in the next game.

We knew that we had a tough draw, but we gave them a battle and contained their super star point guard pretty well until the fourth quarter. Next up? The Kentlake Falcons started five D1 athletes who all played multiple sports. They were 23-2 and some had them the favorite.

After the close encounter with Kennewick, our sponsors took us out for pizza and games at this spacious restaurant overlooking the harbor in Tacoma. It was fun as the girls were given tokens to play and they sure ate lots of pizza and salads. It was cool that the sponsors invited the entire Monroe contingent: the coaches, the wives, Banger (stats), Mark Zaremba and Larry Roberson (our loyal fans) and volunteer managers. These eating events always provided great memories beyond the lines of the basketball court. Another key volunteer was "shooting coach" Doug Van Wyk – he also was the lead statistician with Banger, Larry, and Mark his assistants.

Once again we arose early to battle Kentlake again at 9:00AM. The game was about as close as could be with fifteen lead changes; unfortunately our Lady Cats lost a close (loser out) game 45-42. Senior forwards Karissa and Kristen played perhaps their best games of their careers and we sure were proud of them. Our sophomores were outstanding in the two tough battles, as well as juniors Kacey, Tianna, and Chelsey. Our future would even be brighter the next few years.

Timeout!

The 2003 state tourney was the only one of seven state appearances where our Monroe squad did not win a game at state. Yet, no regrets here – we lost close battles with our youthful squad against two of the best teams in the Northwest. Their foundation was built with a promise of more to come.

Chapter 34

Expectations rose rapidly for the Monroe girls program in 2004. Blessed with the outstanding talent returning from the previous season, we now added three outstanding frosh and another top quality (potential D1) transfer from Mariner. It was late spring and our roster was perhaps one of the deepest in the state: Kirsten (a 6'6" post), Sarah Morton (9th grade point guard), Chelsey Zimmerman our senior all league point guard, and our new wing (6'1") who was perhaps the best free-throw shooter and three-point scorer I ever coached (boys or girls). Brittany would usually make 30 free throws in a row at our end of practice free throw shooting contest. To be honest, it was in rare occasion when she would miss one.

These players were all labeled D-1 recruits by the college coaches contacting me. In addition, Kacey Kolrud, Tianna, Dani and Chelsea Drivstuen, Jordan Battle and Marjani Muhammad were all potential college recruits. We were ten deep and I was able to use a variety of starting rotations without a drop off. We just played a little different style with each group.

Timeout!

God was certainly good to this coach; He gave me the talent to have fun developing. Now I felt repaid for the two transfers that I lost to the private schools in Seattle.

I received numerous recruiting calls on my school phone as well as my home phone. These calls started that spring and did not let up for two years. Listen, I charted every call and followed up with calling back the college coaches, often telling them of our other girls that they may look at.

In addition, my school and home email was loaded with college coaches' letters of intent in our players. Those Monroe followers that really know me understand that no other high school girls coach worked harder than me at promoting our Lady Cats to the next level!

I will never forget that Monday night practice during the second week of the season. The girls utilized the upper gym on Mondays rather than have late practices. It was about three o'clock and coach Rod Phillips came busting into the coaches office where I was finishing the pre-practice meeting with the assistant coaches while Rod began stretching drills.

"Coach Dickson, the upper gym is loaded with D-1 coaches. We need more chairs up there!"

I knew University of Connecticut and Stanford coaches would be there, but nine others showed up that day. "It's like the who's who of college coaches lining the gym!" I have to admit I was instantly excited – this was the kind of basketball atmosphere that I dreamed of having for our Monroe Community!

Now it must be said that most high school programs didn't get this kind of attention and we probably won't always draw such a following, but we wanted to benefit as much as possible. All of our varsity girls gained college exposure, right during our regular practices. These constant visiting coaches was a stimulus for the girls to go all out at practice – as most of our players desired to play at the next level.

As a coach who strongly desired to see his players achieve their dreams, I was able to expand my contacts and increase my ability to connect my players to various college programs. Another benefit was my opportunity to pick the minds of some of the brightest coaches: Stanford, U. Conn, Notre Dame, Gonzaga, U. Texas,

Florida State, Arizona State, Washington, and Washington State, Southern California, and several other universities were constant visitors.

I will never forget how Tara of Stanford spent over an hour after practice teaching me some of her favorite rebounding drills. I loved connecting with such bright, seasoned coaches. June Daugherty and I also spent time talking about offensive sets, etc. during her visits and when I worked their camps at the University of Washington in the summers.

The first game of the season was against an athletic, full court pressing team from Rainier Beach. We struggled early against their pressure defense, but in the second quarter we inserted our promising ninth grade point guard Sarah Morton. With Chelsey and Sarah bringing the ball up we blitzed right through their full court defense for many uncontested layins.

Unbelievable anticipation surrounded this 2003-2004 team. I had added two assistant coaches (Doug Van Wyk and Judy Irving) to assist with our newly founded sophomore squad and also help the varsity girls at practice. Our practices were designed to keep moving and cover all the fundamentals as well as our team offenses and defensive sets for the next opponent. Then when college coaches visited our practices would all run like clockwork – and we utilized the clock at practice to keep things moving. Having those top college coaches at practice sure benefitted me as I would ask them to critique our practice plans and execution. Their input was complimentary and most invaluable.

Since I did most of the teaching during the offense and defense team instruction, my assistants and managers would visit with the college coaches at that time. During the warm ups, I would get to chat informally with the visiting coaches as my assistants would often run the first part of practice. We became a smooth running machine after thirteen years together.

The Lady Cats did not disappoint during the regular season finishing 19-1. The only loss was in game number two against

Snohomish, our next-door neighbors and rival. It was a very close game with Snohomish pulling it out at the end 63-58. However, we met again later that season and defeated them soundly 58-46.

In the District 1 playoffs we were stunned by Lake Stevens in our gym 38-32. Nevertheless, we won the next three loser-out games and fought our way back to playing Lake Stevens again "Winner to State" game. This time our girls followed our carefully laid game plan and won decisively 54-36. We played a defense that I never tried before. I assigned our toughest defensive forward (Kacey Kolrud) to guard their 6'4" center and the rest of the girls playing a match-up four-person zone. Our 6'6" post (Kristen) was stationed on left baseline to sweep up all the rebounds. The other girls all moved around more to match –up with their players. Kacey was to meet their post at half court and bump her and keep hands on her continually. It worked and if we gave game balls, Kacey would have gotten the game ball that night.

At the conclusion of the game, Daryl Hart, our principal at Monroe walked out in the court and greeted me with an enthusiastic comment: "Coach Dickson, that was the best game plan I have seen in a long time!"

Timeout!

Words are powerful! That comment by our principal
really encouraged me to always prepare like that. It
gave me a rekindling of my passion as we all need
that in whatever field we have been placed.

It was state tournament time and Monroe drew the favorite (Prairie 24-1). Both teams came out strong, but Prairie's outside shooting took over in the second half and we lost our first game at state. Remember what these girls did in the District 1 tourney? Well, they repeated that comeback at state and won the next three games to earn the fifth place trophy. Our season record was solid at 26-3 – Monroe High's best overall record in girls hoops.

Chapter 35

With the graduation of seniors Kolrud, Zimmerman and Moriarity, the Lady Cats would certainly be missing some solid performers. Yet, there certainly was enough talent for the Monroe squad to expect a sate birth and some more hardware to put into the trophy case. Chelsey went on to having a great four-year career at the D2 level. There was interest in her at the D1 level, but she was very content playing for the coach at Southern Oregon. Presently she is serving as an assistant coach at Portland State for that same coach.

Another great beginning of the season for Monroe as they won their first nine games. It seemed like we did a great job in preseason preparation – year after year. Our staff was very committed to conditioning and game preparation. It really helped having the same assistants for all my Monroe years. Each year we tried to do a better job than the previous years.

In 2004 we introduced the "triangle offense" to utilize Kirsten's strong inside presence. In 2005 we hoped to fine-tune this offense even more. In addition, we always had the motion offense to utilize our talented perimeter players. I felt it was a formidable package along with our twelve set plays that had been so effective at the high school level.

Timeout!

I will have to admit that I spent untiring hours studying
college offenses from tapes that I purchased at coaches
clinics after listening to lectures from some of the top
coaches in America. This was my position that God gave
me and I was not going to fail Him or my players. Just as I
expected my players to do, I was going to give my very best!
Also, I was committed and loyal to all my players. We were
all family; yet, I realized like all families some took more
fathering than others. However, I loved them all the same.

Kirsten Thompson was recruited by every major university in
the nation. In the end she committed to Arizona State. My only
concern that was their offense was totally motion and Kirsten
was not a perimeter player. Notre Dame and coach Muffet ran a
triangle offense, similar to ours and they would have been a good fit.
However, I really liked the staff at Arizona State and thought they
would do a great job of developing Kirsten as a player and a person.
I have to admit that since I grew up in the South Bend, Indiana area
I would have been thrilled to send a player to that famous university.

Kirsten Thompson at the season's end was named to the famous
McDonald's All American squad for the West. She was the first
player ever selected from the state of Washington!

After completing the season at 18-2, the Monroe squad entered
the tough District playoffs with hopes of making their seventh
state tournament under coach Dickson. After easily defeating
Mountlake Terrace in the opening round, the Lady Cats faced a
tough Meadowdale squad in a winner to state contest.

When our team approached the gymnasium area at the
Marysville High School, I noticed that the parking lots were full
and the crowd noise was (emanating) from the huge field house.

It was going to be high school tournament action at its best. This atmosphere was one of the reasons I loved high school basketball, and to be playing a role in the action was unbelievable.

Just as I expected the game was a physical battle for all four quarters. At the very end of the last quarter Meadowdale held a three point lead, but we had the ball. A failed three-point attempt left the ball bouncing toward the baseline and a Meadowdale girl and our six-foot-six inch center went scrambling and fighting for it. No foul or jump ball was called and the game ended right there. My thoughts went immediately to challenge ahead; we now would need to win two games in the consolation round to make it back to the state tournament.

A day after that tough battle with Meadowdale the tape of that game was sent to our school and the newspapers by a rival school that depicted Kirsten pulling the ponytail of the Meadowdale player. Our game tape did not show anything since this incident occurred as the game was ending. The Monroe administrators wanted to know what I was going to do about the situation. My answer was very direct – I would not comment until I watched the video and met with my center. My relationship with my players was based on trust and loyalty, and before I disciplined a player's action I needed to look at the entire picture. The press and most of our opponents were not aware of the tactics employed by some players and teams to get under Kirsten's skin as she was quite a force on the court. To take her out of her game was the goal of many opponents.

Kirsten worked as hard in the off-season as any player that I ever coached. She was the only player (boy or girl) that I coached who had a better hook shot than I did. We had a great relationship and I loved the progress that she made in her three years in our program. However, due to the excessive rough play at the end of the Meadowdale game, I chose to have her sit out the remaining district games. At our conference she understood the situation and accepted the disciplinary action. This was the toughest call that I ever made as a coach. She knew it was my call and I was so impressed how she handled it.

Without Thompson, Dani Drivstuen stepped up her leadership roll and the Cats defeated Jackson soundly 64-52. The biggest fan on the bench was Kirsten as she cheered continually for thirty-two minutes. Next up was Lake Stevens and we knew that they would come to play.

Many thoughts came to play in my mind, as I got ready to deliver the pregame speech. This was the game that would get us back to state and our All American center would be with us again. I had to pull myself together and not think about my cancer tests and upcoming therapy. My mind was also wandering back to my best friend and brother-in-law who just passed away. The doctors did not want me to leave the area until tests were completed. My heart tugged back and forth as I thought of my players, my family and the uncertainty of my future.

Nevertheless, I was able to step through the controversy and brushed aside the pain. It was time to talk to my team. It was game time!

My captains told me that it was a speech unlike any that I ever delivered.

"I don't even remember what he said," senior guard Dani Drivstuen said. "It sparked too much adrenaline inside."

The team burst out of the locker room and sprinted onto the court at Marysville-Pilchuck High School like their season was on the line. Which, in reality it was. A win meant a berth in the 4-A state tournament for Monroe. Monroe won 45-41!

While playing Jackson at districts, I decided to utilize my cancer battle to encourage others. After the conclusion of the game, I was meeting with reporters and I knew this was the right time. The following picture was printed in the papers the next day:

Monroe ended the 2005 campaign with another strong showing at state by winning two games and taking the seventh place trophy. The team fought through the controversy of their coach battling a serious cancer diagnosis and playing two loser-out district games without their star center. That season of basketball taught us how to face adversity and fight through it!

Chapter 36

After the 2004-2005 season I really focused on the cancer battle ahead of me. The doctors game me 2-5 years to live. I needed to fight the good fight of faith. Listen as I wrote about earlier in this memoir, God had instantly healed me at a wonderful, faith filled church service in Troy, Michigan. In addition, I witnessed several healings that took place in my home church (Apostolic Temple) in South Bend, Indiana. Why not one more miracle, God?

God delivered me from a heart attack in October 2003, right before the basketball season began. I was playing intense hoops with some of the boys varsity players and a few coaches. Just a few weeks later I was fully recovered and ready to open the basketball season.

Although my prognosis was dire and the term "incurable" didn't give me a lot of hope; my hope came from my trust in the Lord and His ability to heal. I never forgot the call from my sister Sharon quoting a verse in the book of John: Jesus answered, "It was not that this man sinned, or his parents, but that the works of God might be displayed in him." (John 9:3)

This scripture then clicked in my mind. "I shall not die, but I shall live, and recount the deeds of the LORD!" (Psalm 118:17) Sharon and I were in agreement – I was going to live and God would get the glory. From this new hope I made my decision to continue coaching and share my "Faith Through the Battle" with all who crossed my path in the years to come.

Deciding to continue my passion to coach high school basketball,

I committed to two more years as head coach at Monroe High. Some changes were made in the responsibilities of the assistant coaches as I tried to lighten all of the off-season duties that I had managed. Marc and Coach Potthast coached some of the summer tourneys and I just observed. It was different, but I enjoyed being there and taking notes on what skills the players needed to master.

Like most strong basketball programs, our junior varsity provided the varsity with players who were ready to contribute each year. The 2005-2006 season would need some of these players to fill in the varsity roster. Our offense would need to rely on more of the perimeter game as most of our top players functioned best in the motion offense. We would utilize miss-matches for our "post up" game. As the season progressed we were 15-5 and seemed to be coming together right before playoffs. Then we were struck with the loss of our flashy point guard, Sarah Morton, for the playoffs. She tore her ACL and would not be available.

The players once again pulled together but we lost a couple very close games in the district tournament and failed to make the state tournament (which would have been our fourth consecutive trip to the state finals).

My health continued to be a challenge; yet and I was blessed to be able to continue as Monroe's Varsity girls basketball coach for at least another season. In my passion to coach basketball and be an encouragement to those who were fighting the "cancer battle", I was eager to get to the next season. Also, we would be returning five seniors who had been a vital part of our program the past three years. I realized in my spirit that I needed to complete another season at Monroe and spend one more year with the seniors.

The 2006-2007 season began with our team ready to get back to the state tournament. My major coaching concern was to develop a skilled point guard to fill in for Sarah as she worked her way back from knee surgery. Sarah's college situation was secure as she signed in November to play for the University of Washington.

Our dilemma was for the first half of the season, we needed to limit Sarah's playing minutes to two quarters a game or a total of sixteen minutes per game. We played her for one-half of each quarter for most of the season. The plan worked well as Monroe went on to win the Wesco North title with a league record of 14-2.

Disaster struck in the playoffs as Sarah suffered another knee injury and would not be available for the winner-to-state game against Lake Stevens. Once again our team pulled together and gave Lake a surprising battle; one that they might not have expected. Keena Hopkins and Morgan Thomas played the point guard position and kept our team in the game. However, a missed shot at the buzzer sealed the Lady Cats doom as they lost a close winner-to state battle.

After that disappointing district loss, I needed time to think and talk with my wife, Chris. The best place to do this was a quiet, friendly Mexican restaurant in Snohomish. Chris and I met there after I rode the team bus back to Monroe.

We were seated and I sat quietly while my mind pieced together all the random thoughts that were bombarding my mind. Then I looked up at Chris and spoke to her: "I know that it is time to step down as coach of the Monroe Bearcats. Maybe I will coach again, but right now I am very certain that I need to close the Monroe basketball chapter of my life."

Chapter 37

Spring came early that year. Instead of planning open gyms and tournament schedules for the Lady Cats basketball team, I was planning family time with Chris and our kids and grandchildren. I still maintained my teaching position at Monroe Middle School and my work as the LAP and ELL teacher sure kept me busy. However, when the fall came around and the winter chills approaching, my body sure longed for the gym.

Grandson T.J. Vaught had just enrolled into the Middle School at Cedar Park Christian School in Bothell. While visiting the campus with my daughter Melissa, I ran into one of the most pleasant men that I had ever met – Bill Bettinger. He was the athletic director at the high school and had a charming personality. He remembered my years of success at Monroe and mentioned that he enjoyed watching us at state. We certainly "hit it off" and our bond continues to this day. Before long, Bill talked me into coaching their eighth grade girls basketball squad. I accepted as my PSA scores were improved and I felt great. After all middle school coaching at a Christian School should not be so stressful compared to the powerhouse program we created at Monroe High.

It was a natural transition to be able to continue my passion of coaching basketball and still be able to focus on my cancer battle. Those two months guiding the eighth grade girls team were fun, and I realized that my gifts in the arena of coaching was still effective.

This assignment enabled me to focus on my players and less on my health battles.

What a difference from coaching in the extremely competitive Wesco 4-A League; yet, I found this middle school league to be challenging and an opportunity to develop a promising eighth grade squad for Cedar Park Christian School. I especially enjoyed the emphasis on prayer and sharing our faith at practice.

Timeout!

During my entire coaching career, prayer was always a part of my personal style as a coach. All the way back to my early years of coaching in Michigan, I found times to include God and prayer. If a player was injured in football or basketball, I would have the team pray for that player. I knew it was important to follow the guidance of the Holy Spirit; as a result, it was never a concern to an administrator. I was modeling a coach that I had in high school who had a strong belief in prayer. Coach Heck was a model Christian and an inspiration leader of our highly talented football team at Mishawaka High School. His visits to my hospital room my sophomore year were full of faith. He was a true man of God. As a coach I wanted to be considered above all things: "A true man of God!"

The opportunity to coach that middle school team at Cedar Park refueled my desire to return to high school varsity coaching. Thank you Bill Bettinger for encouraging me to take the helm of that young team!

Later that spring my cancer battle was doing remarkably well – so well in fact that I approached Chris about my returning to coach at the varsity level. My dear wife, who walked so closely with me through this tremendous battle, had one comment.

"Alan, if you go back, it has to be a small Christian School!"

With that restricted green light, I daily checked the W.I.A.A. website and one job showed up in a few days. The Bear Creek School in Redmond, was looking for a varsity girls coach. This was a highly academic, classical Christian school that competed at the 2-B level. It would be different than Monroe High, but it might be a rewarding experience.

At the interview I was impressed with the quality of academics and the involvement of parents in the school activities. The director (head master) of the school was wondering why I would be interested in taking over such a small program compared to what I developed at Monroe. My response was that I would love to build another successful program. I was ready for another challenge.

I asked for the weekend to decide as they offered me the position that day. My big concern was the commute to Redmond was thirty-five minutes versus the ten-minute drive I was used to at Monroe. Another concern was that I always loved getting my family involved. Daughter Allison "Ally" and son Marc both assisted at times when I coached the eighth graders at Cedar Park. I hoped to get them involved again at Bear Creek. On Monday I accepted the job and Marc accepted the junior varsity position. Ally offered to assist in the summer program.

The challenge of building the program at Bear Creek was difficult at first. At our team meeting late that spring I was able to recruit only five players for team camp. We went anyway and actually with only a few practices before camp, the team competed very hard and beat a 4A school from Oregon. We finished the camp at University of Portland with four and one-half players as one girl was injured the first game.

That young lady had her big toe nail ripped off and she returned form the trainers office with it protected by a metal cover and all taped up ready to play. I loved the grit of these young ladies.

On that note at the initial team meeting I loved the attitude of our two returning starters form the previous season. Tajel and Megan were willing to step up and recruit and be our leaders on the court for the next two years. I told them while the younger players were developing, they would have to average thirty points between them and play "all out" at "all times".

I will never forget Megan blurting out at the end of that meeting, "I'm so excited for next year!" I knew she bought in and the others would follow!" Megan and Tajel made all league the next two seasons and the younger players developed nicely. Kendall, Maddie, Nikki, Morgan and others contributed to make the Bear Creek team one to not take lightly.

That fall I attended volleyball games to recruit more players and I was able to pick up a couple of solid athletes who developed rapidly during the season. At the end of the season we were very competitive in our league.

Losing only one player off that 2008-2009 squad, the next season was very promising. In the 2009-2010 season we won sixteen games and advanced all the way to the winner-to-state game in the districts. That game was close all the way and a couple missed free throws in the final seconds kept us from state. It was a disappointed team in the locker room; yet they were able to look at the progress made and the near miss to state.

The foundation was laid at Bear Creek and next years team would be adding two exceptionally talented frosh: a much-needed 5'10" point guard and a 6' athletic post. This team would have the potential to compete at any level in our state. We had a very successful summer competing in local tournaments and a wonderful team camp experience at N.B.C.'s team camp in Oregon. We took two squads there and both teams were very competitive.

Timeout!

NBC is a national Christian basketball camp that I encouraged so many of my former players to attend. Fred Crowell founded the program nearly forty years ago, and developed a beautiful blend of leadership training, faith and basketball skills development. One summer I had twenty-one Monroe girls, grades 4-10, attend the camp.

At the team camp in LaGrande, Oregon I had some very inspiring conversations with the director Danny Beard. Since both of us had suffered through cancer battles, our faith encouraged each other. Danny and I both were fighting the good fight of faith – to reverse what Satan meant for evil to God's glory.

The fall was soon in full swing with basketball season soon approaching. The program at Bear Creek was so promising and all was set for this coach to take another school to state and maybe win a trophy or two the next two seasons. Then, a phone call came form my friend and director of athletics at Cedar Park Christian Schools. Bill Bettinger was so excited to be able to offer me the head girls coaching position at their growing school. "Now what?" I thought. The Bear Creek program was ready to roll, but I felt a "calling" to check out the Cedar Park program.

Full Timeout!

Reflecting on the decision to uproot my family and our obvious material security back in 1984, changed my entire outlook on life. Following the leading of the Holy Spirit was forever first and foremost for my family and me. Once again I recognized the calling. It was so clear in my spirit as I heard the inner voice: "Alan, you are to move forward and answer the call at Cedar Park."

It didn't matter how hard I worked to build up the program at Bear Creek. It was not about me. They would do well. A new coach would step up. So many thoughts penetrated my mind.

I met with Cedar Park's administration and the plans they had for me were just what I desired. They recognized my desire to serve at a Christian School. After all, I moved out here following the call to the Community Chapel Christian School. Now, my voyage was coming full circle. My life's calling would be completed. At Cedar Park Bothell I could substitute teach, maybe assist in administrative duties, and most importantly establish another top quality girls basketball program. It was a total family environment and I was excited to join.

The Bear Creek team and administration totally understood my decision to join Cedar Park. It was much closer to home; two grandsons were attending there, and they were willing to get me involved in the school's curriculum. This was what I truly desired – I wanted to be an active part of the entire educational experience at Cedar Park.

My two years at the Bear Creek School were a great experience. I was totally impressed with the curriculum and the quality of the players and their families. I need to share one story:

On a team camp trip to the University of Portland (my second summer) I was blessed with a full team, which included some of the incoming ninth graders. All twelve players contributed and we made it to the championship round of the camp tournament. We needed to match the other teams physical play, so I inserted Kendall (the daughter of the Seahawk great linebacker, Dave Wyman). She set some ferocious screens to set up our point guard. One of the refs commented to me: "Coach, that was the toughest screen that I have ever seen in this tournament – and it was legal!" My response was simple: "what do you expect, out of the daughter of Dave Wyman?"

I left the Bear Creek program with great memories, but most importantly, I was excited that one of the coaches of the boys program was willing and excited to take over the program. His daughter was on my team for two years and the team was in great hands with him at the helm.

With the return of Maddie, Kendall, Megan, and Nikki and the addition of the outstanding frosh Bear Creek was ready to bloom. And they did with a trip to state and I was so blessed to be a part of their development. They have a top-flight athletic director and he selected a wonderful coach for the team in Greg Cheever.

Chapter 38

"Delight yourself in the LORD, and he will give you the desires of your heart." (Psalms 37:4)

After forty years of serving in the public schools where God definitely called me to minister, I now was being given the opportunity to serve in a thriving Christian School. Cedar Park Christian School was one of the largest fundamental Christian schools with five campuses.

At the interview with the administrators at C.P.C.S. in Bothell, they were impressed with my longtime desire to contribute and serve in a Christian school. They valued my experiences and I certainly respected the growth and educational excellence of their schools. I remember Dr. Behrends, the superintendent, stating: "Alan, what took you so long to get here?" I certainly felt welcomed and valued.

In addition to recruiting me to work there, they had a strong interest in my daughter Allison, as she had been a top elementary teacher in the Monroe School District. Of course, I did some bragging as a proud dad. She had experience coaching basketball and was gifted in the musical field – both qualities that would be an asset at Cedar Park Christian Schools.

In order for me to get a quick feel for the school, I was asked to substitute on the day we were to sign my coaching contract. It was an awesome experience as I had most of the returning players in the classes that day. Since it wasn't official yet, I was careful to avoid disclosing that fact. It was great getting to know the girls and allowing them to become familiar with me. At the end of the day, I was quite impressed with the student/athletes that I would be coaching.

In my conversations with the players I soon was convinced that they had high expectations. This certainly fit my philosophy.

There was a nice blend of older, experienced players and some promising ninth graders. I really liked the positive attitude of one ninth grader, Madison who looked me directly in the eyes and said, "I will be one of your varsity players."

When I left Bear Creek to take the position, one of the coaches there told me that I would be inheriting a player who had tremendous potential. He was correct. Rachel Staudacher was a thoroughbred. One of my new assistant coaches gave me some tapes of last year's games. I was excited to have the opportunity to help develop a potential D1 college player. In addition, Michaela, a very athletic point guard was returning and had been a starter for three years. There were others returning that showed skill and determination on the tapes. It was going to be really fun to develop another program and watch players develop as players and leaders in the community.

In a few weeks they asked me to teach part time as the instructor of the weight training class. It was a perfect set up as I would arrive at 11:30 am and teach two classes and then be here for practice. Half of my team was in my classes that semester, therefore, I certainly had the opportunity to get to know them on a personal level. To me this was so important when coaching high school girls basketball.

Cedar Park Christian School was such a warm environment; it had a real family flavor on campus. On Fridays parents often dropped off a mocha for me to enjoy. The staff was encouraging and very helpful. Needless to say, Bill Bettinger always "lit up" the classroom when he stopped by. The kids enjoyed him as much as I did. He was a great leader as you wanted to please him and make him proud.

The season was soon to begin as the beautiful fall that year was beginning to bring chilly air. Football and Volleyball were winding down and there was excitement in the air for the new basketball season.

The preseason practices were well organized and my new staff was really dedicated and enthusiastic. Sherri Staudacher (Rachel's mom) had also coached as an assistant for a number of years at the high school level. They both liked my pressure defense and fast break style of hoops.

I was right in my early evaluation. We had a great blend of frosh talent to fill some gaps with the experienced varsity returners Laura Goodnight, a 6-1 center showed a soft touch on her jumper. Since I had helped develop so many talented posts at Monroe, I was able to see her potential. You can't teach height they say. However, you can teach jump hooks, power post moves, and elbow and short corner jumpers.

The season began and in three weeks we were 8-0 and ranked in the top ten in state. Our fast break was red hot as we spent forty minutes per practice on it. The girls readily picked up my package of multiple defenses. They were bright and eager to play the game the right way!

The parents of Cedar Park's student/athletes are very involved in all aspects of the school. Basketball was sure no exception. Pregame meals were provided before all home games, and the away games were provided with bag dinners. It was a genuine family environment.

That first season went very well at Cedar Park. Our team won twenty games, finished second in the league to a strong, experienced Bellevue Christian team. The girls won three games in the playoffs, but lost a winner to state game in the districts. It was a heart breaking loss as we battled and fought only to fall short in an overtime game. Our season ended with a solid 20-6 record.

Year two at Cedar Park was going to be another fine year. Allison had resigned from Monroe to join the elementary staff at Cedar Park. She would be available to assist the varsity team and that would certainly add to our staff. Sheri was a very enthusiastic assistant who could really push the girls to go all out on the daily drills, and Glenn complimented our staff by developing a strong junior varsity program. Ally would be well liked by the girls and she had an in depth understanding of my motion basketball concepts. I was excited as my health was strong and it would be an exciting challenge to get these girls to the state tournament.

We lost two starters to graduation Erin and Michaela, but we had ten returners. We were excited for the next season.

In the summer Ally, Sheri and I organized a summer camp that drew nearly fifty girls ages 7-14. It was an excellent experience and also it taught leadership skills to the varsity players. These camps are so valuable to a high school program.

Rachel was receiving numerous letters from D1 schools in the northwest and as far away as Montana. Therefore, I made sure that I went to the Oregon City Tournament to chat with some of those coaches who would be there scouting the players. Just as I did at Monroe, I would work hard to promote any of my players who had the talent to play at the next level. I enjoyed trying to help players achieve their dreams – especially since one of my high school coaches made my dreams come true.

November soon came and the 2011-12 season was another successful one. For the first time in school history, the girls varsity beat Bellevue Christian 51 to 47 in Bellevue. The season concluded with Cedar Park Christian and Bellevue Christian tied for the Emerald City League title, both with 13-1 records!

Rachel Staudacher finished the season as the top scorer in the Seattle area at 21.2 points per game and was named to the All State team by *Seattle Times*. She signed to play for the University of Montana with a full ride scholarship.

However, the highlight of the season was the teams return to the state playoffs. A very daunting task awaited there as they drew the defending state champs, Freeman.

Since Freeman was known to pressure teams early and try to knock them out in the first quarter, our plan would be to smack them in the face with our own pressure. It worked for a quarter and a half. We took an early lead and held on until midway through the second quarter. Then their pressure got to our guards and we lost in this regional battle at Wenatchee High School.

Perhaps the pressures of the competition began to affect my body as I began to feel the pain of the prostate cancer. It was a struggle to coach that game, but I had Sherri, Glenn, and my daughter Ally to assist.

It was during the drive back home that I was having serious thoughts that this might be the end of my basketball-coaching career. Would the pain decrease and would the tumor begin to shrink? I was believing for a miracle.

Chapter 39

There was nothing more beautiful than the following summer in Chelan at our summerhouse we shared with Melissa and Todd. I loved waking early and taking my coffee and walking to the park bench across the street at River Walk Park. The pristine water glistened as the sun would light up the lake. Sailboats, motorboats, and people on boogie boards, and kayaks would soon fill the lake. Much of my writing for this book was completed as I sat on that park bench.

Soon the cooler winds would prevail as fall began approaching. Yet the afternoons were so warm and beautiful. I soon would be starting my second fall season as the eighth grade girls coach at Manson Middle School. I took this position originally to help develop a solid foundation for their girls team at the high school. Perhaps in the future there would be an opportunity to continue with these girls and transform the high school program into a contender for their league and the playoffs. In my mind I was excited about this possibility.

My first season with the Manson girls was five wins and five losses. One of the players told me that they hadn't won a game in three years. We certainly turned that around. However this season was going to be special. We had seven or eight girls returning and there were some talented athletes in the group. Baylee and Maddie were starters for me last year and both went to N.B.C. basketball camp last summer. They would definitely be improved. Azalea and Daicy both were returners who loved the game and had great promise. The center position would be alternated between Julia and Alyssa both strong rebounders.

I really fine-tuned the practices to take these girls to the next level. And they developed quite nicely. We had installed an aggressive full court press that took most of the teams by surprise. On offense our players really blossomed – if the fast break was not there, they learned to pull the ball out and set up our motion offense or run a set play.

It was so much fun as these kids were so eager to be successful. I think that I took this coaching as serious as I did my high school coaching. I really wanted them to taste an undefeated season!

About halfway through that fall basketball season my fall paradise in Chelan was greatly disturbed. Cancer's attack on my body returned like a raging bull.

"Why now?" I was so enjoying this fall, I thought to myself.

My sleep was interrupted as I got up every hour (at least) and paced the floor to relieve pain. Pain pills helped some but I was determined to finish this season and beat this attack on my body. I reached out for prayer from family members and friends who prayed for me. With subbing and coaching at Manson I was so content that this would be a perfect retirement just as soon as I finished coaching at Cedar Park.

Continuing on with my coaching I noticed that the pain would vanish when I was on the court coaching at practice. I received great satisfaction watching these aspiring hoopsters develop daily with their court skills. Manson was a close-knit community where many of the parents worked in the apple business that surrounded that small town.

The town itself was nestled on the shores of Lake Chelan just a few miles from the city of Chelan. The families were very supportive of the school sports and our middle school team had great support for our late afternoon games. They were great family oriented people and I loved the respect and gratitude they showed me as their coach.

One kind mother always showed up to the home games with some home made tacos for me to enjoy before the eighth grade game.

It was a "storybook season" as the girls stayed focused for the two-month season and we played extremely well that second year at Manson Middle School. I used this coaching experience to experiment with plays that my varsity team at Cedar Park could utilize. As a motivational tool I had a chips and ice cream party for the girls during the last week of the season. The girls brought chips and I bought enough ice cream for the varsity and our junior varsity squads. Our entertainment would be watching "Hoosiers". It was such a treat for me to narrate this movie for the girls as I did play those years at Butler, and I did meet Bobby Plump my frosh year there.

We finished that season 10-0! Our defense was stifling as we held most teams under thirty-five points. Azalea was on the ball and she would totally harass the other team's point guard. Daicy and Baylee would defend the wings and Maddie served as the interception with our center back as safety. This 1-2-1-1 three-quarter press stunned most of our opponents. Nearly half of our offense came from this pressure.

It was a really fun experience coaching that young team and planting some dreams into their young minds. I told them preseason that if they believed and worked really hard we would be very successful – and we were!

I finished that coaching assignment on a Thursday and began my varsity coaching at Cedar Park Christian School that next Monday. In my mind and spirit I was excited for the challenge awaiting at Cedar Park. However, my body was still under attack as the cancer battle was still raging with increased bladder and bone pain. My hope for healing kept me going as I did not consider stepping down at that point.

At the preseason coaching meeting that Sunday afternoon, I carefully went over our practice plan for that first week of tryouts. Allison would play a bigger role as Sherri would be out of town a lot watching Rachel play for Montana. Todd Jurdana, who had showed enthusiasm and an eagerness to grow as a coach agreed to serve as the junior varsity coach. As a new staff we worked well together the previous summer. We all looked forward to continue a tradition of excellence on and off the court for Cedar Park Christian School – Bothell.

It would be tough replacing Rachel, Brie and the four other seniors (Ty, Morgan, Emily and MiKayla) but I had confidence in the young players returning. Of course our standout sophomore center, 6-1 Laura Goodnight would be a force to build around. And the next year our squad would include some very talented frosh that were still in eighth grade. The future for Cedar Park was bright – the foundation was laid.

One dark cloud loomed over our season. My strength was waning and the pains were becoming unbearable. Quitting was not part of my vocabulary. When you know you are in God's will, "Why can't He just heal you and make it all right?" My mind was strong; I felt young at heart, but my body was failing.

After four games I took a three-day retreat to the ocean and turned the coaching over to my assistants with practice plans and goals for them. I needed to be alone with God and just walk the ocean beaches. I would meet the team at the next game. Dr. Behrends agreed to oversee the program and attend that away game against Seattle Christian.

After a restful trip with Chris I returned to the bench and basically took over that night at Seattle Christian. We got there early as it was on our way home from the ocean. As I looked back I realized that those wonderful players really cared for me – even more than winning basketball games. Inadvertently, it affected their play. I was struggling to be the coach that I had been for so many years. What should I do?

That next week I asked for a meeting with the athletic director and Dr. Behrends, C.P.C.S. Superintendent.

Instead of asking for a leave, I asked the athletic director to assume my duties as I sensed that he had an interest in coaching varsity basketball. He did take over on an interim basis and we agreed to meet again in two days.

At the conclusion of that meeting I felt led to ask Dr. Clint Behrends to seek God about my decision and advise me at the next meeting. By the way, he let the decision be totally mine as he said, "the job was mine until I decided to no longer continue". I appreciated his support.

However, I did decide that I no longer had the energy needed to serve as the head varsity girls' coach. I stepped down. It was a sad day for me as I was unable to build an everlasting girls' basketball program for Cedar Park – Bothell.

I supported the girls and showed up for a few practices and some key games. However, the cancer battle became more serious than I had experienced in the first six years of fighting stage 4 prostate cancer. During the next 4 years I endured surgery, radiation, chemotherapy along with the hormone therapy that I had been enduring for nearly seven years.

I still subbed at Monroe Schools when I was strong enough. I needed to be around the youth as that was my calling – plus the pay helped with my natural treatments that I used to supplement my medical treatments.

During winter break the athletic director asked me to coach the "Kings Christmas Tournament" as he had tickets to vacation in California with his family – they were going to watch his son play for the Cedar Park boys basketball squad. I coached the tourney, but it wasn't pain free. One of the parents assisted me on the bench and continually got me fresh ice packs to relieve the pain in the small of my back. She sure blessed me and we also had a good win in the tourney! Lisa was a big help as a coach and trainer! That was my final game as a varsity girls basketball coach.

Chapter 40

Looking back at my life, I clearly see a pattern: God held my hand and He was there when I slipped. As I looked back over the events described in this book, everything made sense – especially in an eternal way.

With no funds saved for college, God orchestrated a full ride academic/athletic scholarship to Butler University, and the opportunity to be a Bulldog on the court and on the gridiron. Every cent of my college was fully paid for four years.

Yet, after nearly two solid years of success at Butler, I joined a fraternity. Not used to the party life, I began to slip in sports and grades!

Then, Chris dropped out to join American Airlines and I was further depressed. My solution was to visit Ball State University and talk to the football coaching staff about a transfer. They remembered me from high school and at Butler and seemed very receptive. They offered me a place to stay with the frosh coach until I could qualify for a scholarship. I finished the full tern at Butler and transferred in time for spring training at Ball State.

A much better choice would have been to stay at Butler and work my way back into the rotation in football and be the best practice player on the basketball team. Then, who knows what could have happened. Well, I didn't stay, but after a semester at Ball State, Chris became pregnant and another decision had to be made. We were to get married.

God was right there, he literally opened up an opportunity to return to my hometown of Mishawaka Indiana and play on the varsity basketball squat at Bethel College with some former high school stars from our area. And I would be reunited with my best friend from high school, Denny Wood.

Bethel had a great coach who was a perfect mentor for me, Tom Granitz. We moved to Mishawaka and I was offered a high paying night manufacturing job at Dodge and played that next year as the power forward on one of Bethel's best teams at the time. Our squad averaged over ninety points per game as we ran the break and were loaded with shooters. My personal stats that year were 14.5 points per game and 10.2 rebounds a game. I was now satisfied that I restored my collegiate athletic career.

We were happily married, and soon I would venture into my calling – teaching and coaching. That journey was described thoroughly in earlier chapters, but I want to emphasize the peace that comes from being in God's will. I was now content and flowing in His will for my life.

This book shared the journey and numerous stories that followed. I am finally convinced that God orchestrated every stop on the way of my journey. I am not special; He has the desire to lead each and every one of His followers (children). It is never too late.

Just remember the following: Don't let things in our lives derail God's bigger purposes for us.

Solomon wrote, "Catch the foxes, for the little foxes that spoil the vineyards for our vineyards are in blossom". Oftentimes it's the little things that keep us from walking fully in God's calling.

Remember when you gave your life to Jesus? Like so many other Christians, your heart was filled with a laser-like purpose. Perhaps you experienced God's healing miracles and you longed to share it with others, maybe you even sensed a calling to ministry. You utilized your position in life to fully express God's love to others.

Then, what happened? Those little foxes crept in and captured your attention and distracted you from God's purpose for your life. A decrease in your anointing and favor soon followed.

However, rejoice! Our God is powerful and a great source of renewed strength and purpose! He will redeem you and place you in positions of ministry –giving you a fresh anointing and even greater influence.

Each day of our life is so precious. The average life span is 25,550 days. Stay focused and make each day a wonderful experience for you and those you encounter.

I can't replay those days that I "messed up" along my journey; however, I can look to a brighter road ahead as I follow the guiding light of His spirit.

Chapter 41

Here I ventured with my family to the great northwest to get involved in Christian education; yet God led me to where I was called – back to the public schools. So glad He directed my path and recovered my purpose. My twenty-four years at Monroe were rich and satisfying.

The basketball program that I developed there was a top tier program for thirteen years. Yet, when I stepped down and had time to think – it wasn't the 232 victories and 7 state appearances that were significant. Rather, it was the relationships that developed and as I later realized they were eternal.

My two years at Bear Creek and two years at Cedar Park were successful, but once again, it was the relationships that stood the test of time.

On June 9, 2013 my former players organized a fund raising alumni game to support me in my cancer battle. I was really struggling and the cancer was no longer affected by my hormone treatments. When my former players got word of this, they proceeded to organize an alumni game to celebrate my years as their coach and to fundraise for my family.

My granddaughter Maddy White (Brittany's daughter) was in the middle of a serious battle of leukemia. Grandson Drew Torres (Allison's son) has had 8 brain surgeries and was facing possibly more surgeries for his hydrocephalus caused by an inoperable brainstem tumor. Also, I have a special needs granddaughter, Taylor Vaught (Melissa's daughter), who is the light of our family as she cheerfully goes through life in a wheel chair and very little ability to talk. Her favorite words are a joy to my ears "Bumpa, Bumpa".

This Alumni event was carefully hid from me. After attending the service at our church in Bothell, I was told by my son, Marc and his wife Jen that a group of former players were scrimmaging at Monroe at 1:00 PM and they wanted me to attend.

Chris and I went out to lunch and pulled up to the gym at 12:50. I was stunned by the number of cars in the lot at Monroe High School. My son-in-law and former assistant, Todd Vaught, came running to our car. "Hurry up", he shouted the television station wants to interview you before you enter the gym. Channel 13 was there in full force with all the cameras and bright lights. Now, I was more than stunned. Soon brightness lit up my spirit and I felt like I was walking on a cloud – not really on this earth. I never felt so good in a long time, maybe never before.

"It's all about relationships", I told the reporter from Channel 13. Now more than ever, I realize how those words describe all those years of coach at Monroe, Bear Creek, Cedar Park Christian School, and Manson Middle School. I should emphatically state that my forty years of teaching and coaching at Avondale Senior High (Michigan), Palatine High (Illinois), and Monroe all provided me with priceless relationships.

The Alumni Game was a huge success. The crowd included innumerable fans, and family members of Monroe girls basketball players. My daughter Ally, and granddaughter Layla along with two other friends started off the game singing '*The Star Spangled Banner*' in my honor. Referees from my coaching days donated their services (L. Ottini, T. Wheatley, and Terry Olson). I hugged each one after I jogged through the two lines of players who stood clapping and high-fiving me as I jogged through the greeting lines. What a celebration! This was a day to remember! Genuine love permeated the gym.

The game was an absolute fun time for all. During the first half I was so impressed with the conditioning and strength of the older Lady Bear Cats, which featured players from my 1996-2002 graduates. I was coaching them in the first half and decided the younger players needed me in the second half. It seemed just as I sat on the bench of the teams of 2003 and up, those players responded to my coaching and went on an extended run to pull ahead of the older squad.

In addition to the Monroe players some of my Cedar Park players joined the scrimmage with the 2003 and up squad. I was so in the moment at this scrimmage; I enjoyed every moment.

Numerous fundraising events were organized for halftime. All the funds went to support the Dickson family battles and my cancer treatments.

The highlight of the halftime events was when T.J. Vaught, my grandson, won the half court shot contest. His prize was $1,200 gift certificate to Grocery Outlet of Monroe. Out of the kindness of his heart he donated it to his Bumpa, such a sweet young man.

To me this Alumni Game was a dream come true. Nearly fifty players attended to support their coach. Some came from out of state. I always considered my players like family and now I knew that they considered me as family also.

A couple of months after this event I was nominated to the Hall of Fame as a coach for Monroe High School. Several of my players wrote beautiful letters supporting my nomination. It was a dreamlike ending for a man who followed his dream as a teacher of over forty years and a coach of nearly thirty-five years.

I am so glad that I put my hand in the hand of the One who stilled the waters and truly He was always there for me and His plan prevailed.

TIMEOUT! (MY LAST)

After all the years recording in journals while teaching and coaching, I now see clearly how God was directing my path. It was never my career choices – all along He had my future planned. Certainly He blessed many of my endeavors (like real estate sales), but He never let it deter me from my purpose in life. Today after such a battle with the prostate cancer that continually threatens my life, I have a peace beyond comprehension that I finally saw that I did His will for my life. There is no greater satisfaction.

<u>OVERTIME</u>

Coaching a varsity high school team was fading from my immediate goals. What would be next for me? I have always led a life that had a purpose. I now felt lonely and without a cause.

Once again God started speaking to me:

"Finish your book and use it as a springboard to reach future athletes as well as students."

Perhaps I can still encourage and motivated these friends. In addition, Facebook postings would be a way to reach all those people that were a part of my coaching and teaching experiences.

Therefore, while putting the finishing touches on my book, I spent time every two weeks giving updates on my cancer battle through Facebook. I would only write when I felt the anointing.

Many times I wept while writing – it was hard to explain, but God's love just seemed to pour through my emotions as I wrote! I really wanted to encourage all my friends who are walking through the fires: people who were hurting needed a connection from God. I was sincere and I think it reached my audiences.

What a rewarding and fun life – as God seemed to always keep me on the path that He laid out for my life.

I believe the words of Psalm 32:8 came alive in my life: "I will instruct you and teach you in the way you should go; I will counsel you with my eye upon you." (Psalm 32:8)

I am so grateful for the support of my children and grandchildren. My journey was indeed a family affair.

Chris the wife of my youth and dreams was uniquely molded by God to give me the most precious, supportive and perfect life partner. Our six children and their spouses and our eighteen grandchildren have definitely enriched the life of this coach/teacher and mentor.

Love, Coach

The following pages contain inspiring Facebook posts I journaled throughout my battle, along with a letter from a former player:

October 11, 2015

Dear Friends and Family,

Thank you so much for the tremendous love and support during my nearly 11 year battle with prostate cancer. I have shared much of this journey with you with hopes of spreading the value of prayer and Faith!! My journey is still going and that is already a miracle as I have been stage 4 from day 1. The battle has intensified lately, but I am believing for another turnaround! I want to do much more with my life:) This morning I am asking for prayer re medical decisions and relief from pain that has attacked my body this week!

Love you, Coach

February 4, 2016

Don't give up when the outlook becomes dimmer! Back in Troy, Michigan while teaching and coaching 3 sports, just 2 years out of college I was struck with bleeding intestines (Acute Ulcerative Colitis). Surgery was scheduled to remove the large intestine. I was so depressed as I was so involved in athletics. My wife suggested that I go to a faith filled church and seek prayer. We were not attending any church as we were too busy. But Chris knew that I grew up in a church in Indiana that had miracles on a regular basis. One of their pastors did our marriage ceremony when we were in college at Butler. We now needed help as the doctor was giving me a dire outlook. I opened the phone book and found Troy Christian Apostolic, I visited, enjoyed the service and received prayer. The next day no bleeding, I was coaching varsity baseball and teaching. I was so excited as the bleeding was severe for nearly a month. Surgery was cancelled and I still have my colon. What a foundation for my faith! In 2004 our Monroe team was ranked no. 2 in 4A state rankings and we're playing Anacortes and losing by 25 pts. AT HALFTIME. We came roaring back and won by 20 pts. Never give up!! Yesterday my report from the cancer marker was alarming to my medical team. The PSA score doubled in 3 weeks to 5,000 and chemo was canceled. I was sent home waiting for oncologists to decide what to do. Yet, I reflected that I am nearing the 11 year mark of stage 4 cancer. Pain comes and goes, I feel like I am moving ahead as I sure enjoyed being back on court at Sultan H.S. last week. I was honored to work with girls so hungry to learn. My former athletic director at Cedar Park said: "Alan, you are not going unless God needs a good coach in heaven." It is so comforting to know the Lord and not fear! I cherish every day! I feel so excited when I wake up with no pain. Friends, A few moments of prayer is so valued as I have more to do. My book has 38 chapters, with a couple to go. Sometimes I just pray for strength to finish. I hope to mentor in hoops in a greater way next year and get back to subbing. Retirement for me is to finish the race!! I pray continually for those who have requested, and I am counting on you...we are a team for life:)

Love, Coach

March 21, 2016

Timeout: I want to update my family and friends:) When diagnosed stage 4 prostate cancer 11 years and 33 days ago, I decided to fight this attack on my body...and make the battle public so I could help others when they might face a similar battle. I have tried to update every month. Little did I know that I would be blessed by all your encouragement and prayers?! Thank you! That last bout to emergency and the days at the hospital were truly overwhelming; yet somehow I recovered and I thank you for helping the miracle happen. My last round of chemo (a much stronger 3 straight days) caused me to nearly bleed to death, needed numerous blood transfusions, my heart became irregular, and my entire body was in a bad state. Some of the treatments to get rid of blood clots were excruciating. After I was home a few days the doctor wanted me to come in for another round. I guess they would watch the platelet counts better. I have decided to continue my vitamin C treatments at naturopath, Shaklee vitamins, and numerous other naturopathic treatments like purified water, with apple cider and baking soda. So much to do, but it is worth it to be around for friends and family. I may or may not continue chemo, but right now I am at peace just gaining my strength. Thanks again for remembering this old coach in prayer. So many of you will enjoy the book I am writing as the journey that God had for me was to be part of your lives. It ended up being 41 chapters and I am writing the final chapter this week. Remember God is good...I cut my grass for the first time in 3 years, but on the tractor.

Love,
Coach

March 25, 2016

Grandparents Day at Cedar Park Christian:) was a beautiful experience today.

I was blessed to attend the service in the church auditorium with worship lead by my daughter Allison -and then visit Drew's class and my daughter, Ally's class.

Tears came to my eyes as I heard numerous parents proclaim how Allison has blessed their child's life.

Love,
Coach

April 15, 2016

Such a blessing :) Your prayers (all from a variety of true friends) lifted me up again. Tuesday I went in for a routine blood check and they discovered right side kidney failure and the left one fading fast. Once again I was rushed to surgery. I came home an hour ago with both kidneys. There was enough improvement to let me come home. With a miracle I can hold on to both kidneys...join me in that prayer.

The doctor said that my decision to get that blood check that day probably saved my life. I was in pain for so many weeks that I thought it was normal for advanced prostate cancer. God covers us even in our ignorance. My friends and family are such a real blessing. Thanks for the prayers, God answers prayer!! "In the Morning, Night and Noon", I learned that song in Sunday school back in my Indiana days.

I am honored to have another chance to share my love for all of you:) And if you need prayer, this is my passion.

Love,
Coach

April 20, 2016

Final Proofreading!! Just got home from a meeting with my doctor and the head of prostate clinic at UW. After their report I am scrambling to finish this 40 yr. project!!

They kindly informed me that there is nothing left for my treatment. They were so sweet as they both told me that they are so glad that I know the Lord!! I really was surprised at their comments:) No politics here...it was a spiritual atmosphere.

Another hospital and their set of doctors gave me a similar talk 3 yrs. ago...that was why I switched to the U.W. Once again I am reaching out for prayer from my faithful family and friends. I want more time and experiences with all of you!! Their 6 months was not enough for me! :)

Love,
Coach

May 24, 2016

Today I was really battled in my mind re the cancer battle. After a few hours I sat up in my chair and said aloud "I will not quit!" The sun came out, and I opened my Facebook to this message from an elementary student in my daughter Ally's class. I have been blessed with prayers from so many of you. "Quitting is not an option!"

Love,
Coach

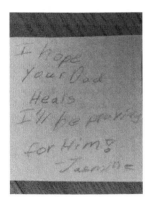

June 12, 2016

Awake and alone in hospital and as I am drawing strength from your messages:) with such a blessed and large family....So much going on over weekend with graduations, sports games...my wife, Chris was busy representing us...My friends you have been with me in your messages...May God bless you all...esp. your prayers.

All of your comments given to me are like messages from God.

Be blessed and isn't it wonderful how God never leaves us alone.... even when people can't be there. Thank you to my children and their families for their support in representing me at all these events I missed. My wife and children stepped up as I missed a grandson's graduation from U.W. and the Dickson twins from Sultan HS. I was there in spirit. I think of you all at lonely times in middle of the night at the hospital. I really believe God has me rebounding! I trust the One who never leaves us alone!!

Love and thanks,
Coach

July 24, 2016

Continued prayers appreciated. I haven't updated in a while. Your prayers are invaluable to me. Last week I had 2 serious falls and am fighting to regain strength. As always we are trusting God to strengthen me and allow me to continue my life in a fruitful way. My book has been finished and my daughter Ally is completing the finishing touches. Pray for the successful completion of this 40 yr.

project. I hope to be able to share the stories with many of you:)
Thanks for the visits and prayers received.

I think of you all often and treasure our friendship.

Love,
Coach

August 5, 2016

Not just hanging on, but moving on.

GOD JUST BLESSED ME WITH A WONDERFUL DAY!! My daughters came over and got me out of the house (first time in 6 weeks). Treated my wife and I to lunch!! With a few grandkids .... it was a real fun time!! Had to get used to walking with a cane... It will be short lived with therapy :) So thankful for friends visits and all your strengthening prayers!! Hope to get to Chelan for bb tourney##

God is so good...Hoping for more opportunities to be with my friends, family and players!! Real friendships are eternal...

Love,
Coach

48275091R00171

Made in the USA
Middletown, DE
14 September 2017